A 2001 HOMETOWN COLLECTION

America's Best Recipes

Oxmoor House®

Book Division of Southern Progress Corporation
P.O. Box 2463, Birmingham, Alabama 35201

ISBN: 0-8487-2385-6
ISSN: 0898-9982

Printed in the United States of America
First Printing 2001

Editor-in-Chief: Nancy Fitzpatrick Wyatt
Senior Foods Editor: Susan Carlisle Payne
Senior Editor, Copy and Homes: Olivia Kindig Wells
Art Director: James Boone

America's Best Recipes: A 2001 Hometown Collection

Editor: Kelly Hooper Troiano
Copy Editor: Donna Baldone
Editorial Assistant: Allison Long Lowery
Copy Assistant: Jane Lorberau
Director, Test Kitchens: Elizabeth Tyler Luckett
Assistant Director, Test Kitchens: Julie Christopher
Recipe Editor: Gayle Hays Sadler
Test Kitchens Staff: Donna Baldone; Rebecca Mohr Boggan; Jennifer A. Cofield; Gretchen Feldtman, R.D.; David C. Gallent; Ana Price Kelly; Jan A. Smith
Senior Photographer: Jim Bathie
Photographer: Brit Huckabay
Senior Photo Stylist: Kay E. Clarke
Director, Production and Distribution: Phillip Lee
Production Coordinator: Leslie Wells Johnson
Production Assistant: Faye Porter Bonner
Publishing Systems Administrator: Rick Tucker

CONTRIBUTORS
Designer: Rita Yerby
Photo Stylist: Connie Formby
Indexer: Mary Ann Laurens
Test Kitchens: Kathleen Royal Phillips; Alyssa Ouverson; Kate M. Wheeler, R.D.
Recipe Consultant: Janice Krahn Hanby
Project Consultant: Jean Wickstrom Liles

Cover: Carrot-Praline Cake *(page 98)*

WE'RE HERE FOR YOU!

We at Oxmoor House are dedicated to serving you with reliable information that expands your imagination and enriches your life. We welcome your comments and suggestions. Please write to us at:

Oxmoor House, Inc.
Editor, *America's Best Recipes*
2100 Lakeshore Drive
Birmingham, AL 35209

To order additional publications, call 1-205-445-6560.

For more books to enrich your life, visit **oxmoorhouse.com**

Contents

Introduction

Join us on a culinary tour across America as you sample the best tried-and-true recipes we've discovered from community cookbooks across the country. Our newest edition of *America's Best Recipes–A 2001 Hometown Collection* brings you the best of regional cuisine as well as recipes handed down from generation to generation. Each recipe is tested by our Test Kitchens staff whose goal is to ensure that each recipe is top-notch in taste, appearance, and technique. Any minor changes from the original recipes reflect simple updates in can or package sizes and cooking procedures.

This all-new edition of *America's Best Recipes* has something for everyone.

- Beginner cooks and busy families will appreciate a special chapter called "Quick and Easy Recipes" that begins on page 37. Each recipe can be on the table in 45 minutes or less and uses only a handful of ingredients–most of which you already have on hand.
- Creative cooks will enjoy the wide variety of classic to contemporary recipes throughout the food category chapters that begin on page 57. They're guaranteed to woo the best cooks in town at covered-dish dinners and supper clubs.
- Cooks of all ages will find favor with this year's special feature chapter called "Classic Comfort Foods" that begins on page 5. These foods will tap vivid childhood memories and create new ones your famliy will cherish for years to come.

In addition, look on page 320 for a list of the charitable organizations that contribute time and money from the sale of their cookbooks in an effort to lend a helping hand to their communities. You'll find addresses to contact these organizations and to place an order for their cookbooks that appear in the pages of *America's Best Recipes.* By purchasing these cookbooks, you'll not only receive family-pleasing recipes but the satisfaction of knowing you've helped support local communities and their charitable causes.

The Editors

Classic Comfort Foods

Buttermilk Cinnamon Rolls, page 12

Classic Comfort Foods

Certain foods and aromas evoke pleasant and vivid memories. Remember the fragrance of freshly baked cinnamon rolls coming from your grandmother's oven or the taste of chicken and dumplings stewing on the stovetop. And how about funnel cakes from the state fair?

Whatever the food, one sure thing is that it comforts your heart and soul. The comforts come as much from memories of the recipe being lovingly prepared and gathering with family and friends around the table as from the food itself. No matter your age, a home-cooked meal symbolizes stability and joy.

To help you create memorable meals in your home, you'll find a sampling of time-honored comfort food recipes from across the country. Some you'll recognize as old favorites and some will surely become new favorites. Our goal is to make meal planning creative and simple for you, so follow the suggestions on the opposite page to help you select recipes that not only taste great together but capture the eye as well. Remember, you're not only making meals—you're creating memories your family will cherish, generation after generation.

Page 12

Page 108

Page 240

Creative Meal Planning

Make your meals look as fabulous as they taste by composing menus with these suggestions in mind.

- **First choose an entrée.**
  Then center the menu around it, planning accompaniments that complement.

- **Let variety be your guide.**
  An assortment of foods prepared by different cooking methods adds interest to the meal.

- **Consider the color, flavor, texture, and size of each menu item that goes on your plate.**
  You'll want to include contrasting colors instead of a monochromatic meal. Garnishes can help in this area, if needed. Simple ideas such as fresh herb sprigs brighted any meal.

- **Don't repeat flavors.**
  It's a good idea to plan only one highly seasoned recipe and one starchy item in a menu. Remember to introduce milder flavors before strong ones. And if you're serving a tomato appetizer, avoid serving tomatoes as a side dish.

- **Serve both hot and cold foods.**
  Cold soups, chilled fruit, and vegetable salads are a welcome contrast to hot entrées. Try chilling the plates for cold foods and warming the serving dishes to keep entrées hot.

- **Vary food shapes.**
  Just as you would contrast the colors and textures of a meal, try not to serve a meal of round foods such as meatballs, new potatoes, and brussels sprouts. Also avoid multiple casseroles in one meal.

- **Consider your schedule when planning a menu.**
  If time is limited, plan quick and easy recipes, taking advantage of convenience products and the supermarket deli.

Apple and Spice Baked French Toast

Tempt those late sleepers out of bed with the appetizing aroma of baked apples, cinnamon, and nutmeg coming from this make-ahead French toast.

1 (1-pound) unsliced French or Italian bread
8 large eggs
1 cup sugar, divided
3½ cups milk
1 tablespoon vanilla extract
6 to 8 medium Granny Smith apples
1 tablespoon ground cinnamon
1 teaspoon ground nutmeg
2 tablespoons butter
Warm maple syrup
Whipped cream
Garnish: fresh mint sprig

Slice bread into 1½-inch-thick slices. Arrange bread slices in a lightly greased 13- x 9-inch baking dish, placing tightly together.

Beat eggs, ½ cup sugar, milk, and vanilla with a wire whisk until blended. Pour half of egg mixture over bread.

Peel, core, and slice enough apples to measure about 8½ cups. Place sliced apple over bread to cover. Pour remaining half of egg mixture over apple. Combine remaining ½ cup sugar, cinnamon, and nutmeg; sprinkle evenly over apple. Dot with butter. Cover and chill at least 8 hours.

Bake, uncovered, at 350° for 1 hour. Remove from oven, and let stand 5 to 10 minutes before serving. Cut into squares, and serve with warm maple syrup; top with whipped cream. Garnish, if desired. Yield: 8 servings.

Diane and Don Crosby

Flavors of Falmouth
Falmouth Historical Society
Falmouth, Massachusetts

Blueberry Coffee Cake

Fresh blueberries awaken the senses in this yummy coffee cake that's drizzled with a powdered sugar icing.

¼ cup firmly packed brown sugar
1 tablespoon all-purpose flour
½ teaspoon ground cinnamon
¾ cup butter or margarine, softened
1½ cups sugar
4 large eggs
3 cups all-purpose flour
1½ teaspoons baking powder
¾ teaspoon baking soda
1 (8-ounce) container sour cream
1 teaspoon vanilla extract
1 pint fresh blueberries (2 cups)
1 cup sifted powdered sugar
2 tablespoons milk

Combine brown sugar, 1 tablespoon flour, and cinnamon; set aside.

Beat butter at medium speed with an electric mixer until creamy; gradually add 1½ cups sugar, beating well. Add eggs, 1 at a time, beating after each addition.

Combine 3 cups flour, baking powder, and soda; add to butter mixture alternately with sour cream, beginning and ending with flour mixture. Mix at low speed after each addition until blended. Stir in vanilla. Pour one-third of batter into a greased and floured 10-inch tube pan. Sprinkle with half of blueberries and half of reserved brown sugar mixture. Repeat layers, ending with batter.

Bake at 350° for 1 hour or until a wooden pick inserted in center comes out clean. Cool 20 minutes in pan on a wire rack. Remove cake from pan, and cool completely on wire rack.

Combine powdered sugar and milk, stirring well; drizzle over cake. Yield: one 10-inch cake. Mary MacDonald

Over the Bridge
Corpus Christie Women's Guild
East Sandwich, Massachusetts

Sour Cream Cornbread

1 cup all-purpose flour
¾ cup plain yellow cornmeal
¼ cup sugar
2 teaspoons baking soda
¾ teaspoon salt
1 (8-ounce) container sour cream
¼ cup milk
2 tablespoons vegetable oil
1 large egg, lightly beaten

Combine first 5 ingredients in a large bowl. Add sour cream and remaining ingredients; stir just until dry ingredients are moistened.

Pour batter into a greased 8-inch square pan. Bake at 400° for 18 minutes or until golden. Yield: 9 servings. Thelma Kouri

We're Cooking Up Something New: 50 Years of Music, History, and Food
Wichita Falls Symphony League
Wichita Falls, Texas

Rich Refrigerator Rolls

Variety is a bonus with these great-tasting rolls. Choose your favorite shape–cloverleaf, miniature, Parker House, or crescent–or make a portion of each!

1 cup water
½ cup butter or margarine
4½ to 5 cups all-purpose flour
½ cup sugar
2 (¼-ounce) envelopes rapid-rise yeast
1 teaspoon salt
3 large eggs

Combine water and butter in a saucepan; heat until butter melts, stirring occasionally. Cool to 120° to 130°.

Combine 2 cups flour, sugar, yeast, and salt in a large mixing bowl. Gradually add liquid mixture to flour mixture, beating at low speed with an electric mixer. Add eggs, beating until moistened. Beat 3 more minutes at medium speed. Gradually stir in enough remaining flour to make a soft dough.

Turn dough out onto a lightly floured surface, and knead 3 or 4 times. Place in a large well-greased bowl, turning to grease top. Cover and chill at least 8 hours.

Punch dough down, and divide dough into fourths. Shape each portion into Cloverleaf, Miniature, Parker House, or Crescent rolls. Yield: dough for about 3 dozen rolls.

Cloverleaf Rolls

Using one-fourth of dough recipe, divide dough into 3 portions. Divide each portion into 6 pieces; shape each piece into a smooth ball. Place 3 balls in each greased muffin pan. Cover and let rise in a warm place (85°), free from drafts, 20 minutes or until doubled in bulk. Bake at 400° for 10 to 12 minutes or until golden. Yield: 6 rolls.

Miniature Rolls

Using one-fourth of dough recipe, divide dough into 3 portions. Divide each portion into 4 pieces; shape each piece into a smooth ball. Place 1 ball in each greased miniature (1¾-inch) muffin pan. Cover and let rise in a warm place (85°), free from drafts, 20 minutes or until doubled in bulk. Bake at 400° for 8 to 10 minutes or until golden. Yield: 1 dozen.

Parker House Rolls

Using one-fourth of dough recipe, roll dough to ¼-inch thickness on a lightly floured surface; cut with a 2-inch biscuit cutter. Brush tops lightly with melted butter. Make an off-center crease in each round, using the dull edge of a knife. Fold each round along crease, with larger half on top. Place folded rolls in rows 2 inches apart on lightly greased baking sheets. Cover and let rise in a warm place (85°), free from drafts, 20 minutes or until doubled in bulk. Bake at 400° for 8 to 10 minutes or until golden. Yield: 10 rolls.

Crescent Rolls

Using one-fourth of dough recipe, roll dough into a ½-inch circle on a lightly floured surface; brush with melted butter. Cut into 10 wedges. Starting with wide end of wedge, roll toward point. Place rolls 2 to 3 inches apart on greased cookie sheets; curve to form a crescent shape. Cover and let rise in a warm place (85°), free from drafts, 20 minutes or until doubled in bulk. Bake at 400° for 8 to 10 minutes or until golden. Yield: 10 rolls.

Black Tie & Boots Optional
Colleyville Woman's Club
Colleyville, Texas

Buttermilk Cinnamon Rolls

2 (¼-ounce) envelopes active dry yeast
¼ cup warm water (100° to 110°)
1½ cups warm buttermilk (110°)
½ cup vegetable oil
3 tablespoons sugar
1 teaspoon salt
½ teaspoon baking soda
4¾ cups all-purpose flour
¼ cup butter or margarine, softened
¾ cup firmly packed brown sugar
1½ teaspoons ground cinnamon
¾ cup raisins (optional)
¼ cup chopped walnuts (optional)
1½ cups sifted powdered sugar
2 to 3 tablespoons milk

Combine yeast and warm water in a 1-cup liquid measuring cup; let stand 5 minutes. Combine buttermilk and next 4 ingredients in a large mixing bowl. Add yeast mixture; mix well. Add 2 cups flour, beating at medium speed with an electric mixer until well blended. Gradually stir in enough remaining flour to make a soft dough.

Turn dough out onto a lightly floured surface, and knead lightly 5 minutes. Cover and let rest 5 minutes.

Roll dough into an 18- x 9-inch rectangle; spread butter over dough. Sprinkle brown sugar and cinnamon over butter. If desired, sprinkle with raisins and walnuts. Roll up dough, starting at long side, pressing firmly to eliminate air pockets; pinch seam to seal.

Slice roll into 12 (1½-inch) slices. Place slices in a greased 13- x 9-inch pan. Cover and let rise in a warm place (85°), free from drafts, 30 minutes or until doubled in bulk.

Bake at 350° for 20 minutes or until golden. Cool 10 minutes.

Combine powdered sugar and enough milk to make a good drizzling consistency; drizzle over rolls. Yield: 1 dozen. Kathy Young

Past to Present: A Pictorial Cookbook
Washington School Restoration Committee
Oakland, Oregon

Beef Stroganoff

This rich, buttery stroganoff is a surefire family favorite.

2 pounds round steak, cut into 2- x ½-inch strips
¼ cup all-purpose flour
⅓ cup butter or margarine
1½ teaspoons salt
⅛ teaspoon pepper
½ cup water
1 (10¾-ounce) can cream of mushroom soup
⅔ cup sour cream
⅓ cup milk
Hot cooked egg noodles

Coat steak with flour; brown meat in butter in a large skillet, stirring occasionally. Add salt, pepper, and water. Cover and simmer 45 minutes or until almost tender, stirring occasionally.

Stir soup into skillet, and simmer, uncovered, 30 minutes or until meat is tender. Stir in sour cream and milk; cook until thoroughly heated. Serve over noodles. Yield: 6 servings. Betty Pawlowski

Our Savior's Lutheran Church 75th Anniversary Cookbook
Our Savior's Lutheran Church
Casper, Wyoming

Swiss Steak

2 pounds top round steak (1 inch thick)
½ cup all-purpose flour
3 tablespoons vegetable oil
1 medium onion, sliced
1 garlic clove, minced
½ cup chili sauce
1 teaspoon dry mustard
2 teaspoons salt
¼ teaspoon pepper
½ cup water

Pound steak with a meat mallet, and cut into serving-size pieces. Coat steak with flour. Brown in hot oil in a large skillet over medium heat; drain well. Place steak in a 13- x 9-inch baking dish, and cover with onions. Combine garlic and remaining 5 ingredients, and pour over steak and onions. Cover and bake at 350° for 1½ to 2 hours or until meat is tender. Yield: 6 servings. Leigh Ann McMahan

Diamond Delights
Diamond Hill Elementary School
Abbeville, South Carolina

Old-Fashioned Beef Stew

4 pounds beef stew meat, cut into 1-inch pieces
2 tablespoons vegetable oil
2 cups water
2 medium onions, sliced
1 garlic clove, minced
2 bay leaves
1 tablespoon salt
1 teaspoon Worcestershire sauce
½ teaspoon paprika
½ teaspoon pepper
6 carrots, quartered
6 potatoes, peeled and quartered
1 pound boiling onions
¼ cup water
2 tablespoons all-purpose flour

Brown beef in hot oil in a large Dutch oven. Add 2 cups water and next 7 ingredients. Bring to a boil; cover, reduce heat, and simmer 1½ hours, stirring occasionally.

Add carrot, potato, and boiling onions; cover and cook 30 to 40 minutes or until meat and vegetables are tender. Discard bay leaves.

Stir together ¼ cup water and flour until smooth. Stir flour mixture into stew, and cook, stirring constantly, 3 minutes or until bubbly. Yield: 15 cups.

John T. Fagan

A Perfect Measurement of Love
Little Flower Children's Services of New York
Wading River, New York

Meat Loaf Winner

No need for potatoes on the side; they're already in this winning meat loaf!

⅓ cup ketchup
2 large eggs
1 tablespoon Worcestershire sauce
1 teaspoon dried basil
1 teaspoon salt
½ teaspoon pepper
1 large potato, peeled and shredded (about 2 cups)
1 small onion, grated
1 green pepper, finely chopped
1 pound ground beef
1 pound ground pork
2 tablespoons ketchup

Combine ketchup, eggs, Worcestershire sauce, basil, salt, and pepper; mix well. Stir in potato, onion, and green pepper. Add beef and pork; mix well. Shape meat mixture into an 11- x 5-inch loaf on a lightly greased rack of a broiler pan. Bake, uncovered, at 350° for 1 hour and 15 minutes, brushing meat loaf with 2 tablespoons ketchup during last 10 minutes of baking time. Let meat loaf stand 15 minutes before slicing. Yield: 6 servings. Terrianne and John Koepp

Today's Special: 25th Anniversary Cookbook from the Kitchens of Empire
Empire State Chapter FMCA
Scotia, New York

Shepherd's Pie

1 pound ground round
1 large onion, chopped
3 medium carrots, chopped
1 large green pepper, chopped
1 medium tomato, chopped
¼ cup chopped fresh parsley
½ cup plus 2 tablespoons chicken broth
1½ teaspoons salt, divided
½ teaspoon pepper, divided
3 tablespoons Worcestershire sauce
1 tablespoon cornstarch
1 tablespoon cold water
1½ pounds baking potatoes, peeled and cubed
2 tablespoons butter
¼ cup milk

Brown beef and onion in a large skillet, stirring until meat crumbles. Add carrot, and cook until tender; drain. Add green pepper, tomato, parsley, broth, ¾ teaspoon salt, ¼ teaspoon pepper, and Worcestershire sauce. Bring to a boil; reduce heat, and simmer, uncovered, 15 minutes.

Combine cornstarch and water, stirring until smooth. Stir into meat mixture. Cook, stirring constantly, until mixture thickens and boils; boil 1 minute, stirring constantly. Remove from heat; keep warm.

While mixture boils, cook potato in boiling water to cover 15 minutes or until tender; drain well. Return to pan. Add butter, and mash with a potato masher. Stir in milk, remaining ¾ teaspoon salt, and remaining ¼ teaspoon pepper. Mash until smooth; keep warm.

Spoon meat mixture into a greased 11- x 7-inch baking dish. Spread potato mixture over meat, sealing edges. Bake, uncovered, at 350° for 30 minutes or until lightly browned. Yield: 6 servings. Laura Perry

Designer's Recipes for Living
East Tennessee Interior Design Society
Knoxville, Tennessee

Sweet 'n' Orange Pork Chops

Long, slow cooking tenderizes these pork chops so much that the meat starts to fall off the bone. Serve the chops over rice to enjoy the gravy.

6 (1-inch-thick) center-cut pork loin chops, trimmed
Salt and pepper to taste
3 tablespoons brown sugar
1 cup orange juice
2 garlic cloves, minced
3 medium oranges, unpeeled and sliced

Season pork chops as desired with salt and pepper. Place chops in a 3½-quart electric slow cooker.

Combine brown sugar, orange juice, and garlic in a small bowl; pour over chops. Place orange slices over chops. Cover and cook on HIGH setting 1 hour. Reduce to LOW setting, and cook 7 to 8 hours. Yield: 6 servings.

Phyllis Sternberg

Culinary Tastes from Blue Mountain Cooks
Grand Terrace Branch Library: Friends
Grand Terrace, California

Southern Spareribs

Dark beer delivers the best flavor to these smoked ribs. And if you want to spice up things a bit, add a sprinkling of ground red pepper or hot sauce to the marinade.

4 pounds spareribs
1 (12-ounce) can beer
¼ cup soy sauce
2 tablespoons brown sugar
2 tablespoons chili sauce
2 tablespoons ketchup
2 tablespoons lemon juice
1 teaspoon onion powder
½ teaspoon salt
¼ teaspoon pepper
Hickory chunks
Vegetable cooking spray

Place ribs in a shallow dish. Combine beer and next 8 ingredients; pour beer mixture over ribs, turning to coat well. Cover and marinate in refrigerator 8 hours.

Soak hickory chunks in water at least 1 hour. Prepare charcoal fire in smoker, and let burn 10 to 15 minutes. Drain chunks, and place on hot coals. Place water pan in smoker, and add water to depth of fill line.

Coat food rack with cooking spray, and place over coals. Place ribs on rack; cover with smoker lid and smoke 5 hours or until ribs are tender, refilling water pan and adding charcoal as needed. Yield 6 servings.

Matt McCarter

Diamond Delights
Diamond Hill Elementary School
Abbeville, South Carolina

Best-Ever Baked Ham

Three ingredients is all it takes to make this ham the best ever!

1 (8- to 10-pound) smoked fully cooked ham half (shank end)
1 (8-ounce) jar Dijon mustard
1 (1-pound) package brown sugar
1 (12-ounce) can cola-flavored beverage

Remove and discard skin from ham. Score fat on ham in a diamond design. Place ham, fat side up, in a 13- x 9-inch baking dish. Coat ham with mustard; pat with brown sugar. Pour cola into baking dish. Bake, uncovered, at 325° for 2½ to 3 hours or until a meat thermometer registers 140°. (Do not baste.)

Carefully remove ham from pan, reserving pan drippings. Let ham stand.

Meanwhile, bring drippings to a boil in a 1½-quart saucepan over medium-high heat. Reduce heat to medium, and simmer, uncovered, 20 minutes or until sauce thickens. Serve sauce with ham. Yield: 16 to 18 servings.

Simply the Best . . . Recipes by Design
Columbus Area Visitors Center
Columbus, Indiana

Crispy Oven-Fried Mexican Chicken

1 (2¼-pound) package assorted chicken pieces, skinned
1 cup vegetable juice
¼ teaspoon hot sauce
½ cup (2 ounces) shredded sharp Cheddar cheese
½ cup crushed cornflakes cereal
1 teaspoon garlic powder
½ teaspoon salt
½ teaspoon ground cumin
½ teaspoon chili powder
½ teaspoon paprika
½ teaspoon pepper

Place chicken in a large heavy-duty, zip-top plastic bag or shallow dish. Combine vegetable juice and hot sauce. Pour over chicken. Seal or cover, and marinate in refrigerator 3 hours, turning often.

Remove chicken from marinade, discarding marinade. Combine cheese and remaining 7 ingredients in a large heavy-duty, zip-top plastic bag; seal and shake well. Place chicken pieces in bag, a few at a time; seal and shake to coat chicken.

Place chicken on a lightly greased baking sheet; sprinkle any remaining cornflake mixture over chicken. Bake, uncovered, at 375° for 40 minutes or until done. Yield: 4 servings. Carl and Carol Sweeden

Past to Present: A Pictorial Cookbook
Washington School Restoration Committee
Oakland, Oregon

Never-Fail Chicken and Dumplings

Nothing says comfort like a helping of homemade chicken and dumplings. Follow these directions for "never-fail" results every time.

1½ cups all-purpose flour
½ teaspoon salt
3 tablespoons shortening
1 large egg, lightly beaten
5 tablespoons cold water
3½ cups chicken broth or 2 (14½-ounce) cans chicken broth
½ teaspoon freshly ground pepper
3 cups chopped cooked chicken or 1 roasted chicken from the deli, meat pulled from bone and shredded

Combine flour and salt; cut in shortening with a pastry blender until mixture is crumbly. Gently stir in egg and cold water; form dough into a ball, and knead 3 or 4 times.

Combine broth and pepper in a Dutch oven; bring to a boil over medium-high heat.

Meanwhile, roll dough to ⅛-inch thickness on a lightly floured surface. Cut dough into 2- x ¾-inch strips; drop several dough strips at a time into boiling broth. Reduce heat to medium, and cook, uncovered, 7 minutes. Add chicken, and cook 4 to 6 minutes or until dumplings are tender and chicken is heated, stirring occasionally. Yield: 4 servings. Sharon Hampton and Harold Mesimer

Note: To make your own broth, combine 3 bone-in chicken breast halves, 8 cups water, ¾ teaspoon salt, and ½ teaspoon freshly ground pepper in a Dutch oven. Bring to a boil; cover, reduce heat, and simmer 30 minutes or until chicken is tender. Remove chicken from broth, reserving broth in Dutch oven; let chicken cool. Remove meat from bone, and shred. Prepare dumplings, and cook in homemade broth as directed above; do not add pepper from original recipe to homemade broth.

Blended Blessings
First Presbyterian Church
Salisbury, North Carolina

Carolina Turkey Pie

Self-rising flour and cornmeal, along with a couple of flavors of canned soups, keep preparation to a minimum for this old-fashioned favorite. The soups also add the salt needed for this dish, so hold off on the shaker. If you're trying to limit sodium intake, use reduced-sodium broth.

1 (10¾-ounce) can cream of celery soup
1 (14½-ounce) can chicken broth
1 cup self-rising flour
¾ cup self-rising cornmeal
2 tablespoons chopped onion
1 teaspoon dried sage
½ teaspoon poultry seasoning
½ teaspoon pepper
1½ cups buttermilk
½ cup butter, melted
4 cups chopped cooked turkey (about 1½ pounds)

Combine soup and broth in a saucepan; bring to boil over medium heat. Reduce heat, and keep warm.

Combine flour and next 5 ingredients in a bowl; stir well. Add buttermilk and butter to flour mixture; stir well.

Place turkey in a greased 13- x 9-inch baking dish. Pour broth mixture over turkey; spread flour mixture evenly on top of broth mixture.

Bake, uncovered, at 425° for 25 minutes or until lightly browned and thoroughly heated. Yield: 8 servings.

Seaboard to Sideboard
The Junior League of Wilmington, North Carolina

Shrimp Gravy

5 slices bacon
1 medium-size green bell pepper, chopped
2 tablespoons minced garlic
1 bunch green onions, sliced
4½ cups sliced fresh mushrooms (about 12 ounces)
1 tablespoon all-purpose flour
¾ cup chicken broth
1½ pounds unpeeled medium-size fresh shrimp
1 teaspoon garlic salt
½ teaspoon pepper
3 cups hot cooked grits

Cook bacon in a large skillet until crisp; remove bacon. Drain skillet, reserving 2 tablespoons drippings. Crumble bacon, and set aside.

Cook green pepper, garlic, and green onions in bacon drippings over high heat, stirring constantly, until tender. Stir in mushrooms, and sauté 3 minutes. Add flour, stirring until smooth. Slowly add broth; bring to a boil. Add shrimp; cover and cook over medium heat 5 minutes or until shrimp turn pink, stirring often. Stir in garlic salt and pepper. Serve over grits, and sprinkle with crumbled bacon. Yield: 3 to 4 servings. Tom Kapp

'Pon Top Edisto
Trinity Episcopal Church
Edisto Island, South Carolina

Oven-Baked Jambalaya

The ease of this one-dish meal will make it a family favorite for years to come. Just combine all the ingredients and bake! Be sure to use converted rice, though, to ensure that the rice cooks evenly in this dish.

2 pounds unpeeled medium-size fresh shrimp
1 pound smoked sausage, sliced
2 cups uncooked converted rice
1 (10½-ounce) can beef broth
1 (10½-ounce) can French onion soup
1 (8-ounce) can tomato sauce
¼ cup water
¼ cup butter or margarine, melted
1 (6-ounce) jar sliced mushrooms, undrained
2 green onions, chopped
½ cup chopped green bell pepper
½ cup chopped celery
3 tablespoons chopped fresh parsley
1 teaspoon dried thyme

Peel shrimp, and devein, if desired. Combine shrimp, sausage, and remaining ingredients in a large bowl; stir well. Pour mixture into a greased 13- x 9-inch baking dish. Cover and bake at 350° for 1½ hours. Yield: 6 to 8 servings. Kathy Gamble

The Art of Cooking
The Muscle Shoals District Service League
Sheffield, Alabama

Kim's Baked Beans

Three kinds of beans and two kinds of meat make this the quintessential casserole to take along to covered-dish suppers.

1½ pounds ground chuck
5 bacon slices
1 small onion, chopped (about ½ cup)
1 (15¼-ounce) can lima beans, drained
1 (31-ounce) can pork and beans, undrained
1 (15¼-ounce) can dark red kidney beans, undrained
2 tablespoons white vinegar
1 tablespoon prepared mustard
½ teaspoon salt
½ cup firmly packed brown sugar
½ cup ketchup

Brown ground chuck in a large skillet, stirring until it crumbles. Drain and set aside.

Cook bacon in a large skillet until crisp; remove bacon, reserving drippings in skillet. Crumble bacon, and set aside.

Cook onion in bacon drippings, stirring constantly, until tender.

Combine beef, bacon, onion, lima beans, and remaining ingredients in a large bowl.

Spoon mixture into a lightly greased 13- x 9-inch baking dish. Cover and bake at 350° for 1½ hours. Yield: 8 servings. Kitty Blair

Sesquicentennially Delicious
Western Pennsylvania Hospital
Pittsburgh, Pennsylvania

Home-Style Green Beans

"Home-style" reflects the flavor and tenderness of these green beans. For crisper beans, simply decrease the simmering time.

¾ pound fresh green beans, trimmed and cut into 2-inch pieces
1½ cups water
6 bacon slices, cooked and crumbled
1 teaspoon seasoned salt

Combine green beans and water in a medium saucepan; bring to a boil. Cover, reduce heat, and simmer 10 minutes or until crisp-tender.

Add bacon and seasoned salt; simmer 10 to 15 more minutes. Serve with a slotted spoon. Yield: 3 servings. Debbie Eperson

Recipes from the Kitchens of Family & Friends
Gresham Women of Elks
Gresham, Oregon

Macaroni au Gratin

Kids enjoy the comforts of "mac 'n' cheese," and adults will, too, when they discover the hint of onion and dry mustard mixed in this favorite blend. Italian-seasoned breadcrumbs cap the casserole with unexpected flavor.

1 (8-ounce) package elbow macaroni (about 1¾ cups)
¼ cup butter or margarine
¼ cup all-purpose flour
2 cups milk
½ (16-ounce) package process American cheese, cubed
1 tablespoon minced onion
½ teaspoon salt
½ teaspoon Worcestershire sauce
¼ teaspoon pepper
¼ teaspoon dry mustard
2 tablespoons Italian-seasoned breadcrumbs
Butter or margarine

Cook macaroni according to package directions; drain. Place in a greased 2-quart baking dish; set aside.

Melt ¼ cup butter in a large heavy saucepan over low heat; whisk in flour until smooth. Cook 1 minute, whisking constantly. Gradually whisk in milk. Cook over medium heat, whisking constantly, until mixture is thickened and bubbly. Reduce heat, and add cheese, onion, salt, Worcestershire sauce, pepper, and mustard; stir until cheese melts. Pour cheese mixture over macaroni, and mix well. Sprinkle with breadcrumbs, and dot lightly with additional butter. Bake, uncovered, at 375° for 30 minutes. Yield: 4 to 6 servings.

Favorite Recipes Taste of Tradition
B.A. Ritter Senior Citizen Center
Nederland, Texas

Chili Fries

Take your pick of chili powder or Cajun seasoning to jazz up these fries.

1 tablespoon olive oil
2 teaspoons chili powder or Cajun seasoning
½ teaspoon salt
½ teaspoon dried oregano
¼ teaspoon garlic powder
¼ teaspoon ground cumin
1½ pounds baking potatoes (about 3 medium), unpeeled

Combine first 6 ingredients in a large bowl. Peel potatoes, and cut into ¼-inch-thick strips. Add potato strips to olive oil mixture; toss gently to coat.

Arrange potato strips in a single layer on a baking sheet lightly coated with cooking spray. Bake, uncovered, at 450° for 25 minutes or until golden brown. Yield: 4 servings. Mary A. Chiasson

Our Favorite Recipes
Claremont Society for the Prevention of Cruelty to Animals
Serving Sullivan County
Claremont, New Hampshire

Blue Cheese Scalloped Potatoes

Blue cheese fans will love these scalloped potatoes. There's a half pound of crumbled cheese between the layers!

4 pounds baking potatoes, peeled (5 to 6 large)
1 teaspoon salt
1 teaspoon freshly ground pepper
¼ teaspoon freshly ground nutmeg
8 ounces crumbled blue cheese
2 cups whipping cream
2 cups milk
3 tablespoons butter

Cut potatoes into ⅛-inch-thick slices. Arrange half of slices in a greased 13- x 9-inch baking dish.

Combine salt, pepper, and nutmeg. Cover slices with half each of seasonings, cheese, and whipping cream. Repeat procedure with remaining potato slices, seasonings, cheese, and cream. Pour milk over potato slices; dot with butter.

Bake, uncovered, at 375° for 1 hour and 10 minutes or until bubbly and golden. Yield: 8 to 10 servings.

Chautauqua Celebrations
Wythe Arts Council, Ltd.
Wytheville, Virginia

Pecan-Crumble Sweet Potatoes

2 tablespoons all-purpose flour
½ cup firmly packed brown sugar
½ teaspoon ground allspice
¼ cup butter or margarine
⅓ cup chopped pecans
2½ pounds sweet potatoes, peeled and sliced
¼ cup maple syrup

Combine first 3 ingredients in a medium bowl; stir well. Cut in butter with a pastry blender until mixture is crumbly; add pecans, and set aside.

Place one-third of sweet potato in a greased 11- x 7-inch baking dish; sprinkle with ½ cup pecan mixture. Layer remaining potato slices, slightly overlapping. Sprinkle remaining pecan mixture over potato. Drizzle with maple syrup. Cover and bake at 350° for 45 minutes. Uncover and bake 30 more minutes or until potato is done. Yield: 6 servings.

Maxine Rollen

Recipes for Champions
Shebas of Khiva Temple Oriental Band
Amarillo, Texas

Great Depression Cake

This moist cake gets its name from the Great Depression era when eggs, milk, and butter were scarce. As you see, none were used for this recipe.

2 cups water
2 cups sugar
2 cups raisins
1 medium apple, peeled, cored, and shredded (we tested with Granny Smith)
½ cup shortening
2 cups all-purpose flour
2 teaspoons baking powder
1 teaspoon baking soda
1 teaspoon ground allspice
1 teaspoon ground nutmeg
1 teaspoon ground cinnamon
1 teaspoon ground cloves
1 cup chopped walnuts

Combine first 5 ingredients in a large saucepan. Bring to a boil; reduce heat, and simmer, uncovered, 10 minutes, stirring occasionally. Cool 10 minutes. (Mixture will be very warm.)

Combine flour and next 6 ingredients in a large bowl, stirring well with a wire whisk. Stir in walnuts.

Combine raisin mixture and flour mixture, stirring well. Pour batter into a greased 13- x 9-inch pan. Bake at 350° for 25 minutes or until a wooden pick inserted in center comes out clean. Cut into squares. Yield: 15 servings.

Donna Walson

Noel Bluffin' We're Still Cookin'
Noel Area Chamber of Commerce
Noel, Missouri

Pumpkin Gingerbread

We liked the addition of pumpkin to this all-time favorite that's quick and easy to prepare.

¼ cup butter or margarine, softened
½ cup firmly packed brown sugar
2 tablespoons sugar
1½ teaspoons grated orange rind
3 egg whites
1 teaspoon vanilla extract
1¼ cups all-purpose flour
1 teaspoon baking soda
½ teaspoon baking powder
½ teaspoon ground ginger
1 teaspoon ground cinnamon
1 cup canned pumpkin
¼ cup plus 2 tablespoons dark corn syrup

Beat butter at medium speed with an electric mixer until creamy. Gradually add sugars and orange rind, beating well. Add egg whites, 1 at a time, beating until blended. Stir in vanilla.

Combine flour and next 4 ingredients.

Combine pumpkin and corn syrup; add to sugar mixture alternately with flour mixture, beginning and ending with flour mixture. Pour into a greased 8-inch square pan. Bake at 350° for 25 to 30 minutes or until a wooden pick inserted in center comes out clean. Cut into squares. Yield: 9 servings. Barbara Brazear

Madalene Cooks–50 Years of Good Taste
Church of the Madalene
Tulsa, Oklahoma

Old-Fashioned Buttermilk Pound Cake

½ cup butter or margarine, softened
½ cup shortening
2 cups sugar
4 large eggs
½ teaspoon baking soda
1 cup buttermilk
3 cups all-purpose flour
⅛ teaspoon salt
1 teaspoon almond extract
⅛ teaspoon lemon extract

Beat butter and shortening at medium speed with an electric mixer 2 minutes or until soft and creamy. Gradually add sugar, beating at medium speed 5 to 7 minutes. Add eggs, 1 at a time, beating just until yellow disappears.

Dissolve soda in buttermilk. Combine flour and salt; add to sugar mixture alternately with buttermilk mixture, beginning and ending with flour mixture. Mix at low speed just until blended after each addition. Stir in flavorings.

Pour batter into a greased and floured 10-inch tube pan. Bake at 350° for 1 hour or until a wooden pick inserted in center comes out clean. Cool in pan on a wire rack 15 minutes; remove from pan. Cool completely on wire rack. Yield: one 10-inch cake. Mary Edington

202's Totally Tempting Treasures
American Legion Auxiliary Green-Pierce Unit 202
Wichita Falls, Texas

Funnel Cake

Bring a taste of the state fair into your home by making these funnel cakes for a fun snack or dessert. To make spiraling the batter easier, put it into a squeeze bottle with part of the tip cut off to ⅜-inch diameter.

1⅓ cups all-purpose flour
2 teaspoons baking powder
½ teaspoon baking soda
¼ teaspoon salt
2 tablespoons sugar
1 large egg, beaten
¾ cup milk
Vegetable oil
Powdered sugar

Combine first 5 ingredients; stir well.

Combine egg and milk; add to dry ingredients, beating at medium speed with an electric mixer until smooth.

Pour oil to depth of 1 inch into a large heavy skillet; heat to 375°. Fill a squeeze bottle, with tip cut off to make a ⅜-inch diameter opening, with batter. Squeeze batter into hot oil, moving both in a slow, circular motion to form a spiral.

Fry each funnel cake 30 seconds or until golden; turn and fry 15 seconds more or until golden. Drain well on paper towels. Repeat procedure with remaining batter. Sprinkle cakes with powdered sugar. Serve warm. Yield: 1 dozen (5-inch) cakes. Susie Bratten

Note: A funnel with a ⅜-inch opening also works but is trickier to maneuver than a squeeze bottle.

Culinary Tastes of Blue Mountain Cooks
Grand Terrace Branch Library: Friends
Grand Terrace, California

Brandy Pecan Pie

A splash of brandy and whipping cream elevates this pecan pie to new heights. Prebaking the crust for this pie works better than starting with an unbaked pastry shell. Shield the crust with strips of aluminum foil as the pie bakes after adding filling to achieve a perfect golden crust.

4 large eggs
1 cup sugar
½ cup dark corn syrup
½ cup whipping cream
2 tablespoons butter or margarine, melted
½ teaspoon salt
¼ cup brandy
1 teaspoon vanilla extract
1 cup chopped pecans
1 baked (9-inch) pastry shell

Combine first 6 ingredients in a large bowl; beat at medium speed with an electric mixer until well blended. Stir in brandy, vanilla, and pecans. Pour into pastry shell; cover edges of pastry with strips of aluminum foil to prevent excessive browning. Bake at 325° for 55 minutes or until set. Cool. Yield: 1 (9-inch) pie. Cleo Catherine Dick

Blended Blessings
First Presbyterian Church
Salisbury, North Carolina

Old-Fashioned Fried Pies

2 cups dried peaches, apples, or apricots
½ cup sugar
2 tablespoons butter or margarine, melted
2 cups all-purpose flour
1 teaspoon salt
⅓ cup shortening
⅔ to 1 cup cold water
Vegetable oil
Powdered sugar (optional)

Place fruit in a medium saucepan; cover with water. Bring to a boil; cook, uncovered, 30 minutes, adding water to cover, if necessary. Drain well. Finely chop fruit; place in a bowl. Stir in sugar and melted butter; set aside.

Combine flour and salt; cut in shortening with a pastry blender until mixture is crumbly. Sprinkle cold water, 1 tablespoon at a time, evenly over surface; stir with a fork until dry ingredients are moistened.

Divide pastry into thirds; roll each portion to ⅛-inch thickness on a lightly floured surface, and cut with a 4½-inch round cutter.

Place 1 heaping tablespoon (about 1½ tablespoons) reserved fruit filling in center of each pastry circle. Moisten edges with water. Fold pastry over filling, pressing edges to seal. Crimp edges with a fork dipped in flour; pierce tops with fork.

Pour oil to depth of 1 inch into a large heavy skillet; heat oil to 400°. Fry pies, 4 or 5 at a time, in hot oil 3 to 4 minutes or until golden, turning once. Drain on paper towels. Sprinkle with powdered sugar, if desired. Yield: 1½ dozen.

Montees Holloway

A Dab of This and a Dab of That
Bethlehem Baptist Church Senior Missionary
Ninety Six, South Carolina

Apple Crisp

2 cups all-purpose flour
1 cup firmly packed brown sugar
¾ cup regular oats, uncooked
¼ teaspoon salt
½ cup butter, softened
7 Granny Smith or other baking apples, peeled and thinly sliced
1 cup water
2 tablespoons cornstarch
1 cup sugar
¾ cup butter

Combine first 4 ingredients; stir well. Cut in ½ cup butter with a pastry blender until mixture is crumbly. Sprinkle half of crumb mixture into a lightly greased 13- x 9-inch pan; set remaining crumb mixture aside. Arrange apple slices over crumb mixture; set aside.

Combine water and cornstarch in a small saucepan; stir well. Add sugar and ¾ cup butter; bring to a boil. Reduce heat, and simmer, uncovered, 4 to 5 minutes or until thickened, stirring occasionally. Pour hot mixture over apple; sprinkle reserved crumb mixture over apple.

Bake at 375° for 50 minutes or until golden. Serve with ice cream or whipped cream. Yield: 6 to 8 servings.

Judy White

Today's Special: 25th Anniversary Cookbook from the Kitchens of Empire
Empire State Chapter FMCA
Scotia, New York

Bread Pudding with Whiskey Sauce

We think you'll agree this is one of the best bread puddings around–so good that it received our highest rating.

1 (1-pound) loaf dry French bread
4 cups milk
4 large eggs, beaten
2 cups sugar
2 tablespoons vanilla extract
1 cup raisins
2 apples, peeled, cored and cubed
1 (8-ounce) can crushed pineapple, drained
¼ cup butter, melted
Whiskey Sauce

Tear bread into small pieces; place in a large bowl. Add milk to bowl; let mixture stand 10 minutes. Stir mixture well with a wooden spoon. Add eggs, sugar, and vanilla; stir well. Stir in raisins, apple, and pineapple. Pour butter in a 13- x 9-inch pan; tilt pan to coat evenly. Spoon pudding mixture into pan. Bake, uncovered, at 350° for 55 to 60 minutes. Remove from oven, and cool slightly. Serve warm with Whiskey Sauce. Yield: 16 servings.

Whiskey Sauce

½ cup melted butter
1 cup sugar
⅓ cup bourbon, divided
1 large egg, beaten

Combine butter and sugar in a heavy saucepan; cook over medium heat until sugar dissolves. Add half of bourbon, and simmer 3 minutes; stirring well. Reduce heat to medium-low, and add egg; stir well. Remove from heat, and let stand 2 minutes. Stir in remaining bourbon. Yield: about 2 cups. Georgia Moncada

Note: To dry out fresh bread, tear bread into small pieces; bake at 200° for 1 hour, turning once.

The Heart of Pittsburgh
Sacred Heart Elementary School PTG
Pittsburgh, Pennsylvania

Chocolate Frostie

Cool off on triple-digit summer days with this frozen chocolate delight that resembles soft-serve ice cream. Serve it with either a spoon or a straw.

1 (14-ounce) can sweetened condensed milk
½ cup instant malted milk powder
1 cup chocolate syrup
6 cups chocolate milk
1 (16-ounce) container frozen whipped topping, thawed

Combine first 4 ingredients; fold in whipped topping. Pour mixture into freezer container of a 1-gallon hand-turned or electric freezer. Freeze according to manufacturer's instructions. Yield: about 4 quarts.

Sharon Craw

Culinary Tastes of Blue Mountain Cooks
Grand Terrace Branch Library: Friends
Grand Terrace, California

Grandma Olund's Oatmeal Cookies

For mailing or road-tripping, be sure to include a batch of these goodies. Their texture holds together well so you won't be disappointed with a box of crumbs at your final destination.

1 cup butter or margarine, softened
2 cups firmly packed brown sugar
2 large eggs
½ teaspoon baking soda
¼ cup hot water
2 cups all-purpose flour
1 teaspoon baking powder
½ teaspoon salt
4 cups regular oats, uncooked
1 cup flaked coconut
1 cup raisins
1 cup chopped pecans

Beat butter at medium speed with an electric mixer until creamy; gradually add brown sugar, beating well. Add eggs; beat well.

Combine soda and water, stirring well. Combine flour, baking powder, salt, and soda mixture; gradually add to butter mixture, beating well. Stir in oats and remaining ingredients.

Drop dough by heaping teaspoonfuls onto greased cookie sheets. Bake at 350° for 14 minutes or until lightly browned. Cool 2 minutes on cookie sheets; remove to wire racks to cool completely. Yield: about 6 dozen.

Pardie Olund

Recipes and Remembrances
Otsego County Historical Society
Gaylord, Michigan

Pound Cake Cookies

These cookies garnered a blue ribbon at a state fair competition. Once you taste these buttery gems, you'll agree that they're a hands-down winner for any occasion.

1 cup butter, softened
1 cup sugar
1 egg yolk
1 teaspoon rum or ½ teaspoon imitation rum flavoring
½ teaspoon vanilla extract
2¼ cups sifted cake flour
½ teaspoon salt
About 42 pecan halves

Beat butter at medium speed with an electric mixer until creamy; gradually add sugar, beating well. Add egg yolk, rum, and vanilla; beat well. Combine flour and salt in a bowl; gradually add to butter mixture, beating well. Cover and chill at least 2 hours or until firm.

Shape dough into 1-inch balls; place 2 inches apart on ungreased cookie sheets. Press 1 pecan half into each cookie.

Bake at 350° for 12 to 14 minutes or until edges are lightly browned. Cool 2 minutes on cookie sheets; remove to wire racks to cool completely. Yield: about 3½ dozen.

Down by the Water
The Junior League of Columbia, South Carolina

Award-Winning North Carolina Pecan Shortbread

"Award-winning" says it all about this spectacular shortbread. You can chill the dough up to two days before cutting and baking the dough, or you can freeze the dough up to a month.

1 cup all-purpose flour
½ cup pecans
¼ teaspoon salt
½ cup butter, softened
¼ cup firmly packed dark brown sugar
½ teaspoon almond extract
¼ teaspoon ground cinnamon

Process first 3 ingredients in a food processor 1 minute or until finely chopped.

Beat butter and sugar at medium speed with an electric mixer until creamy; add almond extract and cinnamon, beating well. Add flour mixture to butter mixture, beating well. Shape dough into a ball; cover and chill at least 8 hours.

Roll dough to ¼-inch thickness on a lightly floured surface. Cut with a 2-inch cookie cutter, and place on ungreased cookie sheets.

Bake at 300° for 25 minutes. Immediately remove cookies to wire racks to cool. Yield: 2 dozen.

Back to the Table
Episcopal Church Women—Christ Church
Raleigh, North Carolina

Quick & Easy Recipes

BLTs with a Twist, page 43

Hot Pepper Jelly Spread

2 cups (8 ounces) shredded sharp Cheddar cheese
1 bunch green onions, chopped (about 1 cup)
½ cup chopped pecans, toasted
2 tablespoons hot jalapeño jelly
1 tablespoon mayonnaise

Combine all ingredients, stirring well. Serve immediately, or cover and chill. Serve with crackers. Yield: 2 cups. Nan Sibley

Madalene Cooks–50 Years of Good Taste
Church of the Madalene
Tulsa, Oklahoma

English Muffin Cheese Snacks

2 cups (8 ounces) shredded sharp Cheddar cheese
1 bunch green onions, finely chopped (about 1 cup)
¼ cup butter or margarine, softened
¼ cup mayonnaise
6 English muffins, split

Combine first 4 ingredients in a medium bowl, stirring well. Spread mixture evenly over English muffin halves; place on a baking sheet. Broil 5½ inches from heat 4 minutes or until bubbly and lightly browned. Cut each muffin half into fourths. Yield: 12 appetizer servings. Claudia Noe

Doggone Good Cookin'
Support Dogs, Inc.
St. Louis, Missouri

Eggnog Punch

The "punch" in this nog comes from the lemon-lime soda. It's the perfect solution to a quick, kid-friendly holiday beverage.

1 quart refrigerated eggnog
1 pint vanilla ice cream, softened
1 (1-liter) bottle lemon-lime soft drink, chilled (we used 7UP)
Ground nutmeg

Combine eggnog and ice cream in a punch bowl, stirring well. Add carbonated beverage just before serving; sprinkle with nutmeg. Serve immediately. Yield: 14 cups. Sharri Hackbarth

The Cookbook Tour
Good Shepherd Lutheran Church
Plainview, Minnesota

Easy Pudding Milk Shake

Kids will love this easy shake! Feel free to substitute your favorite pudding mix and ice cream flavors.

3 cups milk
1½ cups chocolate ice cream, softened
1 (3.9-ounce) package chocolate instant pudding mix

Process all ingredients in container of an electric blender on low until smooth, stopping occasionally to scrape down sides. (Blender will be very full.) Serve immediately, or cover and chill up to 8 hours. Stir well before serving. Yield: 5 cups. Ashley Ockey

Panthers' Pantry
Children's Educational Foundation
Madera, California

Butter-Me-Nots

Just stir the three ingredients and bake. Muffins don't get any better than this!

2 cups self-rising flour
1 (8-ounce) carton sour cream
1 cup butter, melted

Combine all ingredients. Spoon batter into lightly greased miniature (1¾-inch) muffin pans, filling full. Bake at 400° for 15 minutes or until golden. Yield: 3 dozen.

Simply Divine
Second-Ponce de Leon Baptist Church
Atlanta, Georgia

Cheese Muffins

For a kick, try sharp Cheddar or pepperjack cheese in place of American.

2 tablespoons butter or margarine, divided
½ cup chopped onion
1½ cups biscuit mix
1 cup (4 ounces) shredded American cheese, divided
½ cup milk
1 large egg, beaten
1 tablespoon sesame seeds, toasted

Melt 1 tablespoon butter in a small skillet over medium-high heat. Add onion; sauté 3 minutes or until tender. Combine onion mixture, biscuit mix, and ½ cup cheese in a medium bowl; make a well in center of mixture. Combine milk and egg; add to dry ingredients, stirring just until moistened. Spoon batter into greased muffin pans, filling half full. Sprinkle with remaining ½ cup cheese and sesame seeds. Dot with remaining 1 tablespoon butter. Bake at 400° for 13 minutes or until muffins are golden. Remove from pans immediately. Yield: 9 muffins.

Lolita Leahy Smith

Noel Bluffin' We're Still Cookin'
Noel Area Chamber of Commerce
Noel, Missouri

Barbecued Flank Steak

1½ pounds flank steak
¼ cup soy sauce
¼ cup vegetable oil
2 tablespoons cider vinegar
2 tablespoons honey
½ teaspoon ground ginger
¼ teaspoon garlic powder

Score steak diagonally across grain at ¾-inch intervals. Place steak in a large heavy-duty, zip-top plastic bag or shallow dish. Combine soy sauce and remaining 5 ingredients. Pour ½ cup marinade over steak; seal or cover, and marinate in refrigerator 8 hours, turning occasionally. Cover and chill remaining marinade.

Remove steak from marinade, discarding marinade. Grill steak, without grill lid, over medium-high heat (350° to 400°) 8 to 10 minutes on each side or to desired degree of doneness, basting with reserved marinade during last 5 minutes. To serve, slice diagonally across grain. Yield: 4 servings. Sharon and Colby Cox

Sharing Our Best
Bull Run Parent Teacher Club
Sandy, Oregon

Honey Pork Tenderloin

⅓ cup soy sauce
½ teaspoon ground ginger
5 garlic cloves, crushed
2 (12-ounce) pork tenderloins
2 tablespoons brown sugar
3 tablespoons honey
2 teaspoons dark sesame oil

Combine first 3 ingredients in a shallow dish. Add pork, turning to coat. Cover and marinate in refrigerator 8 hours, turning occasionally.

Remove tenderloins from marinade, discarding marinade.

Combine sugar, honey, and oil in a saucepan; cook over low heat until sugar dissolves. Grill pork, covered with grill lid, over medium heat (300° to 350°) 20 minutes or until a meat thermometer inserted in thickest part registers 160°, turning once and basting occasionally with honey mixture. Yield: 4 servings. Blythe Orr Bowman

Beyond Cotton Country
The Junior League of Morgan County
Decatur, Alabama

Sausage, Peppers, and Mushrooms

This chunky blend doubles as a one-dish meal served with a knife and fork or as a sandwich filling spooned over French rolls.

1 (1¼-pound) package Italian sausage links
1 cup dry white wine
1 medium onion, sliced
1 garlic clove, minced
2 medium-size green bell peppers, cut into strips
1 (8-ounce) package sliced fresh mushrooms
2 (8-ounce) cans tomato sauce

Brown sausage in a 10-inch cast-iron skillet; add wine. Bring to a boil; cover, reduce heat, and simmer 10 minutes or until sausage is done. Uncover, bring to a boil, and reduce wine by two-thirds. Remove sausage, reserving drippings in skillet; set sausage aside, and keep warm.

Add onion, garlic, green pepper, and mushrooms to skillet; sauté until tender. Return sausage to skillet; add tomato sauce. Simmer 10 minutes or to desired consistency. Yield: 5 servings. John Lamantia

Tutto Bene
Salvatore Mancini Lodge #2440
North Providence, Rhode Island

Fettuccine al Mascarpone

1 (16-ounce) package dried fettuccine
2 tablespoons unsalted butter, softened
5 thin slices prosciutto, coarsely chopped (about 4 ounces)
12 fresh basil leaves, chopped
¼ cup freshly grated Parmesan cheese
¾ teaspoon freshly ground pepper
½ teaspoon salt
4 ounces mascarpone cheese

Cook pasta according to package directions; drain.

Toss hot pasta with softened butter in a serving bowl. Sprinkle prosciutto and next 4 ingredients over pasta; toss well. Add mascarpone; toss until well blended. Yield: 6 servings. Fran Holland

Rave Reviews
Ogunquit Playhouse
Ogunquit, Maine

BLTs with a Twist

The novelty behind this bacon, lettuce, and tomato sandwich is using dried tomatoes, fresh basil, and goat cheese. It's also a unique way to make one large sandwich that serves four.

8 bacon slices
1 (1-pound) French bread loaf (not baguette)
¼ cup chopped fresh basil
6 ounces goat cheese
½ cup (about 3 ounces) dried tomatoes in oil, drained and chopped
4 lettuce leaves
½ small purple onion, thinly sliced

Cook bacon in a large skillet until crisp; drain on paper towels. Set aside.

Slice bread in half horizontally. Sprinkle basil over cut side of bottom half of loaf; crumble goat cheese over basil. Sprinkle tomatoes over goat cheese. Top with top half of loaf. Place loaf on a baking sheet; bake at 325° for 10 minutes.

Remove loaf from oven; remove top half of loaf. Arrange bacon, lettuce, and onion over tomatoes; replace top half of loaf. Yield: 4 servings.

Gary Moon

Bread from the Brook
The Church at Brook Hills
Birmingham, Alabama

Chicken à la King

- **1 (10-ounce) package frozen puff pastry shells**
- **½ cup chopped green bell pepper**
- **2 tablespoons butter, melted**
- **1 (10¾-ounce) can cream of chicken soup, undiluted**
- **½ cup milk**
- **2 cups chopped cooked chicken (about 4 skinned and boned chicken breast halves)**
- **1 (2-ounce) jar diced pimiento, drained**

Bake pastry shells according to package directions.

Meanwhile, sauté green pepper in butter in a large skillet until tender. Add soup and milk; stir until smooth. Stir in chicken and pimiento. Cook over medium-high heat, stirring constantly, until heated. Spoon chicken mixture into pastry shells. Yield 4 to 6 servings.

Simply the Best . . . Recipes by Design
Columbus Area Visitors Center
Columbus, Indiana

Home Run Nuggets

No more drive-thru dinners for your family once they taste these winning nuggets. And don't forget to add a dipping sauce!

- **1½ pounds skinned and boned chicken breast halves**
- **1 large egg**
- **2 tablespoons water**
- **1 (1-ounce) envelope onion soup mix**
- **¾ cup fine, dry breadcrumbs (store-bought)**
- **¼ cup butter, melted**

Cut chicken into 1-inch squares. Combine egg and water. Combine soup mix and breadcrumbs. Dip chicken in egg mixture; dredge in breadcrumb mixture. Arrange chicken on a lightly greased shallow roasting pan. Drizzle chicken with melted butter. Bake at 400° for 15 minutes or until done, turning once. Yield: 4 to 6 servings.

It's a Snap!
The Haven of Grace
St. Louis, Missouri

Turkey Cutlets Française

1 pound turkey cutlets
1 large egg
1 tablespoon water
2 tablespoons grated Parmesan cheese
⅓ cup all-purpose flour
½ teaspoon salt
¼ teaspoon ground white pepper
4 teaspoons margarine, divided
¼ cup lemon juice
2 tablespoons chopped fresh parsley

Pat cutlets dry with paper towels.

Combine egg and water; beat well. Stir in Parmesan cheese. Combine flour, salt, and pepper. Dip cutlets in egg mixture; dredge in flour mixture.

Heat 2 teaspoons margarine in a large skillet over medium-high heat. Add half of cutlets; sauté 2 minutes on each side or until lightly browned. Transfer to a serving platter; keep warm. Repeat procedure with remaining margarine and cutlets.

Add lemon juice to skillet; deglaze skillet by scraping particles that cling to bottom. Pour over cutlets. Sprinkle with chopped parsley. Yield: 3 servings.
Barbara Ruderman

We Cook Too
Women's Committee, Wadsworth Atheneum
West Hartford, Connecticut

Baked Orange Roughy

4 (6-ounce) orange roughy fillets (1 inch thick)
3 tablespoons freshly shredded Parmesan cheese
1 teaspoon dried dillweed

Arrange fillets in a single layer in a lightly greased 15- x 10-inch jellyroll pan. Combine Parmesan cheese and dillweed. Sprinkle over fillets. Bake at 450° for 7 to 9 minutes or until fish flakes with a fork. Yield: 4 servings.
Cindy DeHaven

Bread from the Brook
The Church at Brook Hills
Birmingham, Alabama

Sidecar Salmon

1 large purple onion, chopped
2 tablespoons olive oil
4 (8-ounce) salmon fillets (about 1½ inches thick)
½ cup reduced-sodium soy sauce

Cook onion in hot oil in a large skillet over medium-high heat, stirring constantly, 5 minutes. Arrange salmon on top of onion. Pour soy sauce over fillets. Bring to a boil; cover, reduce heat, and simmer 10 minutes or until fish flakes with a fork. Transfer fish to a serving platter, and keep warm.

Cook onion mixture over medium-high heat 5 minutes or until liquid evaporates. Spoon onion mixture over salmon. Yield: 4 servings.

Mary Baker Robbins

Victorian Secrets
The Chiselers, Inc.
Tampa, Florida

Betty's Scallop Fettuccine

1½ pounds bay scallops
1 tablespoon olive oil
1 tablespoon butter, melted
½ cup whipping cream
2 tablespoons chopped fresh parsley
½ teaspoon minced fresh garlic
8 ounces dried fettuccine, uncooked
¾ cup freshly shredded Parmesan cheese
½ teaspoon salt
Freshly ground pepper

Sauté scallops in hot oil and butter in a large skillet 2 to 3 minutes. Drain scallops, reserving ½ cup liquid. Add cream, parsley, garlic, and reserved scallop liquid. Bring to a simmer; remove from heat.

Cook fettuccine according to package directions, and drain. Combine fettuccine, Parmesan cheese, and salt in a large bowl. Toss scallop mixture with fettuccine mixture. Sprinkle with pepper. Yield: 4 servings.

Wende Waggoner Berryhill

St. Andrew's Cooks Again
Presbyterian Women of St. Andrew
Beaumont, Texas

Sautéed Shrimp with Lemon Sauce

1 pound unpeeled large fresh shrimp, peeled and deveined
3 tablespoons olive oil
2 large garlic cloves, minced
3 to 4 tablespoons fresh lemon juice
1 tablespoon finely chopped fresh parsley
½ teaspoon salt
⅛ teaspoon ground white pepper or ¼ teaspoon ground black pepper

Sauté shrimp in hot oil in a large skillet over medium-high heat just until shrimp turn pink; reduce heat to medium. Add garlic, lemon juice, and parsley; cook 1 minute. Sprinkle with salt and pepper. Serve with French bread or pita bread. Yield: 2 servings.

Bay Tables
The Junior League of Mobile, Alabama

Easy Chiles Rellenos

2 (4.5-ounce) cans chopped green chiles, undrained
1 pound Monterey Jack cheese, cut into ½-inch cubes
1 (2¼-ounce) can sliced ripe olives, drained
4 large eggs, lightly beaten
½ cup milk
½ teaspoon dry mustard
¼ teaspoon salt

Layer one-third each of green chiles, cheese, and olives in a greased 11- x 7-inch baking dish. Repeat layers twice. Combine eggs and remaining 3 ingredients in a medium bowl; pour over cheese mixture.

Bake, uncovered, at 325° for 35 minutes. Remove from oven, and let stand 5 minutes before serving. Cut into squares to serve. Yield: 4 to 6 servings.

The Dining Car
The Service League of Denison, Texas

Wild Mushroom and Fontina Pizza

3 large shallots, thinly sliced
2 tablespoons olive oil
8 ounces shiitake mushrooms, stems removed
3 large plum tomatoes, chopped
2 tablespoons chopped fresh thyme
2 tablespoons red wine vinegar
¼ teaspoon salt
¼ teaspoon pepper
1 (16-ounce) Italian bread shell (we tested with Boboli)
10 ounces fontina cheese, grated and divided
½ cup freshly grated Parmesan cheese

Sauté shallots in oil in a skillet over medium-high heat 1 minute or until tender. Add mushrooms; cook, stirring constantly, 2 minutes. Stir in tomato and next 4 ingredients; remove from heat. Place bread shell on a 12-inch pizza pan. Top with three-quarters of fontina cheese and all of vegetable mixture. Sprinkle with remaining cheeses. Bake at 500° for 12 minutes. Yield: 4 servings. Amy Boettcher

Tried and True from Riverview
Riverview Hospital Auxiliary
Wisconsin Rapids, Wisconsin

Chili of the '90s

Black beans and picante sauce pinpoint the origin of this popular southwestern-style chili.

1 pound ground chuck
1 large onion, chopped
3 cups water
2 (14½-ounce) cans diced chili-style tomatoes, undrained
2 (15-ounce) cans black beans, rinsed and drained
1 (16-ounce) jar picante sauce
½ teaspoon ground cumin
Shredded Cheddar cheese

Brown beef and onion in a Dutch oven, stirring until it crumbles; drain. Stir in water and next 4 ingredients. Bring to a boil; reduce heat, and simmer, uncovered, 10 minutes, stirring occasionally. Sprinkle each serving with cheese. Yield: 11 cups. Judy Rust

St. Andrew's Cooks Again
Presbyterian Women of St. Andrew
Beaumont, Texas

Kiwifruit Ambrosia

1 kiwifruit
1 (20-ounce) can pineapple slices in heavy syrup, undrained
1 (11-ounce) can mandarin orange sections, drained
¼ cup flaked coconut

Peel kiwifruit, and cut into ½-inch chunks; set aside. Drain pineapple, reserving syrup. Cut pineapple slices into chunks. Combine mandarin oranges, kiwifruit, pineapple, reserved syrup, and flaked coconut in a medium bowl. Let stand 15 minutes before serving. Yield: 4 to 6 servings. Loretta Ainsworth

Down Home Dining in Mississippi
Mississippi Homemaker Volunteers, Inc.
Water Valley, Mississippi

Phyllis's Favorite Carrot Salad

Celery and walnuts add crunch, while raisins and pineapple sweeten this vitamin-packed salad.

2 cups grated carrot (about 5 carrots)
1 (8-ounce) can pineapple tidbits in heavy syrup, undrained
½ cup raisins
½ cup sliced celery
½ cup chopped walnuts
¼ cup mayonnaise
1 tablespoon fresh lemon juice
¼ teaspoon salt

Toss together all ingredients in a medium bowl. Cover and chill. Yield: 4 to 6 servings. Phyllis Shelton

NPT's Community Cookbook
Neighborhood Pride Team
Portland, Oregon

Raspberry-Spinach Salad

2 tablespoons raspberry vinegar
2 tablespoons seedless raspberry jam
⅓ cup corn oil
4 cups torn fresh spinach, tightly packed (about 5 ounces)
1 (3.5-ounce) jar lightly salted macadamia nuts, chopped
1 cup fresh raspberries
3 kiwifruit, peeled and sliced

Process vinegar and jam in container of an electric blender until smooth, stopping once to scrape down sides. With blender on high, gradually add oil in a slow, steady stream; blend until thickened.

Combine spinach and remaining 3 ingredients in a large bowl. Drizzle with dressing, and toss gently. Yield: 6 servings.

Tested by Time
Porter Gaud Parents Guild
Charleston, South Carolina

Green Beans with Bacon and Mushrooms

1 (12-ounce) package sliced bacon
1 small onion, chopped
3 (9-ounce) packages frozen whole green beans, thawed
2 (4½-ounce) cans sliced mushrooms, drained
1 tablespoon sugar

Cook bacon in a large skillet until crisp; remove bacon, reserving 1 tablespoon drippings in skillet. Crumble bacon, and set aside.

Cook onion in reserved bacon drippings, stirring constantly, until tender. Stir in greens beans, mushrooms, and sugar; cover and cook over medium heat 10 minutes. Spoon green beans into a serving dish; sprinkle with bacon. Yield: 8 to 10 servings. Becky Welborn

Cooking Up Memories
The Tazewell County Genealogical and Historical Society
Pekin, Illinois

Peas and Cashews

2 (10-ounce) packages frozen sweet green peas in butter
½ cup sliced fresh mushrooms
½ cup chopped celery
3 green onions, sliced
¼ cup butter or margarine, melted
½ cup salted cashews

Cook peas according to package directions.

Meanwhile, sauté mushrooms, celery, and green onions in butter until tender. Stir vegetables into peas; cook until thoroughly heated. Sprinkle with cashews. Yield: 6 servings. Chuck and Jackie Moore

North Country Cooking
51st National Square Dance Convention
St. Paul, Minnesota

Rice Pilaf

This simple side dish pairs nicely with a high-flavored entrée.

1 tablespoon olive oil
1 cup uncooked long-grain rice
2½ cups chicken broth
½ cup coarsely chopped walnuts or pecans, toasted

Heat olive oil in a large skillet over medium-high heat until hot. Add rice; sauté 3 to 5 minutes or just until rice is light brown.

Meanwhile, bring broth to a boil in a large saucepan. Gradually add rice to broth; cover, reduce heat, and simmer 25 minutes or until liquid is absorbed and rice is tender. Stir in walnuts. Yield: 4 servings.

Out of the Ordinary
The Hingham Historical Society
Hingham, Massachusetts

Saffron Rice

1 small onion, chopped
½ cup butter, melted
2 cups uncooked long-grain rice
¼ teaspoon ground saffron
1 (32-ounce) carton chicken broth
¼ teaspoon freshly ground pepper
½ cup raisins

Sauté onion in butter in a Dutch oven 5 minutes. Stir in rice and saffron; sauté 5 minutes.

Add broth and pepper; bring to a boil. Cover, reduce heat, and simmer 20 minutes or until liquid is absorbed and rice is tender. Remove from heat, and stir in raisins. Cover and let stand 5 minutes. Yield: 6 servings.

The Cookbook of the Museum of Science, Boston
The Volunteer Service League of the Museum of Science, Boston
Boston, Massachusetts

Banana Pudding Cake

Cake and pudding mixes lend a helping hand in the preparation of this dessert that's similar to pound cake.

1 (18.25-ounce) package yellow cake mix (we tested with Duncan Hines)
1 (3.4-ounce) package vanilla instant pudding mix
4 large eggs
1 cup water
½ cup mashed ripe banana (about 1 medium)
¼ cup vegetable oil

Combine all ingredients in a mixing bowl. Beat at medium speed with an electric mixer until blended. Pour into a greased 10-inch tube pan. Bake at 350° for 50 to 55 minutes or until a wooden pick inserted in center comes out clean. Cool in pan on a wire rack 15 minutes; remove from pan, and let cool completely on wire rack. Yield: 1 (10-inch) cake.

The Tastes and Tales of Moiliili
Moiliili Community Center
Honolulu, Hawaii

No-Bake Blueberry Pie

Blueberries simmer on the cooktop into a thick, rich filling for this easy pie. No-bake in the title refers to the filling, but you'll need to bake the pie shell to make it crisp and golden.

4 cups fresh blueberries, divided
1 cup sugar
¾ cup hot water
2 tablespoons cornstarch
¼ teaspoon salt
¼ teaspoon ground cinnamon
2 tablespoons fresh lemon juice
1 baked 9-inch pastry shell
Sweetened whipped cream

Combine 1 cup blueberries, sugar, and next 4 ingredients in a saucepan. Cook, stirrring constantly, over medium-high heat until mixture thickens. Add remaining 3 cups blueberries and lemon juice; stir gently. Spoon into pastry shell; cover and chill 1 hour or until set. Serve pie with sweetened whipped cream. Yield: 1 (9-inch) pie.

Out of the Ordinary
The Hingham Historical Society
Hingham, Massachusetts

Real Easy Chocolate Pie

For a smooth and silky pie, use a plain milk chocolate bar.

1 (7-ounce) milk chocolate bar with almonds (we tested with Hershey's)
2 tablespoons water
1 (8-ounce) container frozen whipped topping, thawed
1 (6-ounce) graham cracker crust

Combine chocolate and water in a microwave-safe bowl. Microwave at MEDIUM (50% power) 1½ to 2 minutes; stir until smooth. Fold in whipped topping; pour into crust. Cover and chill 8 hours. Yield: 1 (9-inch) pie.

Lea Fortgang

Best and Blessed
Sweet Spirit Singers
Liberty, Mississippi

Lillian Fuller's Lemon Pie

1 (14-ounce) can sweetened condensed milk
¼ cup fresh lemon juice (about 2 lemons)
1 cup whipping cream, whipped
1 (6-ounce) graham cracker crust

Fold condensed milk and lemon juice into whipped cream; pour into crust. Cover and chill 4 hours or until pie is firm. Yield: 6 to 8 servings.

Lillian Fuller

A Cookery & Memories from Old Bourne
The Bourne Society for Historic Preservation
Bourne, Massachusetts

Turtle Cookies

2 cups all-purpose flour
1 cup firmly packed brown sugar
½ cup butter or margarine, softened
1 cup pecan halves
⅔ cup butter
½ cup firmly packed brown sugar
1 cup milk chocolate morsels

Combine first 3 ingredients in a mixing bowl; beat well. Pat mixture firmly into an ungreased 13- x 9-inch pan. Arrange pecans over crust.

Combine ⅔ cup butter and ½ cup brown sugar in a saucepan. Bring to a boil over medium heat, stirring constantly; cook 3 minutes, stirring constantly. Spoon mixture over pecans. Bake at 350° for 15 to 17 minutes or until golden and bubbly.

Remove from oven; sprinkle top with chocolate morsels. Let stand 2 to 3 minutes or until slightly melted. Gently swirl chocolate with a knife, leaving some morsels whole (do not spread); let cool. Cut into squares. Yield: 20 cookies.

Helen Kelly

Over the Bridge
Corpus Christie Women's Guild
East Sandwich, Massachusetts

Black Bottom Special

This ice cream shake is sweet and chocolaty enough to double as dessert. Substitute 1/4 teaspoon ground cinnamon for the coffee granules, if you'd like.

3/4 cup chocolate syrup
1 quart vanilla ice cream, softened
1 1/2 cups milk
1 tablespoon instant coffee granules
Shaved chocolate (optional)

Spoon 3 tablespoons chocolate syrup into each of 4 glasses. Stir ice cream to soften; quickly stir in milk and coffee. Pour evenly over chocolate syrup. Sprinkle with shaved chocolate, if desired. Yield: 4 servings.

Bonnie Scherer

Our Heritage Cookbook
First Baptist Church
Billings, Montana

Quick Chocolate Mousse

For an added flavor boost, stir 1 to 2 teaspoons coffee liqueur or orange liqueur into the melted chocolate mixture. Look for good quality dark chocolate on the candy or baking aisle of your supermarket.

5 ounces dark chocolate, chopped (we tested with Perugina by Nestle)
1 1/4 cups whipping cream

Combine chocolate and whipping cream in a heavy saucepan. Cook over medium-low heat, stirring constantly, until chocolate melts and mixture is smooth. Remove from heat, and let cool completely. Cover and chill at least 8 hours.

Just before serving, beat chocolate mixture at medium-high speed with an electric mixer until mixture thickens to desired consistency. Spoon into individual dessert dishes. Yield: 5 servings.

Made in the Shade
The Junior League of Greater Fort Lauderdale, Florida

Easy Homemade Vanilla Ice Cream

No ice cream is easier–no cooking or chilling in advance is required!

1 (14-ounce) can sweetened condensed milk
1 quart half-and-half
1 tablespoon vanilla extract

Pour all ingredients into freezer container of a 4-quart hand-turned or electric freezer. Freeze according to manufacturer's instructions.

Pack freezer with additional ice and rock salt, and let stand 1 hour before serving. Yield: 6 cups.

Fresh Fruit Ice Cream

Decrease half-and-half to 3 cups. Add 1 to 1½ cups fresh fruit puree, such as peaches, strawberries, bananas, or raspberries. Yield: 7 cups.

Mint Chocolate Chip Ice Cream

Decrease half-and-half to 2 cups and omit vanilla. Add 2 teaspoons peppermint extract, 2 cups whipping cream, and ¾ cup miniature semisweet chocolate morsels. Add a few drops of green food coloring, if desired. Yield: 7 cups.

Picnics, Potlucks & Prizewinners
Indiana 4-H Foundation
Indianapolis, Indiana

Strawberries Jessica

½ cup heavy whipping cream
½ cup sour cream
2 tablespoons sugar
1 tablespoon lemon juice
3 pints strawberries, sliced

Combine first 4 ingredients; stir well. Spoon cream mixture over sliced strawberries. Yield: 6 servings. Joanna Conti Pritchard

Generations of Good Food
Jeannette Public Library
Jeannette, Pennsylvania

Appetizers & Beverages

Honey Chicken Wings, page 66

Coyote Caviar

- **1 (15-ounce) can black beans, rinsed and drained**
- **1 (4¼-ounce) can chopped ripe olives**
- **1 (4½-ounce) can chopped green chiles**
- **1 small onion, finely chopped**
- **1 garlic clove, minced**
- **¼ cup chopped fresh cilantro**
- **2 tablespoons vegetable oil**
- **2 tablespoons lime juice**
- **2 teaspoons chili powder**
- **1 teaspoon black pepper**
- **¼ teaspoon salt**
- **¼ teaspoon dried crushed red pepper**
- **¼ teaspoon ground cumin**
- **1 (8-ounce) package cream cheese, softened**
- **2 hard-cooked eggs, peeled and chopped**
- **2 tablespoons chopped green onions**
- **Tortilla chips**

Stir together first 13 ingredients in a bowl. Cover and chill at least 2 hours.

To serve, spread softened cream cheese on a round serving platter. Spoon bean mixture over cream cheese. Sprinkle egg around edge of bean mixture. Sprinkle green onions over bean mixture. Serve with tortilla chips. Yield: 12 appetizer servings. Patti Hunter

Southern Elegance: A Second Course
The Junior League of Gaston County
Gastonia, North Carolina

That Junior League Pesto Mold

The title of this recipe hints that it's the talk of the party whenever it's served, and we understand why. Not only does it taste exceptional, but it's easy to make ahead and it unmolds to make a stately presentation with ribbons of pretty green pesto layered between cream cheese whipped with butter.

2 (8-ounce) packages cream cheese, softened
1 pound unsalted butter, softened
¼ cup pine nuts, toasted
2 or 3 garlic cloves
1 cup tightly packed fresh spinach leaves
1 cup tightly packed fresh basil
½ cup fresh parsley, stems removed
½ teaspoon salt
½ cup olive oil
3 cups freshly grated Parmesan cheese (about ¾ pound)
3 tablespoons butter, softened
Garnish: fresh parsley sprigs

Beat cream cheese and 1 pound butter at medium speed with an electric mixer until smooth; set aside.

Process pine nuts, garlic, spinach, basil, parsley, and salt in a large food processor until smooth, stopping once to scrape down sides. Gradually pour olive oil through food chute with processor running; process until well blended. Add Parmesan cheese and 3 tablespoons butter; process just until blended.

Line a 6-cup mold with an 18-inch piece of cheesecloth or heavy-duty plastic wrap, smoothing any wrinkles. Place one-fourth of cream cheese mixture in an even layer in prepared mold; top with one-fourth of pesto mixture. Repeat layers three times, using remaining cream cheese and pesto mixtures. Fold cheesecloth or plastic wrap over top, and pack down lightly. Chill at least 8 hours.

About 30 minutes before serving, unfold cheesecloth or plastic wrap, and invert mold onto a serving platter. Carefully peel away cheesecloth or plastic wrap. Garnish platter, if desired. Serve with water crackers or thinly sliced baguettes. Yield: 24 to 30 appetizer servings.

Gracious Gator Cooks
The Junior League of Gainesville, Florida

Cold Smoked Salmon Soufflé

Cream cheese and sour cream spiked with Madeira and fresh dill create a heavenly base to lace with smoked salmon. Cream cheese and gelatin make this mold a little denser than a traditional soufflé and perfect for spreading on bagel chips or Belgian endive.

2 envelopes unflavored gelatin
¼ cup Madeira
½ cup chopped purple onion
3 shallots, chopped
1 (16-ounce) container sour cream
2 (8-ounce) packages cream cheese, softened
2 tablespoons grated lemon rind
½ cup minced fresh dill
1 teaspoon salt
½ teaspoon ground white pepper
1 pound thinly sliced smoked salmon, finely chopped
Garnishes: fresh dill sprigs, grated lemon rind

Sprinkle gelatin over Madeira in a small microwave-safe bowl; stir and let stand 1 minute. Microwave at HIGH 15 seconds; stir until gelatin dissolves. Set aside.

Process onion and shallots in a food processor until very finely chopped, stopping once to scrape down sides. Add sour cream, cream cheese, lemon rind, dill, salt, pepper, and reserved gelatin mixture; process until well blended, stopping once to scrape down sides. Transfer mixture to a large bowl; fold in salmon.

Pour salmon mixture into a lightly oiled 8-cup mold lined with plastic wrap. Cover and chill 4 hours or until firm.

About 30 minutes before serving, invert mold onto a platter, and peel away plastic wrap. Garnish, if desired. Serve with bagel chips, pumpernickel squares, or Belgian endive. Yield: 7½ cups (about 30 appetizer servings).

Lore M. Dodge

De Nuestra Mesa: Our Food, Wine, and Tradition
New Hope Charities, Inc.
West Palm Beach, Florida

Artichoke Loaf

A dense and cheesy artichoke mixture bakes inside shells made from pumpernickel bread loaves. Cut the bread removed from the loaves into serving-size pieces to use as dippers.

2 (7-inch-round) loaves pumpernickel bread
2 tablespoons butter or margarine, softened
1½ cups (6 ounces) shredded Cheddar cheese, divided
2 (14-ounce) cans artichoke hearts, drained and chopped
1 (4.5-ounce) can chopped green chiles
1 (6-ounce) jar marinated artichoke hearts, undrained
2 tablespoons mayonnaise
¼ teaspoon paprika
Tortilla chips

Using a serrated knife, slice off top one-third of 1 bread loaf. Hollow out bottom of loaf, leaving a ½-inch shell. Cut top of loaf and hollowed-out portions into bite-size pieces; set aside. Repeat with remaining bread loaf. Place loaves on a large baking sheet.

Spread 1 tablespoon softened butter into bottom of each bread shell. Sprinkle ½ cup cheese over bottom of each bread shell. Sprinkle chopped artichokes over cheese. Sprinkle green chiles over artichokes.

Drain marinated artichoke hearts, reserving 1 teaspoon marinade. Chop marinated artichokes; combine with 1 teaspoon marinade. Sprinkle marinated artichokes over green chiles. Spread 1 tablespoon mayonnaise over top layer of each bread loaf. Sprinkle each loaf evenly with remaining cheese and paprika.

Bake at 350° for 30 minutes or until slightly bubbly. During last 5 minutes of baking, toast reserved bread cubes on a baking sheet. Serve loaf with toasted bread cubes and tortilla chips. Yield: 14 to 16 appetizer servings.

Secrets of Amelia
McArthur Family Branch YMCA
Fernandina Beach, Florida

Sandy's Pizza Dip

Dip into melted mozzarella to discover your favorite pizza toppings sprinkled underneath.

1 (8-ounce) package cream cheese, softened
½ cup sour cream
1 teaspoon dried oregano
⅛ teaspoon garlic powder
⅛ teaspoon dried crushed red pepper
½ cup pizza sauce
½ cup chopped pepperoni
¼ cup chopped onion
¼ cup chopped green pepper
½ cup (2 ounces) shredded mozzarella cheese

Stir together first 5 ingredients; spoon into a 9-inch pieplate. Spread pizza sauce over cream cheese mixture. Sprinkle pepperoni, onion, and green pepper over sauce. Bake at 350° for 10 minutes. Sprinkle with mozzarella cheese; bake 5 more minutes or until cheese melts. Serve warm with breadsticks, melba toast rounds, baguette slices, or crackers. Yield: 10 to 12 appetizer servings.

Hearthside: A Country Community Cookbook
Christ Community Church
Weare, New Hampshire

Mushroom Pâté

Crumbled bacon adds crunch to this warm mushroom spread that's delicious simply served with melba toast or crackers.

4 slices bacon
1 cup chopped onion
1 (8-ounce) package cream cheese
8 ounces fresh mushrooms, chopped
½ cup sour cream
Ground white pepper (optional)

Cook bacon in a Dutch oven until crisp. Remove bacon, and crumble, reserving drippings in Dutch oven; set bacon aside.

Sauté chopped onion in bacon drippings 4 minutes or until onion is tender. Reduce heat to medium, and add cream cheese; cook, stirring constantly, until cream cheese melts. Add chopped mushrooms, and cook until mixture is thoroughly heated. Remove from heat. Stir in sour cream, crumbled bacon, and pepper, if desired. Spoon mixture into a 1-quart baking dish; bake at 325° for 30 minutes. Serve immediately with melba toast or crackers. Yield: 3 cups (12 appetizer servings).

Jan Dolfi

We Cook Too
Women's Committee, Wadsworth Atheneum
West Hartford, Connecticut

Bleu Cheese Ball

The belle of this ball is the whole package of crumbled blue cheese that's mixed with black olives and cream cheese and then rolled in crunchy pecans.

1 (8-ounce) package cream cheese, softened
1 (4-ounce) container crumbled blue cheese
½ cup chopped ripe olives
1 teaspoon Worcestershire sauce
1 cup finely chopped pecans

Combine first 4 ingredients in a bowl, stirring until blended. Shape into a ball, using wet hands; roll in pecans. Cover and chill thoroughly. Yield: 8 to 10 servings.

Gator Championship Recipes
Florida Goal-Liners
McIntosh, Florida

Parmesan-Coated Brie

Enhance a round of Brie with this coating of Parmesan cheese and Italian breadcrumbs. It's cooked to a golden crunch which warms the cheese inside perfectly for spreading over French bread or crackers.

1 large egg, lightly beaten
1 tablespoon water
½ cup Italian-seasoned breadcrumbs
¼ cup freshly grated Parmesan cheese
1 (15-ounce) round Brie cheese with herbs
¼ cup vegetable oil
Garnish: fresh rosemary sprigs

Combine egg and water in a shallow dish; set aside. Combine breadcrumbs and Parmesan cheese in a shallow dish. Dip Brie round in egg mixture, turning to coat all sides. Dredge in breadcrumb mixture, turning to coat all sides. Repeat procedure. Chill at least 1 hour for coating to set.

Heat oil in a small skillet over medium heat. Cook Brie round in hot oil 2 minutes on each side or until golden. Garnish, if desired. Serve with sliced French bread or crackers. Yield: 10 to 12 appetizer servings.

Southern . . . On Occasion
The Junior League of Cobb-Marietta
Marietta, Georgia

Fried Mozzarella Sticks

You won't keep these cheesy snacks around for long! Serve with marinara sauce for dipping.

1 pound mozzarella cheese
½ cup all-purpose flour
¼ teaspoon salt
¼ teaspoon pepper
2 large eggs, lightly beaten
1 cup Italian-seasoned breadcrumbs
Vegetable oil

Cut mozzarella into 18 (3½- x ½-inch) sticks. Combine flour, salt, and pepper. Dip cheese sticks into egg; dredge in flour mixture, and dip again in egg. Roll in breadcrumbs; press firmly so crumbs adhere. Place on wax paper, and chill 30 minutes.

Pour oil to depth of 1 inch into a large heavy skillet; heat to 350°. Fry cheese sticks until golden; drain on paper towels. Serve immediately. Yield: 18 cheese sticks.

Tutto Bene
Salvatore Mancini Lodge #2440
North Providence, Rhode Island

Sugared Walnuts

These sweet nuts are great for gift giving! Enjoy them by themselves or sprinkle them over a salad for added crunch.

8 cups water
4 cups walnut halves or pieces
½ cup firmly packed brown sugar
Vegetable oil
¼ teaspoon salt

Bring water to a boil in a large saucepan. Add walnuts, and boil 1 minute; drain well. Combine walnuts and brown sugar in a bowl; stir until sugar melts.

Pour oil to depth of 1 inch into a large heavy skillet; heat to 320°. Fry walnuts in two batches for 2 minutes each. Drain on a rack over paper towels. Sprinkle with salt. Yield: 4 cups. Sandy Maskaly

Our Family's Favorite Recipes
University Family Fellowship
Sparks, Nevada

Almond-Bacon-Cheese Crostini

1 French baguette
4 slices bacon, cooked and crumbled
1 cup (4 ounces) shredded Monterey Jack cheese
⅓ cup mayonnaise
¼ cup sliced almonds, toasted
1 tablespoon chopped green onions
¼ teaspoon salt
Garnish: toasted sliced almonds

Slice baguette into 36 (¼-inch-thick) slices. Arrange slices on an ungreased baking sheet; bake at 400° for 6 minutes or until golden.

Combine bacon and next 5 ingredients in a small bowl; stir well. Spread cheese mixture on slices; bake at 400° for 5 minutes or until cheese melts. Garnish, if desired. Serve immediately. Yield: 3 dozen.

The Dining Car
The Service League of Denison, Texas

Honey Chicken Wings

16 chicken wings (about 3½ pounds)
1 cup honey
½ cup ketchup
½ cup soy sauce
2 teaspoons vegetable oil
¼ teaspoon pepper
2 large garlic cloves, minced

Cut off and discard wingtips; cut wings in half at joint. Place wings, skin side down, in a single layer in a lightly greased 15- x 10-inch jellyroll pan.

Combine honey and remaining 5 ingredients in a medium bowl, stirring well. Pour honey mixture over chicken. Turn chicken, skin side up, brushing with honey mixture to coat.

Bake, uncovered, at 375° for 1 hour or until done, basting every 15 minutes. Yield: 8 appetizer servings. Eva Buckler

Tasty Treasures
Immanuel Lutheran Church Ladies Aid
Leland, Michigan

Stuffed Grape Leaves

It takes a little time to stuff these grape leaves with a ground lamb mixture, but they're probably the tastiest we've ever had and definitely worth the effort. Plan ahead and make these the day before; refrigerate until ready to serve. You can find grape leaves in the international section of larger supermarkets.

1 pound lean ground lamb
1 (16-ounce) canned crushed plum tomatoes, undrained
3 cups loosely packed fresh mint leaves, chopped
2 cups chopped green onions (about 2 bunches)
1 cup uncooked long-grain rice
¾ cup olive oil
½ teaspoon salt
50 medium-size bottled grape leaves
⅓ cup fresh lemon juice

Combine first 7 ingredients in a bowl; stir well.

Rinse grape leaves with cold water; drain well, and pat dry with paper towels. Remove and discard stems.

Spoon 1 rounded tablespoon of lamb mixture onto center of each grape leaf. Bring 2 opposite points of leaf to center, and fold over filling. Beginning at 1 short side, roll up leaf tightly, jellyroll fashion.

Place stuffed grape leaves, seam side down, in a Dutch oven. Pour lemon juice over leaves, and add enough water to almost cover. Weight leaves with a heavy plate. Bring water to a boil; cover, reduce heat, and simmer 35 minutes or until a thermometer inserted in center of bundles registers 180°. Yield: about 4 dozen. Wendy Garf-Lipp

A Taste of Tradition
Temple Emanu-El
Providence, Rhode Island

Irresistible Sausage Bites

We think they're irresistible, too! Monterey Jack and ground sausage are spooned into crisp pastry shells made from wonton wrappers.

48 wonton wrappers
Vegetable cooking spray
1 pound ground pork sausage
1 medium onion, diced
1 red bell pepper, diced
2 teaspoons olive oil
2 cups (8 ounces) shredded Monterey Jack cheese
½ teaspoon salt
½ teaspoon dried oregano
½ teaspoon pepper

Place wonton wrappers in greased miniature (1¾-inch) muffin pans, pressing wrappers down to cover bottoms of cups. Coat each wrapper lightly with cooking spray. Bake at 350° for 4 to 5 minutes or until golden. Remove wonton cups from muffin pans, and place on baking sheets; set aside.

Brown sausage, onion, and diced red pepper in 2 teaspoons oil, stirring until sausage crumbles. Drain and cool to room temperature. Stir in cheese and remaining 3 ingredients.

Spoon 1 rounded tablespoon sausage mixture into each reserved wonton cup. Bake at 350° for 4 to 5 minutes or until cheese melts. Serve hot. Yield: 4 dozen.

Bay Tables
The Junior League of Mobile, Alabama

Gourmet Stuffed Mushrooms

24 large fresh mushrooms
2 tablespoons butter or margarine, melted
1 (3-ounce) package cream cheese, softened
¾ cup sour cream
6 slices bacon, cooked and crumbled
½ teaspoon seasoned pepper

Wash and remove stems from mushrooms, reserving half of stems; set caps aside. Finely chop reserved stems. Cook chopped stems in butter in a large skillet over medium-high heat, stirring constantly, until tender.

Combine cream cheese and sour cream; stir in cooked mushrooms, bacon, and seasoned pepper. Spoon about 1 tablespoon cream cheese mixture into each mushroom cap. Place caps on a lightly greased large baking sheet.

Broil 5½ inches from heat 6 minutes or until mushrooms begin to brown. Serve immediately. Yield: 2 dozen. Jim Kleissle

Cooking with Pride
Madison Park/Camelview PTO
Phoenix, Arizona

Shiitake Mushroom Napoleons

Serve this recipe as an elegant first course at your next dinner party.

½ (17¼-ounce) package frozen puff pastry, thawed
1¼ pounds shiitake mushrooms
¼ cup butter or margarine
¾ cup Marsala
½ cup whipping cream
¼ teaspoon salt
¼ teaspoon pepper
¼ teaspoon dried oregano
1 (8-ounce) round Camembert or Brie cheese

Cut puff pastry into 8 (4- x 2-inch) rectangles. Sprinkle baking sheet with water, and shake off excess water. Place pastry on baking sheet; bake at 400° for 13 to 15 minutes or until puffed and golden. Gently remove pastry from baking sheet, and cool completely on a wire rack.

Remove mushroom stems and discard. Slice caps into ¼-inch-thick slices.

Melt butter in a large skillet over medium heat. Add mushrooms, and sauté 5 minutes. Add Marsala, and simmer 5 minutes or until liquid is reduced by half. Add cream and next 3 ingredients; reduce heat to low, and simmer 3 minutes or until liquid is reduced by half.

Slice Camembert into ¼-inch-thick slices; set aside.

Split each puff pastry rectangle into 2 layers, using a serrated knife. Place bottom halves of pastry on serving plates. Layer with cheese and mushrooms, and top with remaining pastry halves. Serve immediately. Yield: 8 appetizer servings.

Tested by Time
Porter Gaud Parents Guild
Charleston, South Carolina

Hot Mulled Fruit Cider

Take the chill off a winter day by sipping a mug of this four-fruit cider. It'll warm your spirit and add a welcoming scent throughout your house.

5 (3-inch) cinnamon sticks
10 whole cloves
10 whole allspice
4 cups apple juice
2 cups cranberry juice
2 cups pineapple juice
2 cups water
2 tablespoons lemon juice

Place first 3 ingredients in a cheesecloth bag. Combine apple juice, spices, cranberry juice, and remaining ingredients in a large Dutch oven. Bring to a boil, and cook 1 minute. Reduce heat, and simmer, uncovered, 45 minutes. Remove and discard spice bag. Serve warm. Yield: 7¼ cups. Jennifer J. Bowles

Silver Spoons
Kaiser Rehabilitation Center
Tulsa, Oklahoma

Coffee Frappé

This recipe serves a crowd, but easily halves, too. And if you want to spike it, just add a little coffee liqueur to the bowl.

1 gallon vanilla ice cream, softened
1 quart double-strength coffee, chilled
1 pint whipping cream, whipped

Combine all ingredients in a large punch bowl; mix well. Serve immediately. Yield: 18 cups. Allison Pelham

Designer's Recipes for Living
East Tennessee Interior Design Society
Knoxville, Tennessee

Holiday Irish Coffee Eggnog

Cheers to this holiday nog! Adding hot brewed coffee and a couple of choice spirits elevates this favorite beverage to a new level.

1¼ cups hot brewed coffee
½ cup sugar
1 quart refrigerated eggnog
⅔ cup Irish cream liqueur
½ cup brandy

Combine coffee and sugar, stirring until sugar dissolves. Stir in eggnog, liqueur, and brandy. Cover eggnog, and chill thoroughly. Yield: 7 cups.

Note: Eggnog may be made up to 3 days ahead.

What Can I Bring?
The Junior League of Northern Virginia
McLean, Virginia

Piedmont Punch

2¼ cups white grape juice, chilled
2¼ cups apple juice, chilled
2 cups pineapple juice, chilled
½ cup cold water
2 tablespoons fresh lemon juice
2 teaspoons fresh lime juice
½ teaspoon almond extract

Combine all ingredients in a large pitcher; stir well. Serve over ice. Yield: 7 cups.

Down by the Water
The Junior League of Columbia, South Carolina

Lynn's Punch

Three frozen fruit concentrates, apricot nectar, plus a splash of peach liqueur stir into a tasty fruit punch that'll enliven your next adult gathering. Just omit the liqueur in a second batch if there'll be children around.

1 (12-ounce) can frozen orange juice concentrate, thawed
1 (12-ounce) can frozen lemonade concentrate, thawed
1 (10-ounce) can frozen strawberry daiquiri, thawed
1½ cups apricot nectar
1½ cups water
⅓ cup peach Schnapps (optional)
1 (2-liter) bottle lemon-lime carbonated beverage, chilled (we used 7UP)

Combine first 6 ingredients in a large punch bowl. Add lemon-lime beverage to bowl, and stir mixture well. Serve immediately. Yield: 16 cups.

Eileen deHaro

Spice It Up!
Baton Rouge Branch of American Association of University Women
Baton Rouge, Louisiana

Tropical Melon Daiquiri

Take advantage of the watermelon crop during the hot days of summer and mix a batch of this refreshing island cooler.

4 cups watermelon cubes, seeded
½ cup light rum
¼ cup orange liqueur or orange juice
2 tablespoons fresh lime juice (about 1 lime)
2 tablespoons fresh lemon juice (about 1 lemon)
Crushed ice
Lime slices
Margarita salt

Cover and freeze watermelon cubes at least 3 hours. Combine watermelon, rum, and next 3 ingredients in container of an electric blender; process until smooth, stopping once to scrape down sides. Add enough ice to bring mixture to 5-cup level; process until smooth.

Rub rims of wide-mouth glasses with a lime slice. Place salt in a saucer, and spin rim of each glass in salt. Pour daiquiri mixture into glasses, and garnish each glass with a lime slice, if desired. Yield: 5 cups.

Made in the Shade
The Junior League of Greater Fort Lauderdale, Florida

Pineapple Aloha Punch

Greet guests at your next party or shower with this creamy concoction, and let the celebration begin!

1 (46-ounce) can pineapple juice, chilled
1 pint vanilla ice cream, softened
1 pint orange sherbet, softened
1 (1-liter) bottle ginger ale, chilled

Combine juice, ice cream, and sherbet in a punch bowl; stir until blended. Slowly stir in ginger ale. Serve immediately. Yield: 12 cups.

St. Philomena's Jr. Beta Delicious Recipes of the Future
St. Philomena School's Junior Beta Club
Labadieville, Louisiana

Italian Slush

This recipe makes a slushy fruit base that you can keep on hand in the freezer to make at a moment's notice, so it's adaptable for a small gathering or a crowd. Just make one batch at a time, and keep the rest in the freezer to use as the need arises.

2 cups sugar
2 cups water
1 (12-ounce) can frozen orange juice concentrate, undiluted
1 (12-ounce) can frozen lemonade concentrate, undiluted
2 cups gin or other liquor
Crushed ice
Ginger ale or other carbonated lemon-lime beverage

Combine sugar and water in a large saucepan; bring to a boil. Boil 15 minutes; cool. Stir in orange juice concentrate and lemonade concentrate. Pour mixture into a half-gallon container. Add gin, and stir well. Freeze at least 24 hours or up to 1 month.

For each 2-quart batch, fill a 2-quart pitcher with crushed ice; add 1 cup slush mixture. Add ginger ale, filling to 2-quart measure. Stir well, and serve immediately. Yield: 8 cups. Kitty Herbert

Note: Slush mixture yields 6 cups and makes 6 (8-cup) batches when diluted.

Generations of Good Food
Jeannette Public Library
Jeannette, Pennsylvania

Breads

South-of-the-Border Bread, page 84

Poppy Seed Bread

Orange juice distinguishes these pretty poppy seed loaves instead of the more familiar lemon flavor.

3 large eggs, beaten
2¼ cups sugar
1½ cups milk
1 cup vegetable oil
1½ teaspoons vanilla extract
1½ teaspoons butter flavoring
3 cups all-purpose flour
1½ teaspoons baking powder
1½ teaspoons salt
1½ teaspoons poppy seeds
¾ cup sugar
¼ cup orange juice
1½ teaspoons butter flavoring
½ teaspoon vanilla extract

Combine first 6 ingredients in a large bowl. Combine flour and next 3 ingredients. Add flour mixture to egg mixture, stirring just until smooth.

Pour batter into 2 greased 8½- x 4½-inch loafpans. Bake at 350° for 1 hour or until a wooden pick inserted in center comes out clean. Cool in pans on wire racks 10 minutes; remove from pans.

Combine ¾ cup sugar and orange juice in a small saucepan. Cook over medium heat, stirring constantly, until sugar dissolves. Remove from heat, and stir in 1½ teaspoons butter flavoring and ½ teaspoon vanilla. Prick holes in each loaf with a wooden pick. Brush glaze over loaves while warm. Let loaves cool completely on wire racks. Yield: 2 loaves.

Shara C. Baggett

Best and Blessed
Sweet Spirit Singers
Liberty, Mississippi

The Best Rhubarb Bread

Don't let April pass without making this moist bread. Rhubarb is sweetest in early spring.

1 large egg, lightly beaten
1½ cups firmly packed brown sugar
1 cup buttermilk
⅔ cup vegetable oil
1 teaspoon vanilla extract
2½ cups all-purpose flour
1 teaspoon baking soda
1 teaspoon salt
2 cups (¼-inch pieces) fresh or frozen rhubarb (about ½ pound)
½ cup chopped pecans
½ cup sugar
½ teaspoon ground cinnamon
1 tablespoon butter or margarine, softened

Combine first 5 ingredients in a large bowl; stir well.

Combine flour, soda, and salt; add to brown sugar mixture, and stir just until blended. Fold in rhubarb and pecans. Pour batter into 2 well-greased 8½- x 4½-inch loafpans.

Combine ½ cup sugar, cinnamon, and butter; stir with a fork until mixture is crumbly. Sprinkle mixture over batter. Bake at 350° for 1 hour or until a wooden pick inserted in center comes out clean. Cool in pans on wire racks 10 minutes; remove from pans, and cool completely on wire racks. Yield: 2 loaves. Arlette J. Hollister

Iowa: A Taste of Home
Iowa 4-H Foundation
Ames, Iowa

Bahamian Banana Pancakes

Banana slices inside and on top of these pancakes can turn any breakfast into a tropical escape.

2 bananas, peeled, and cut into ¼-inch slices
1¼ cups all-purpose flour
4 teaspoons baking powder
⅛ teaspoon salt
2 tablespoons sugar
2 large eggs, separated
1 cup milk
2 tablespoons butter, melted
2 tablespoons vanilla extract
Ground nutmeg (optional)
Maple syrup

Set aside one-fourth of banana slices.

Combine flour, baking powder, salt, and sugar in a medium bowl; set aside.

Lightly beat egg yolks with a fork; stir in milk, butter, vanilla, and remaining banana slices. Add milk mixture to flour mixture, stirring just until dry ingredients are moistened.

Beat egg whites at high speed with an electric mixer until stiff peaks form; gently fold into batter.

Pour about ¼ cup batter for each pancake onto a hot, lightly greased griddle. Cook pancakes until tops are covered with bubbles and edges look cooked; turn and cook other side.

Sprinkle pancakes with nutmeg, if desired. Serve with reserved banana slices and maple syrup. Yield: 14 pancakes. Dorothy Keach

'Pon Top Edisto
Trinity Episcopal Church
Edisto Island, South Carolina

Orange Waffles

3 cups all-purpose flour
4 teaspoons baking powder
¼ teaspoon salt
½ cup sugar
4 large eggs, separated
⅓ cup butter, softened
2 cups milk
1 tablespoon grated orange rind (about 1 orange)
1 teaspoon vanilla extract

Combine first 4 ingredients in a large bowl. Add egg yolks and butter; stir until blended. Add milk, orange rind, and vanilla; stir until blended. Beat egg whites until stiff peaks form; gently fold into batter.

Spread 1¼ cups batter onto a preheated, oiled waffle iron; spread batter to edges. Bake until lightly browned. Repeat procedure with remaining batter. Yield: 16 (4-inch) waffles.

A Taste of Washington State
Washington Bed & Breakfast Guild
Seattle, Washington

Cheese Blintz Muffins with Blueberry Sauce

Surprise your family with this unique alternative to French toast.

1 (15-ounce) container part-skim ricotta cheese
3 large eggs, lightly beaten
2 tablespoons sour cream or yogurt
¼ cup butter or margarine, melted
½ cup reduced-fat biscuit mix
⅔ cup sugar, divided
1 tablespoon cornstarch
⅓ cup water
2 tablespoons lemon juice
2 cups fresh or frozen blueberries
Sour cream

Combine first 5 ingredients and ⅓ cup sugar in a large bowl; beat at medium speed with an electric mixer or with a wire whisk until blended. Spoon batter into greased muffin pan, filling three-fourths full. Bake at 350° for 30 to 33 minutes or until edges are golden; cool muffins 5 minutes in pan. Run a small knife around edges of muffins in pan; turn muffins out onto a wire rack.

Meanwhile, stir together cornstarch and water in a medium saucepan. Stir in remaining ⅓ cup sugar, lemon juice, and blueberries. Bring to a boil over medium heat, stirring until mixture thickens.

Place muffins on individual serving plates; top each muffin with blueberry sauce, and dollop with sour cream. Serve immediately. Yield: 1 dozen.
Caroline and Jim Lloyd

Flavors of Falmouth
Falmouth Historical Society
Falmouth, Massachusetts

French Breakfast Puffs

These sweet little muffins taste like cinnamon bread. Enjoy them for breakfast or dessert.

⅓ cup butter, softened
½ cup sugar
1 large egg
1½ cups all-purpose flour
1½ teaspoons baking powder
½ teaspoon salt
¼ teaspoon ground nutmeg
½ cup milk
½ cup sugar
1 teaspoon ground cinnamon
6 tablespoons butter, melted

Beat ⅓ cup butter at medium speed with an electric mixer until creamy. Gradually add ½ cup sugar, beating well. Add egg, beating mixture well.

Combine flour and next 3 ingredients; add to butter mixture alternately with milk, beginning and ending with flour mixture. Mix at low speed after each addition until blended.

Place paper baking cups in muffin pans, and coat with cooking spray; spoon batter into cups, filling two-thirds full. Bake at 400° for 14 to 15 minutes or until golden. Remove muffins from pan.

Combine ½ cup sugar and cinnamon in a bowl; stir well. Dip tops of muffins into melted butter; roll buttered tops in cinnamon mixture. Yield: 1 dozen.

Ruth Kolker

NPT's Community Cookbook
Neighborhood Pride Team
Portland, Oregon

Ginger Scones

Crystallized ginger makes these scones a refreshing addition to any afternoon gathering.

2¾ cups all-purpose flour
2 teaspoons baking powder
½ teaspoon salt
½ cup sugar
¾ cup butter
⅓ cup chopped crystallized ginger
1 cup milk

Combine first 4 ingredients in a large bowl; cut butter into flour mixture with a pastry blender until crumbly. Stir in ginger. Add milk, stirring just until dry ingredients are moistened. Turn dough out onto a lightly floured surface, and knead 10 to 15 times. Pat or roll dough to ¾-inch thickness; shape into a round, and cut dough into 8 wedges. Place wedges on a lightly greased baking sheet.

Bake at 400° for 18 to 22 minutes or until barely golden. Cool slightly on a wire rack. Serve warm. Yield: 8 scones. Tina L. Benbough

Cookin' in the Canyon
Jarbidge Community Hall
Jarbidge, Nevada

Lazy Maple Crescent Pull Aparts

Thumbs up for convenience! We gave these yummies a high rating for tastiness and the innovative use of refrigerated rolls. When inverted onto a serving plate, a golden maple nut topping drenches the sweet rolls.

¼ cup firmly packed brown sugar
¼ cup butter or margarine
2 tablespoons pure maple syrup
¼ cup chopped pecans
1 (8-ounce) package refrigerated crescent dinner rolls
1 tablespoon sugar
½ teaspoon ground cinnamon

Combine brown sugar, butter, and syrup in an 8-inch round cakepan. Bake at 375° for 5 minutes or until butter melts; stir gently to blend ingredients. Sprinkle pecans over butter mixture.

Remove dough from package (do not unroll dough). Slice roll into 12 slices. Combine 1 tablespoon sugar and cinnamon. Dip both sides of each slice of dough into sugar mixture. Arrange slices, cut side down, in prepared pan. Sprinkle with remaining sugar mixture. Bake at 375° for 18 minutes or until golden. Invert pan immediately onto a serving platter. Serve immediately. Yield: 1 dozen. Jim and Ruth Larson

North Country Cooking
51st National Square Dance Convention
St. Paul, Minnesota

Breakfast Roll

Starting the morning off with one of these bacon- and cheese-endowed rolls will save time without sacrificing the luxury of a fresh baked breakfast.

1¾ cups biscuit mix
⅓ cup cold water
1 (3-ounce) package cream cheese, softened
¾ cup (3 ounces) shredded Cheddar cheese
½ pound bacon cooked and crumbled (8 slices)
1 large egg, beaten
½ teaspoon poppy seeds

Combine biscuit mix and water in a medium bowl; stir until a soft dough forms. Turn out onto a lightly floured surface, and knead 10 times. Roll into a 12-inch square.

Spread cream cheese over dough, leaving a ¼-inch border. Sprinkle with cheese and bacon. Roll up dough, pressing firmly to eliminate air pockets; pinch seam to seal. Place dough, seam side down, on a lightly greased baking sheet. Brush dough with egg, and sprinkle with poppy seeds.

Cut slices at 1-inch intervals to, but not through, bottom of roll. Bake at 400° for 30 minutes or until rolls are golden. Serve warm. Yield: 4 servings.

Stephanie Winborn

The Art of Cooking
The Muscle Shoals District Service League
Sheffield, Alabama

Apple-Cheddar Cornbread

1 cup yellow cornmeal
1 cup all-purpose flour
1 tablespoon baking powder
½ cup sugar
1 large egg, beaten
1 cup milk
¼ cup butter or margarine, melted
2 small tart red apples, chopped (we tested with McIntosh)
½ cup (2 ounces) shredded sharp Cheddar cheese

Combine first 4 ingredients; make a well in center of mixture. Combine egg, milk, and butter; add to dry ingredients, stirring just until moistened. Stir in apple and cheese.

Place a well-greased 9-inch cast-iron skillet or 9-inch square pan in a 425° oven for 5 minutes or until hot. Remove from oven; pour batter into hot skillet. Bake at 425° for 25 minutes or until golden. Yield: 9 servings.

Sarah Hardin

A Thyme to Remember
Dallas County Medical Society Alliance
Dallas, Texas

Flat Bread

1 (¼-ounce) envelope active dry yeast
2 cups warm water (100° to 110°), divided
⅓ cup sugar
2 tablespoons vegetable oil
1 tablespoon salt
½ cup rye or whole wheat flour
5½ to 6 cups all-purpose flour, divided

Dissolve yeast in ½ cup warm water in a large mixing bowl; let stand 5 minutes. Add remaining water, sugar, and next 3 ingredients. Add 2 cups all-purpose flour, and beat at medium speed with an electric mixer 2 minutes. Stir in enough remaining all-purpose flour to make a soft dough. Turn out onto a well-floured surface, and knead until smooth and elastic (about 8 minutes). Place in a well-greased bowl, turning to grease top. Let rise in a warm place (85°), free from drafts, 1 hour or until doubled in bulk.

Punch dough down, and divide in half. Place each half on a greased baking sheet; flatten each half into a ½-inch-thick circle. Prick each round with a fork. Cover and let rise in a warm place, free from drafts, 25 minutes or until almost doubled in bulk.

Bake at 375° for 25 minutes or until golden. Yield: 2 loaves.

Simply the Best . . . Recipes by Design
Columbus Area Visitors Center
Columbus, Indiana

South-of-the-Border Bread

This bread bakes into two beautiful golden braids speckled with cheese and minced jalapeño pepper.

½ cup butter or margarine
¾ cup finely chopped onion
1 cup buttermilk
6½ cups all-purpose flour, divided
1 cup plain yellow cornmeal
2 (¼-ounce) envelopes active dry yeast
1 tablespoon sugar
1 tablespoon salt
½ teaspoon baking soda
2 large eggs
1½ cups (6 ounces) shredded sharp Cheddar cheese
1 cup canned cream-style corn
¾ cup finely chopped green bell pepper
1 jalapeño pepper, seeded and minced
2 tablespoons butter or margarine, melted

Combine ½ cup butter and onion in a small saucepan; place over medium-low heat until butter melts, stirring occasionally. Add buttermilk, and heat to 120° to 130°.

Meanwhile, combine 2 cups flour, cornmeal, and next 4 ingredients in a large mixing bowl. Gradually add warm liquid mixture to flour mixture, beating at high speed with a heavy-duty electric mixer. Beat 2 more minutes at medium speed. Add eggs and next 4 ingredients; beat 3 minutes. Gradually stir in enough remaining flour to make a soft dough.

Turn dough out onto a floured surface, and knead until smooth and elastic (about 10 minutes). Place in a well-greased bowl, turning to grease top. Cover and let rise in a warm place (85°), free from drafts, 45 minutes or until doubled in bulk.

Punch dough down; turn out onto a lightly floured surface, and knead lightly 4 or 5 times. Divide dough into thirds. Shape 1 portion of dough into 3 (14-inch-long) ropes, keeping remaining dough covered with a damp cloth. Shape ropes into a braid, tucking ends under, and place on a greased baking sheet. Repeat procedure with a second portion of dough, placing braid on a second greased baking sheet.

Divide remaining portion of dough in half. Shape 1 half into 3 (9-inch-long) ropes. Shape ropes into a small braid, tucking ends under, and center on top of first large braid. Repeat procedure with remaining portion of dough, placing on top of second large braid.

Cover and let rise in a warm place, free from drafts, 30 minutes or until doubled in bulk.

Bake at 350° for 30 minutes or until loaves sound hollow when tapped. Remove bread from baking sheets immediately. Brush with melted butter, and cool on wire racks. Yield: 2 loaves.

Picnics, Potlucks & Prizewinners
Indiana 4-H Foundation
Indianapolis, Indiana

Onion and Rosemary Bread

Rosemary is the herb of remembrance. Combined with onion, it makes this savory bread unforgettable.

1 (¼-ounce) envelope rapid-rise yeast
1 tablespoon sugar
1½ cups warm water (100° to 110°)
2 teaspoons salt
½ cup chopped onion
4 cups all-purpose flour
2 tablespoons vegetable or olive oil
1½ tablespoons fresh rosemary leaves
½ teaspoon coarse salt or ¼ teaspoon salt

Stir together first 3 ingredients in a large bowl, and let stand 5 minutes. Stir in 2 teaspoons salt, onion, and enough flour to form a soft dough. Turn dough out onto a floured surface, and knead until smooth and elastic (about 10 minutes). Place in a well-greased bowl, turning to grease top. Cover and let rise in a warm place (85°), free from drafts, 45 minutes or until doubled in bulk.

Punch dough down. Shape into a 12-inch round on a greased baking sheet. Cover and let rise in a warm place, free from drafts, 30 minutes or until doubled in bulk. Drizzle with oil; sprinkle with rosemary and salt.

Bake at 400° for 25 minutes or until golden. Serve warm. Yield: 8 servings.

Always in Season
The Junior League of Salt Lake City, Utah

Marble Swirl Bread

Cocoa, coffee, and rye flour create a marbled bread that will dazzle your friends.

3¼ cups all-purpose flour, divided
¼ cup sugar
1 (¼-ounce) envelope active dry yeast
1 teaspoon salt
1⅓ cups plus 1 tablespoon water, divided
¼ cup butter or margarine
1 large egg
2 tablespoons molasses
2 teaspoons cocoa
1 teaspoon instant coffee granules
1¼ cups rye flour
1 egg yolk

Combine 1½ cups all-purpose flour, sugar, yeast, and salt in a large mixing bowl.

Combine 1⅓ cups water and butter in a saucepan; heat until butter melts, stirring occasionally. Cool to 120° to 130°. Gradually add butter mixture to flour mixture, beating at low speed with an electric mixer until blended. Beat 2 more minutes at medium speed. Add egg and ½ cup all-purpose flour; beat until blended. Beat 2 more minutes at medium speed.

Transfer half of batter to another bowl. Stir in enough remaining all-purpose flour to make a stiff dough; set aside.

Stir molasses, cocoa, and coffee granules into remaining half of dough. Add rye flour to make a stiff dough.

Cover both bowls; let rise in a warm place (85°), free from drafts, 1 hour or until doubled in bulk.

Punch down light-colored dough; turn out onto a lightly floured surface, and knead lightly 4 or 5 times. Cover and let rise 10 minutes. Repeat with remaining dark dough.

Roll light-colored dough into a 12- x 9-inch rectangle on a lightly floured surface. Roll dark dough into a 12- x 8-inch rectangle on a lightly floured surface.

Place dark dough on top of light-colored dough. Roll up doughs together, starting at long side, into a 12- x 4-inch rectangle, pressing firmly to eliminate air pockets; pinch ends and seam to seal. Place dough, seam side down, on a well-greased baking sheet, tucking ends under. Cover and let rise in a warm place, free from drafts, 45 minutes or until doubled in bulk.

Combine remaining 1 tablespoon water and egg yolk; stir well with a wire whisk. Cut 3 (½-inch) slashes across top of dough; brush loaf with egg mixture. Bake at 350° for 35 to 40 minutes or until loaf sounds hollow when tapped. Remove from baking sheet; cool on wire rack. Yield: 1 loaf. Jami Sieger

Iowa: A Taste of Home
Iowa 4-H Foundation
Ames, Iowa

Swedish Rye Bread

Serve this hearty bread with a bowl of your favorite soup for the perfect end to a long winter day.

2 cups milk
2 tablespoons brown sugar
2 tablespoons shortening
2 tablespoons molasses
2 teaspoons salt
1 (¼-ounce) envelope active dry yeast
¼ cup warm water (100° to 110°)
4 cups rye flour
1¾ cups all-purpose flour

Combine first 5 ingredients in a heavy saucepan; cook over medium-low heat until shortening melts. Remove from heat; cool to 100° to 110°.

Combine yeast and warm water in a small bowl; let stand 5 minutes. Combine yeast mixture and milk mixture in a large bowl. Combine flours, and add to yeast mixture, stirring until smooth.

Turn dough out onto a floured surface, and knead 10 minutes or until smooth and elastic. Place in a well-greased bowl, turning to grease top. Cover and let rise in a warm place (85°), free from drafts, 1 hour or until doubled in bulk.

Punch dough down and divide in half; roll 1 portion of dough into a 12- x 9-inch rectangle. Roll up dough, jellyroll fashion, starting at short side; pinch ends to seal. Repeat procedure with remaining portion of dough. Place loaves, seam side down, into 2 greased 9- x 5-inch loafpans. Cover and let rise in a warm place, free from drafts, 1 hour or until doubled in bulk.

Bake at 350° for 40 minutes or until loaves sound hollow when tapped. Yield: 2 loaves. Betty Hilliard

Keittokirja: Kaleva Centennial Cookbook
Project Kaleva/Kaleva Historical Society
Kaleva, Michigan

Cream Cheese and Chocolate Danish

Store these loaves in the freezer to have on hand for unexpected guests. Thaw them completely before frosting.

½ cup water
½ cup milk
¼ cup butter or margarine
4 to 5 cups all-purpose flour, divided
¾ cup sugar, divided
1 teaspoon salt
2 (¼-ounce) envelopes active dry yeast
2 large eggs
1 (8-ounce) package cream cheese, softened
1 egg yolk
Favorite chocolate frosting

Combine water, milk, and butter in a small saucepan; heat to 120° to 130° (butter does not need to melt).

Combine ¼ cup flour, ½ cup sugar, salt, and yeast in a large mixing bowl. Gradually add warm milk mixture to flour mixture, beating 2 minutes at medium speed with an electric mixer. Add 2 eggs and ½ cup flour; beat at medium speed until mixture thickens. Beat 2 more minutes; using a wooden spoon, gradually stir in enough remaining flour to make a soft dough.

Turn dough out onto a lightly floured surface, and knead until smooth and elastic (about 8 minutes). Place in a well-greased bowl, turning to grease top. Cover and let rise in a warm place (85°), free from drafts, 1 hour or until doubled in bulk.

Beat cream cheese and remaining ¼ cup sugar at medium speed with mixer until fluffy. Add egg yolk; beat well.

Punch dough down; turn out onto a lightly floured surface, and knead lightly 4 or 5 times. Divide dough into 4 equal portions. Roll 1 portion of dough into a 16- x 6-inch rectangle. Spread one-fourth of cream cheese mixture over dough, leaving a 1-inch border. Roll up dough, starting at short side, pressing firmly to eliminate air pockets; pinch ends to seal. Place dough, seam side down, on a lightly greased baking sheet. Repeat procedure.

Cut slits in top of each loaf at 1-inch intervals. Cover and let rise in a warm place, free from drafts, 50 minutes or until doubled in bulk.

Bake at 350° for 18 to 20 minutes or until lightly browned. Cool completely on wire racks. Spread tops of loaves with chocolate frosting. Yield: 4 loaves.

Lighthouse Secrets: A Collection of Recipes from the Nation's Oldest City
The Junior Service League of St. Augustine, Florida

Cinnamon Swirl Bread

A perfect combination of cinnamon, chocolate, and pecans makes this loaf prepared in a bread machine great for a late breakfast or an afternoon tea.

1 cup milk
3 tablespoons butter or margarine
1 large egg
1½ teaspoons salt
3 tablespoons sugar
2 tablespoons instant nonfat dry milk powder
3 cups bread flour
¾ teaspoon ground cinnamon
2½ teaspoons bread-machine yeast
½ cup semisweet chocolate morsels
½ cup chopped pecans
¼ cup semisweet chocolate morsels
1 tablespoon butter or margarine
⅓ cup sifted powdered sugar
1 tablespoon water

Combine first 9 ingredients, in order listed, in a large capacity bread machine. Set machine according to manufacturer's instructions to add ½ cup chocolate morsels and pecans during kneading process. (If your machine does not have this feature, add ½ cup chocolate morsels and pecans after 7 minutes of kneading.)

Bake bread according to manufacturer's instructions. When bread is done, remove from pan, and cool completely on a wire rack.

Combine ¼ cup chocolate morsels and remaining 3 ingredients in a small saucepan. Cook over low heat, stirring constantly with a small wire whisk, until chocolate and butter melt and mixture is smooth. Drizzle glaze over bread. Yield: 1 (1¾-pound) loaf.

Dining by Design: Stylish Recipes, Savory Settings
The Junior League of Pasadena, California

Grandmom Rice's Rolls

You'll wish Grandmom Rice was a relative of yours when you taste her tender potato rolls.

1 medium baking potato
2 (¼-ounce) envelopes active dry yeast
1 cup warm water (100° to 110°)
4 large eggs
1 cup milk (110° to 110°)
3 tablespoons shortening
8 to 8¾ cups all-purpose flour, divided
¾ cup plus 2 tablespoons sugar
1 teaspoon salt

Cook potato in boiling water to cover 30 minutes or until done. Peel and mash with a potato masher.

Combine yeast and warm water in a large mixing bowl; let stand 5 minutes. Add eggs, milk, shortening, and mashed potato; beat at medium speed with a heavy-duty electric mixer until combined. Gradually add 8 cups flour, sugar, and salt, kneading with a dough hook until a soft dough forms, adding remaining ¾ cup flour as needed to make a soft dough.

Cover and let rise in a warm place (85°), free from drafts, 35 minutes or until doubled in bulk.

Punch dough down, and divide into thirds; shape each portion into 12 (1½-inch) balls. Place 2 inches apart on greased baking sheets. Cover and let rise in a warm place, free from drafts, 30 minutes or until doubled in bulk.

Bake at 375° for 15 minutes or until golden. Yield: 3 dozen.

A Century of Serving
The Junior Board of Christiana Care, Inc.
Wilmington, Delaware

Bread Machine Rolls

Homemade rolls have never been easier or tastier. Your bread machine takes care of the kneading; you're in charge of the baking and, of course, the eating.

¾ cup plus 2 tablespoons water
1 large egg
3⅓ cups all-purpose flour
¼ cup sugar
3 tablespoons instant nonfat dry milk powder
1½ teaspoons salt
5 tablespoons butter
2 teaspoons bread-machine yeast

Combine all ingredients in a bread machine according to manufacturer's instructions. Select dough cycle; start machine. Remove dough from machine; punch dough down. Cover and let rest 20 minutes.

Lightly grease muffin pans. Shape dough into 2-inch balls; place 1 ball in each muffin cup. Cover and let rise in a warm place (85°), free from drafts, 40 minutes. Bake at 350° for 15 minutes or until golden. Yield: 22 rolls.

Elsie King

Recipes for Champions
Shebas of Khiva Temple Oriental Band
Amarillo, Texas

Whole Wheat Spirals

This recipe spiraled its way through our Test Kitchens with our highest rating.

2 (¼-ounce) envelopes active dry yeast
1¾ cups warm water (100° to 110°)
½ cup sugar
2 teaspoons salt
½ cup butter or margarine, melted and divided
1 large egg, lightly beaten
2¼ cups whole wheat flour
2¼ to 2½ cups all-purpose flour

Combine yeast and warm water in a 2-cup liquid measuring cup; let stand 5 minutes.

Combine yeast mixture, sugar, salt, ¼ cup melted butter, egg, and whole wheat flour in a large mixing bowl; beat at medium speed with an electric mixer until well blended. Gradually stir in enough all-purpose flour to make a soft dough.

Turn dough out onto a well-floured surface, and knead until smooth and elastic (about 5 minutes). Place in a well-greased bowl, turning to grease top.

Cover and let rise in a warm place (85°), free from drafts, 30 minutes or until doubled in bulk.

Punch dough down, and divide in half; shape each portion into a 14- x 7-inch rectangle. Cut each rectangle into 12 (7- x 1-inch) strips. Roll each strip into a spiral, and place in well-greased muffin pans.

Cover and let rise in a warm place, free from drafts, 20 minutes or until doubled in bulk.

Bake at 400° for 8 to 10 minutes or until golden. Remove from pans, and cool on wire racks. Brush with remaining ¼ cup melted butter. Yield: 2 dozen.

Linda Brown

Blended Blessings
First Presbyterian Church
Salisbury, North Carolina

Cakes

Pecan and Blueberry Pound Cake, page 108

Amish Apple Pie Cake

This chunky apple cake defies the traditional wooden pick test for doneness. Rather, it's delightfully gooey (like a pudding cake) and at its peak when served warm with a hefty scoop of ice cream.

¾ cup butter or margarine, softened
2 cups all-purpose flour
1 teaspoon baking soda
¼ teaspoon salt
2 teaspoons ground cinnamon
2 cups sugar
2 large eggs
4 cups peeled, chopped Granny Smith apple (about 3 medium)
1 cup chopped pecans

Beat butter at medium speed with an electric mixer until creamy. Combine flour and next 4 ingredients; add flour mixture and eggs to butter, beating well. Fold in apple and pecans. Pour batter into a lightly greased 9-inch square pan.

Bake at 350° for 1 hour, shielding with aluminum foil after 40 minutes to prevent excessive browning. Serve warm with ice cream. Yield: 9 servings.

Jodie Gouthier

Favorite Recipes Taste of Tradition
B.A. Ritter Senior Citizen Center
Nederland, Texas

Upside-Down Chocolate-Mango Cake

Golden orange slices of juicy mango and spicy-sweet bits of crystallized ginger give this chocolate cake an exotic aura.

¼ cup firmly packed brown sugar
2 tablespoons butter or margarine
1 medium mango, sliced
¾ cup all-purpose flour
1 teaspoon baking soda
¾ cup sugar
⅓ cup cocoa
¼ teaspoon salt
¾ cup buttermilk
¼ cup vegetable oil
1 large egg
3 tablespoons finely chopped crystallized ginger
1 teaspoon vanilla extract
¼ cup peach jelly
1 tablespoon chopped pistachios or blanched almonds

Combine brown sugar and butter in a small saucepan. Cook over medium heat until sugar and butter melt, stirring often. Immediately pour mixture into an 8-inch square pan, and spread over bottom of pan. Arrange mango slices on top of mixture. Set aside.

Stir together flour and next 4 ingredients. Combine buttermilk and next 4 ingredients. Add buttermilk mixture to flour mixture; beat at low speed with an electric mixer 1 minute. Increase to medium speed, and beat 2 more minutes. Pour batter over mango in pan.

Set oven rack in lower third of oven. Bake at 350° for 35 minutes or until a wooden pick inserted in center comes out clean.

Meanwhile, combine jelly and pistachios in a small saucepan. Cook over medium heat until jelly melts, stirring occasionally.

Run a knife around edge of pan to loosen cake. Invert cake onto a serving plate. Brush jelly mixture over cake. Serve warm, or let cool. Yield: 9 servings.

Flavors of Hawaii
Child and Family Service Guild
Honolulu, Hawaii

Pineapple Party Cake

Friends will appreciate the sweet and easy nature of this pineapple-topped loaf cake. Make it the day before your next casual get-together. Chilling the cake allows the flavors to meld and makes it easy to slice.

½ cup butter or margarine, softened
1 cup sugar
2 egg yolks
2 cups graham cracker crumbs (about 20 rectangle crackers)
2 teaspoons baking powder
¼ teaspoon salt
1 cup milk
½ cup chopped pecans
1 tablespoon vanilla extract
2 egg whites
1 cup sugar
1 (8-ounce) can crushed pineapple, undrained

Beat butter at medium speed with an electric mixer until creamy; gradually add 1 cup sugar, beating well. Add egg yolks, 1 at a time, beating until blended after each addition. Combine graham cracker crumbs, baking powder, and salt; add to butter mixture alternately with milk, beginning and ending with crumb mixture. Beat at low speed until blended after each addition. Stir in pecans and vanilla.

Beat egg whites at high speed until stiff peaks form. Gently fold into butter mixture. Pour batter into a greased and floured 9- x 5-inch loafpan.

Bake at 350° for 55 to 60 minutes or until cake pulls away from sides of pan. Let cool in pan on a wire rack 10 minutes. Remove from pan, and place on rack while you prepare topping.

Stir together 1 cup sugar and pineapple in a small saucepan; bring to a boil. Boil 10 minutes. Spoon over warm cake. Let cool completely. Cover tightly, and chill 8 hours. Yield: 1 loaf.

Simply Divine
Second-Ponce de Leon Baptist Church
Atlanta, Georgia

Down East Blueberry Cake

2 cups plus 2 tablespoons all-purpose flour
2 teaspoons baking powder
1¼ cups fresh blueberries
½ cup butter or margarine, softened
1¼ cups sugar, divided
2 large eggs
½ cup half-and-half
¼ teaspoon ground nutmeg

Stir together 2 cups flour and baking powder; set aside. Gently toss blueberries with remaining 2 tablespoons flour. Set aside.

Beat butter at medium speed with an electric mixer until creamy. Gradually add 1 cup sugar, beating well. Add eggs, 1 at a time, beating until blended after each addition.

Add flour mixture alternately with half-and-half, beginning and ending with flour mixture; beat at low speed after each addition until blended. Gently fold in floured blueberries. Pour batter into a lightly greased 13- x 9-inch pan.

Stir together remaining ¼ cup sugar and nutmeg; sprinkle over batter.

Bake at 350° for 30 minutes or until a wooden pick inserted in center comes out clean. Cut into squares. Serve warm, or let cool to room temperature in pan on a wire rack. Yield: 15 servings.

A Taste of Tradition
Temple Emanu-El
Providence, Rhode Island

Carrot-Praline Cake

Buttery bits of homemade pecan praline punctuate each layer of this stunning carrot cake. See it on the cover of this book.

1 tablespoon butter
3 tablespoons sugar
½ cup chopped pecans
1¼ cups sugar
¾ cup vegetable oil
1 teaspoon vanilla extract
3 large eggs
2 cups all-purpose flour
1¼ teaspoons baking soda
¼ teaspoon salt
½ teaspoon ground cinnamon
1 (8-ounce) can crushed pineapple in juice, undrained
2 cups shredded carrot
1 (8-ounce) package cream cheese, softened
¼ cup butter, softened
¼ cup firmly packed brown sugar
1 teaspoon vanilla extract
3 cups sifted powdered sugar
1 cup chopped pecans
1 (8-ounce) can pineapple tidbits in syrup, drained
Garnish: Pecan halves

Melt 1 tablespoon butter in skillet; add 3 tablespoons sugar, and cook over low heat until mixture bubbles. Stir in ½ cup pecans; cook until pecans are coated and sugar begins to caramelize. Pour onto a sheet of wax paper; cool. Break into small pieces.

Beat 1¼ cups sugar, oil, and 1 teaspoon vanilla at medium speed with an electric mixer 1 minute. Add eggs, 1 at a time; beat until blended after each addition. Combine flour and next 3 ingredients; add to oil mixture, beating at low speed until blended after each addition. Stir in crushed pineapple, carrot, and praline pieces. Pour into 2 greased and floured 9-inch round cakepans. Bake at 350° for 30 minutes or until a wooden pick inserted in center comes out clean. Cool in pans on wire racks 10 minutes. Remove from pans; cool completely on wire racks.

Beat cream cheese and ¼ cup softened butter at medium speed until creamy; gradually add brown sugar and 1 teaspoon vanilla, beating well. Add powdered sugar, ½ cup at a time, beating well after each addition. Spread frosting between layers and on top and sides of cake. Press 1 cup chopped pecans into frosting on sides of cake. Press pineapple tidbits into frosting around top edge of cake. Garnish, if desired. Yield: 1 (2-layer) cake. Karen Myers

Cooking Up Memories
The Tazewell County Genealogical and Historical Society
Pekin, Illinois

Maggie's Prizewinning Chocolate Chiffon Cake

⅔ cup butter or margarine, softened
1¾ cups sugar
4 (1-ounce) unsweetened chocolate squares, melted and cooled
1 teaspoon vanilla extract
1¾ cups all-purpose flour
1¼ teaspoons baking soda
¼ teaspoon baking powder
1 teaspoon salt
1¼ cups water
3 large eggs
2 (4-ounce) sweet chocolate bars, divided
¾ cup butter or margarine
½ cup chopped pecans
2 cups whipping cream, whipped

Grease 4 (9-inch) round cakepans; line with wax paper. Grease and flour wax paper.

Beat ⅔ cup butter at medium speed with an electric mixer until creamy; gradually add sugar, beating well. Add melted unsweetened chocolate and vanilla, beating well. Combine flour and next 3 ingredients; add to butter mixture alternately with water, beginning and ending with flour mixture. Beat at low speed until blended after each addition. Add eggs, 1 at a time, beating until blended after each addition. Pour batter into prepared pans (layers will be thin).

Bake at 350° for 15 minutes or until a wooden pick inserted in center comes out clean. Cool in pans on wire racks 10 minutes; remove from pans, and peel off wax paper immediately after inverting. Cool layers completely on wire racks.

Melt 1½ sweet chocolate bars and ¾ cup butter in a heavy saucepan over low heat. Cool 10 minutes. Stir in pecans.

Place 1 cake layer on a cake plate; spread half of chocolate filling on cake layer. Place second layer over filling; spread half of whipped cream on second layer. Repeat layers, using remaining filling and whipped cream (do not frost sides of cake).

Make chocolate curls with remaining ½ sweet chocolate bar by pulling a vegetable peeler along narrow edge of bar. Sprinkle chocolate curls on top of cake. Yield: 1 (4-layer) cake. Maggie Carey

Our Family's Favorite Recipes
University Family Fellowship
Sparks, Nevada

Peanut Butter-Lovers' Cake

3/4 cup butter or margarine, softened
2 cups sugar
5 large eggs, separated
1 cup creamy peanut butter
2 cups all-purpose flour
1 teaspoon baking soda
1/2 teaspoon salt
1 cup buttermilk
1 teaspoon vanilla extract
Peanut Butter Frosting
1/2 cup chopped peanuts

Beat butter at medium speed with an electric mixer until creamy; gradually add sugar; beating well. Add egg yolks, 1 at a time, beating until blended after each addition. Add peanut butter, and beat until smooth.

Combine flour, baking soda, and salt; add to butter mixture alternately with buttermilk, beginning and ending with flour mixture. Beat at low speed after each addition until blended. Stir in vanilla.

Beat egg whites at high speed until stiff peaks form. Gently fold one-third beaten egg whites into batter; fold in remaining two-thirds egg whites. Pour batter into 3 greased and floured 9-inch round cakepans.

Bake at 350° for 25 to 28 minutes or until a wooden pick inserted in center comes out clean. Cool in pans on wire racks 10 minutes; remove from pans, and cool completely on wire racks. Spread Peanut Butter Frosting between layers and on top and sides of cake. Sprinkle peanuts on top of cake. Yield: 1 (3-layer) cake.

Peanut Butter Frosting

3/4 cup butter or margarine, softened
1 cup creamy peanut butter
4 1/2 cups sifted powdered sugar
1/3 cup milk
1 teaspoon vanilla extract

Beat butter at medium speed with an electric mixer until creamy; add peanut butter, beating until blended. Gradually add powdered sugar, beating until light and fluffy. Add milk, and beat until spreading consistency. Stir in vanilla. Yield: 4 cups.

Picnics, Potlucks & Prizewinners
Indiana 4-H Foundation
Indianapolis, Indiana

Pineapple-Meringue Cake

½ cup butter or margarine, softened
½ cup sugar
4 large eggs, separated
½ cup plus 2 tablespoons sifted cake flour
1 teaspoon baking powder
¼ teaspoon salt
¼ cup milk
¾ cup sugar
1 teaspoon vanilla extract
¾ cup chopped pecans
Filling
1 (15½-ounce) can crushed pineapple, drained (about 1 cup crushed pineapple)

Line 2 (8-inch) round cakepans with wax paper; set aside.

Beat butter at medium speed with an electric mixer until creamy; gradually add ½ cup sugar, beating well. Add egg yolks, 1 at a time, beating until blended after each addition.

Combine flour, baking powder, and salt in a bowl; add to butter mixture alternately with milk, beginning and ending with flour mixture. Beat at low speed until blended after each addition. Pour batter into prepared pans.

Beat egg whites at high speed until foamy. Add ¾ cup sugar, 1 tablespoon at a time, beating until stiff peaks form and sugar dissolves (2 to 4 minutes). Fold in vanilla. Spread meringue evenly over cake batter; sprinkle pecans evenly over meringue.

Bake at 325° for 20 minutes. Cool in pans on wire racks 1 minute; remove from pans. Peel off wax paper immediately after inverting. Cool layers completely, meringue side up, on wire racks.

Place 1 cake layer on cakeplate, meringue side down. Spread filling on layer. Sprinkle drained pineapple over filling. Top with remaining layer, meringue side up. Chill at least 1 hour. Yield: 1 (2-layer) cake.

Filling

½ cup whipping cream
1½ tablespoons powdered sugar
½ teaspoon vanilla extract

Beat whipping cream until foamy; gradually add powdered sugar, beating until soft peaks form. Gently fold in vanilla. Yield: 1 cup.

Generations of Good Food
Jeannette Public Library
Jeannette, Pennsylvania

Almond Streusel Cake

1 cup firmly packed brown sugar
1 cup sliced natural almonds
¼ cup all-purpose flour
3 tablespoons butter or margarine, melted
2 teaspoons grated orange rind, divided
½ cup butter or margarine, softened
½ cup sugar
3 large eggs
½ teaspoon vanilla extract
2 cups all-purpose flour
1 teaspoon baking powder
½ teaspoon baking soda
⅔ cup fresh orange juice
Glaze

Combine first 3 ingredients in a medium bowl. Stir in melted butter and 1 teaspoon orange rind; set streusel mixture aside.

Beat ½ cup butter at medium speed with an electric mixer until creamy; gradually add sugar, beating well. Add eggs, 1 at a time, beating until blended after each addition. Stir in remaining 1 teaspoon rind and vanilla.

Combine flour, baking powder, and baking soda; add to butter mixture alternately with orange juice, beginning and ending with flour mixture. Beat at low speed until blended after each addition.

Pour half of batter into a greased 10-inch tube pan; sprinkle with half of streusel mixture. Repeat layers once. Bake at 350° for 35 to 37 minutes or until a long wooden skewer inserted in center comes out clean. Cool completely in pan on a wire rack.

Loosen cake from sides of pan, using a narrow metal spatula; remove from pan. Transfer cake to a serving plate; drizzle with glaze. Yield: 1 (10-inch) cake.

Glaze

2½ teaspoons fresh orange juice
½ cup sifted powdered sugar

Combine orange juice and sugar; stir until mixture is smooth. Yield: 3 tablespoons.

Hearthside: A Country Community Cookbook
Christ Community Church
Weare, New Hampshire

Black Russian Bundt Cake

This bodacious Bundt cake borrows two of its ingredients, vodka and coffee liqueur, from the popular Black Russian cocktail.

1 (18.25-ounce) package yellow cake mix (we tested with Duncan Hines)
½ cup sugar
1 (3.9-ounce) package chocolate instant pudding mix
1 cup vegetable oil
4 large eggs
¼ cup vodka
½ cup coffee liqueur, divided
½ cup sifted powdered sugar
Additional sifted powdered sugar

Combine first 6 ingredients in a large mixing bowl; add ¼ cup liqueur. Beat at low speed with an electric mixer 1 minute; increase speed to medium, and beat 4 more minutes. Pour batter into a greased and floured 12-cup Bundt pan.

Bake at 350° for 50 to 60 minutes or until a long wooden skewer inserted in center comes out clean. Cool in pan on a wire rack 15 minutes; invert onto a serving plate.

Combine remaining ¼ cup liqueur and ½ cup powdered sugar, stirring until smooth. Prick warm cake at 1-inch intervals with a long wooden skewer. Brush liqueur mixture over top and sides of cake; cool completely. Sprinkle additional powdered sugar over cake. Yield: 1 (10-inch) cake.

Myra McDonald

Recipes for Champions
Shebas of Khiva Temple Oriental Band
Amarillo, Texas

Danish Orange Cake

An infusion of orange essence comes from the fragrant sauce poured over this warm date cake.

3 cups all-purpose flour
1½ teaspoons baking soda
1 teaspoon salt
1 (8-ounce) package whole pitted dates, chopped
1 cup chopped pecans
1 cup shortening
1¾ cups sugar
3 large eggs
1½ tablespoons grated orange rind
⅓ cup fresh orange juice
1 cup buttermilk
Sauce

Combine first 3 ingredients. Stir together 1 cup flour mixture, dates, and pecans.

Beat shortening and sugar at medium speed with an electric mixer until creamy. Add eggs, 1 at a time, beating until blended after each addition. Stir in date mixture, orange rind, and orange juice. Add remaining flour mixture alternately with buttermilk, beginning and ending with flour mixture. Beat at low speed until blended after each addition. Pour batter into a lightly greased 10-inch tube pan.

Bake at 350° for 1 hour and 10 minutes or until a long wooden skewer inserted in center comes out clean. Place pan on a wire rack. Pour warm sauce over warm cake; cool completely in pan on rack. Yield: 1 (10-inch) cake.

Sauce

1 cup sugar
1 cup fresh orange juice
1⅓ tablespoons grated orange rind

Combine all ingredients in a small saucepan. Bring to boil. Yield: 1½ cups.

Colleen McMahan

Diamond Delights
Diamond Hill Elementary School
Abbeville, South Carolina

White Wine Cake

½ cup finely chopped pecans, divided
1 (18.25-ounce) package yellow cake mix (we tested with Pillsbury)
1 (3.4-ounce) package vanilla instant pudding mix
¾ cup water
¾ cup vegetable oil
¼ cup dry white wine
4 large eggs
¼ cup sugar
¼ cup firmly packed brown sugar
2 teaspoons ground cinnamon
¼ cup butter or margarine
½ cup sugar
2 tablespoons water
2 tablespoons dry white wine

Grease and flour a 12-cup Bundt pan; sprinkle ¼ cup pecans evenly in pan.

Combine remaining ¼ cup pecans, cake mix, and next 8 ingredients in a large mixing bowl; beat at low speed with an electric mixer until blended. Beat at medium speed 2 more minutes. Pour batter into prepared pan.

Bake at 350° for 1 hour or until a long wooden skewer inserted in center comes out clean. Cool in pan on a wire rack 25 minutes; invert cake onto a serving plate.

Immediately combine butter and remaining 3 ingredients in a small saucepan; bring to a boil over medium-high heat, stirring occasionally. Brush evenly over warm cake, and cool completely. Yield: 1 (10-inch) cake.

A Century of Serving
The Junior Board of Christiana Care, Inc.
Wilmington, Delaware

German Chocolate Pound Cake

1 (4-ounce) sweet chocolate bar, chopped
1 cup butter or margarine, softened
½ cup shortening
3 cups sugar
5 large eggs
3 cups all-purpose flour
1 teaspoon baking powder
½ teaspoon salt
1 cup milk
1½ teaspoons vanilla extract
½ teaspoon lemon extract
1 cup chopped pecans (optional)
Chocolate Frosting

Microwave chocolate in a glass bowl at MEDIUM (50% power) 2 minutes or until melted, stirring twice.

Beat butter and shortening at medium speed with an electric mixer about 2 minutes or until creamy. Gradually add sugar, beating 5 to 7 minutes. Add eggs, 1 at a time, beating just until yellow disappears. Stir in melted chocolate.

Combine flour, baking powder, and salt; add to butter mixture alternately with milk, beginning and ending with flour mixture. Beat at low speed just until blended after each addition. Stir in flavorings. Fold in pecans, if desired. Pour batter into a greased and floured 10-inch tube pan.

Bake at 350° for 1 hour and 30 minutes or until a long wooden skewer inserted in center comes out clean. Cool in pan on a wire rack 15 minutes; remove from pan, and cool completely on wire rack. Spread Chocolate Frosting over cooled cake. Yield: 1 (10-inch) cake.

Chocolate Frosting

2 (1-ounce) unsweetened chocolate squares
1 (16-ounce) package powdered sugar, sifted
½ cup butter or margarine, softened
¼ cup milk
1 teaspoon lemon juice

Microwave chocolate in a glass bowl at MEDIUM (50% power) 3 minutes or until melted, stirring twice. Combine chocolate, sugar, and remaining ingredients in a mixing bowl; beat at medium speed until spreading consistency. Yield: 2 cups. Bettie Weathersby

Down Home Dining in Mississippi
Mississippi Homemaker Volunteers, Inc.
Water Valley, Mississippi

Lemon-Sour Cream Pound Cake

1 cup butter, softened
3 cups sugar
6 large eggs, separated
3 cups all-purpose flour
¼ teaspoon baking soda
1 (8-ounce) container sour cream
1 teaspoon lemon extract

Beat butter at medium speed with an electric mixer about 2 minutes or until creamy. Gradually add sugar, beating 5 to 7 minutes. Add egg yolks, 1 at a time, beating just until yellow disappears.

Combine flour and baking soda; add to butter mixture alternately with sour cream, beginning and ending with flour mixture. Beat at low speed just until blended after each addition. Stir in lemon extract.

Beat egg whites at high speed until stiff peaks form; gently fold into batter. Pour batter into a greased and floured 10-inch tube pan.

Bake at 325° for 1 hour and 30 minutes or until a long wooden skewer inserted in center of cake comes out clean. Cool in pan on a wire rack 15 minutes; remove cake from pan, and cool on wire rack. Yield: 1 (10-inch) cake.

Mattie Lee Hill

A Dab of This and a Dab of That
Bethlehem Baptist Church Senior Missionary
Ninety Six, South Carolina

Peach and Blueberry Pound Cake

Here's a summertime stunner. Juicy ripe peaches and succulent fresh blueberries abound in this cream cheese pound cake. It takes on even more flavor from the fruits if allowed to set overnight before slicing.

½ cup unsalted butter, softened
½ (8-ounce) package cream cheese, softened
2 cups sugar
5 large eggs
¼ cup peach brandy, peach schnapps, or peach nectar
2 cups all-purpose flour
1 teaspoon baking powder
¼ teaspoon salt
1¼ cups diced fresh ripe peaches
1 cup fresh blueberries

Generously grease and sugar a 10-inch tube pan; set aside.

Beat butter and cream cheese at medium speed with an electric mixer about 2 minutes or until creamy. Gradually add sugar, beating 5 to 7 minutes. Add eggs, 1 at a time, beating just until yellow disappears. Stir in brandy.

Combine flour, baking powder, and salt; add to butter mixture, beating at low speed just until blended. Fold in peaches and blueberries. Pour batter into prepared pan.

Bake at 325° for 1 hour and 25 minutes or until a long wooden skewer inserted in center of cake comes out clean. Cool in pan on a wire rack 15 minutes; remove from pan, and cool on wire rack. Yield: 1 (10-inch) cake. Lois Tyler

Sharing Our Best
The Arrangement Hair Salon
Columbus, Ohio

Chocolate-Coconut Cheesecake

1½ cups chocolate wafer crumbs (about 30 wafers)
3 tablespoons sugar
¼ cup butter or margarine, melted
4 (8-ounce) packages cream cheese, softened
1 cup sugar
3 large eggs
1 (14-ounce) package flaked coconut
1 (11.5-ounce) package milk chocolate morsels
1 cup slivered natural almonds, toasted and divided
1 teaspoon vanilla extract
½ cup (3 ounces) semisweet chocolate morsels

Stir together first 3 ingredients; press mixture in bottom of a 10-inch springform pan. Bake at 350° for 8 minutes; cool.

Beat cream cheese at high speed with an electric mixer until creamy; gradually add 1 cup sugar, beating well. Add eggs, 1 at a time, beating until blended after each addition. Stir in coconut, milk chocolate morsels, ½ cup almond slivers, and vanilla. Pour batter into prepared pan.

Bake at 350° for 55 to 60 minutes or until cheesecake is almost set. Remove from oven; cool to room temperature in pan on a wire rack. Cover and chill at least 8 hours. Remove sides of pan.

Place semisweet chocolate morsels in a small heavy-duty, zip-top plastic bag, and seal. Submerge bag in hot water until chocolate melts. Snip a tiny hole in 1 corner of bag, and drizzle melted chocolate over cheesecake. Sprinkle with remaining ½ cup almond slivers. Yield: 16 servings.

Jan Moon

Bread from the Brook
The Church at Brook Hills
Birmingham, Alabama

Frozen Peppermint Cheesecake

Crushed peppermint candy imbues this no-bake cheesecake with holiday spirit. For a classic pairing, serve slices in puddles of rich chocolate sauce.

1¼ cups chocolate wafer crumbs (about 25 wafers)
¼ cup sugar
¼ cup butter or margarine, melted
1 (8-ounce) package cream cheese, softened
1 (14-ounce) can sweetened condensed milk
1 cup crushed hard peppermint candy
2 cups whipping cream

Stir together first 3 ingredients; press mixture in bottom and 1 inch up sides of a 9-inch springform pan. Set aside.

Beat cream cheese at medium speed with an electric mixer until creamy. Gradually add milk, beating until smooth. Stir in candy.

Beat whipping cream until soft peaks form; gently fold whipped cream into cream cheese mixture. Pour into prepared pan. Cover and freeze 6 hours or until firm. Remove sides of pan just before serving. Yield: 12 servings.

Picnics, Potlucks & Prizewinners
Indiana 4-H Foundation
Indianapolis, Indiana

Chocolate-Almond Flourless Torte

Not to worry if, when removed from the oven, this torte takes a bit of a tumble and cracks. It's supposed to. A dusting of powdered sugar, a dollop of whipped cream, and a sprinkle of fresh berries dress it up.

10 (1-ounce) bittersweet chocolate squares, broken into pieces (we tested with Ghirardelli)
½ cup sugar, divided
½ cup unsalted butter, softened
5 large eggs, separated
⅓ cup blanched almonds, finely ground
2 tablespoons Cognac
Sifted powdered sugar
Whipped cream
Fresh raspberries

Melt chocolate in a heavy saucepan over low heat, stirring until smooth. Let cool slightly.

Combine ¼ cup sugar and butter in a large mixing bowl; beat at medium speed with an electric mixer until creamy. Add egg yolks, and beat 1 minute. Add ground almonds and Cognac, and beat 2 more minutes. Stir in melted chocolate.

Beat egg whites at high speed until foamy. Gradually add remaining ¼ cup sugar, 1 tablespoon at a time, beating until stiff peaks form and sugar dissolves (2 to 4 minutes). Gently fold ¼ cup chocolate mixture into beaten egg whites; gradually fold egg white mixture into remaining chocolate mixture. Pour into a greased and parchment paper-lined 9-inch springform pan.

Bake at 300° for 40 minutes or until top begins to lose its shine. Cool in pan on a wire rack 30 minutes. (Cake will fall during this time.) Loosen torte from sides of pan, using a narrow metal spatula, and remove sides of pan. Cool torte completely on wire rack. Sprinkle with powdered sugar. Serve with whipped cream and raspberries. Yield: 8 to 10 servings.

Bea Westin

. . . And It Was Very Good
Temple Emeth
Teaneck, New Jersey

Chocolate Truffle Torte

1 cup (6 ounces) semisweet chocolate morsels
½ cup butter or margarine
½ cup all-purpose flour
4 large eggs, separated
½ cup sugar
1 (2½-ounce) package hazelnuts, chopped and divided (about ½ cup)
Chocolate Truffle Filling

Grease 2 (9-inch) round cakepans; line with parchment paper. Grease and flour parchment paper.

Melt chocolate morsels and butter in a heavy saucepan over low heat until smooth. Cool 5 minutes. Stir in flour until smooth. Add egg yolks, 1 at a time, stirring just until blended after each addition.

Beat egg whites at high speed with an electric mixer until foamy. Gradually add sugar, 1 tablespoon at a time, beating until stiff peaks form and sugar dissolves (2 to 4 minutes). Gently fold beaten egg whites and ¼ cup hazelnuts into batter. Pour into prepared pans.

Bake at 325° for 20 to 22 minutes or until a wooden pick inserted in center comes out clean. Cool in pans on wire racks 10 minutes; remove layers from pans, and cool completely on wire racks.

Spread Chocolate Truffle Filling between layers and on top and sides of torte. Press remaining hazelnuts into frosting around top edge of torte. Yield: 8 to 10 servings.

Chocolate Truffle Filling

2 cups (12 ounces) semisweet chocolate morsels
½ cup butter or margarine
½ cup heavy whipping cream

Melt chocolate morsels and butter in a heavy saucepan over low heat until smooth. Remove from heat. Stir in whipping cream. Cover and chill 30 minutes or until filling is thick enough to mound and to hold its shape. Yield: about 3 cups.

Donna Aberle

Cooking with Class
Timber Lake Booster Club
Timber Lake, South Dakota

Cookies & Candies

Tiger Butter, page 126

Starlight Mint Surprises

1 cup butter, softened
1 cup sugar
½ cup firmly packed brown sugar
2 large eggs
1 teaspoon vanilla extract
3 cups all-purpose flour
1 teaspoon baking soda
½ teaspoon salt
2 (4.67-ounce) packages chocolate mint wafer candies (we tested with Andes)

Beat butter at medium speed with an electric mixer until creamy; gradually add sugars, beating well. Add eggs, 1 at a time, beating until blended after each addition. Stir in vanilla.

Combine flour, soda, and salt; add to butter mixture, beating well.

Drop dough by teaspoonfuls 2 inches apart onto ungreased cookie sheets. Press 1 candy on top of each mound of dough; cover with 1 teaspoonful dough. Bake at 375° for 11 minutes or until golden. Immediately remove to wire racks to cool. Yield: about 4 dozen.

Tasty Treasures
Immanuel Lutheran Church Ladies Aid
Leland, Michigan

Zucchini Cookies

1 cup sugar
½ cup butter or margarine, softened
1 large egg
2 cups all-purpose flour
1 teaspoon baking soda
½ teaspoon salt
1 teaspoon ground cinnamon
1 cup grated zucchini, undrained
1 cup raisins
½ cup chopped pecans

Beat sugar and butter at medium speed with an electric mixer until creamy. Add egg; beat well. Combine flour and next 3 ingredients. Add to butter mixture; beat well. Stir in zucchini, raisins, and pecans.

Drop dough by teaspoonfuls onto lightly greased cookie sheets. Bake at 375° for 15 minutes. Cool 1 minute on cookie sheets; remove to wire racks to cool. Yield: 3 dozen. Ann Gillis

Noel Bluffin' We're Still Cookin'
Noel Area Chamber of Commerce
Noel, Missouri

Coconut Scotchies

Butterscotch morsels melt throughout these crisp cookies.

½ cup butter or margarine, softened
½ cup sugar
½ cup firmly packed brown sugar
2 large eggs
1 teaspoon vanilla extract
2 cups all-purpose flour
½ teaspoon baking soda
½ teaspoon salt
1 cup (6 ounces) butterscotch morsels
½ cup chopped pecans
1½ cups flaked coconut

Beat butter at medium speed with an electric mixer until creamy; gradually add sugars, beating well. Add eggs and vanilla; beat well.

Combine flour, soda, and salt; add to butter mixture, and beat well. Stir in butterscotch morsels and pecans.

Place flaked coconut in a shallow dish. Drop dough by rounded teaspoonfuls into coconut, rolling to coat dough with coconut while shaping dough into balls. Place balls on greased cookie sheets. Bake at 350° for 10 minutes. Immediately remove to wire racks to cool. Yield: 4 dozen.

Darwin Shea

Cookbook Seasoned with Love
Upsala Community Presbyterian Church
Sanford, Florida

The Best Cookies

For an extra sweet touch, roll each ball in sugar before flattening.

1 cup butter or margarine, softened
1 cup sugar
1 cup firmly packed brown sugar
1 large egg
1 cup vegetable oil
1 cup uncooked regular oats
1 cup cornflakes cereal, crushed
½ cup flaked coconut
½ cup chopped pecans or walnuts
3½ cups all-purpose flour
1 teaspoon baking soda
1 teaspoon salt
1 teaspoon vanilla extract

Beat butter at medium speed with an electric mixer until creamy; gradually add sugars, beating until light and fluffy. Add egg; beat well. Add oil; beat until smooth. Stir in oats, cereal, coconut, and pecans. Combine flour, soda, and salt; add to butter mixture, mixing until well blended. Stir in vanilla.

Shape dough into 1-inch balls, and place 2 inches apart on ungreased cookie sheets. Flatten cookies in a crisscross pattern with a fork. Bake at 350° for 10 to 12 minutes or until lightly browned. Cool 2 minutes on cookie sheets; remove to wire racks to cool. Yield: 6½ dozen. Peggy Wood, Phyllis Simpson, and Billie English

St. Andrew's Cooks Again
Presbyterian Women of St. Andrew
Beaumont, Texas

Fattigman (Poor Man)

Cardamom's spicy-sweet flavor and pungent aroma make it a favorite in Scandinavian cooking. Ground cinnamon may be substituted.

¼ cup shortening
¾ cup sugar
6 egg yolks
¾ cup heavy whipping cream
1 tablespoon brandy
½ teaspoon lemon extract
3¾ cups all-purpose flour
¼ teaspoon salt
½ teaspoon ground cardamom
Vegetable oil
Sifted powdered sugar

Beat shortening at medium speed with an electric mixer until creamy; gradually add ¾ cup sugar, beating well. Add egg yolks; beat well. Add cream, brandy, and lemon extract; beat well. Combine flour, salt, and cardamom; add to shortening mixture, beating well.

Pour oil to depth of 2 inches into a large heavy skillet; heat to 375°. Meanwhile, roll half of dough to ⅛-inch thickness on a lightly floured surface; cut into 3- x 2-inch diamonds; make a ¾-inch lengthwise slit in the center of each diamond. Gently thread top of diamond down through slit and back up to its original position. (Folding sides in toward center while threading will help prevent tearing.)

Drop 6 to 8 pieces of dough at a time into hot oil. Cook 2 minutes or until golden. Drain on a rack over paper towels, turning once. Repeat rolling, shaping, and cooking procedure with remaining half of dough. Cool completely, and sprinkle with powdered sugar. Yield: 7 dozen.

Sweet Memories
Holy Covenant United Methodist Women
Katy, Texas

Chocolate Shortbreads

Team these pleasingly bitter chocolate shortbreads with a cup of foamy cappuccino or heaping bowlfuls of your favorite ice cream.

2 cups all-purpose flour
1 cup sifted powdered sugar
½ cup cocoa
¼ teaspoon salt
1 cup cold butter, diced
1 teaspoon vanilla extract

Process first 4 ingredients in a food processor until blended. Add butter and vanilla; process until mixture forms a ball, stopping often to scrape down sides.

Roll dough to ¼-inch thickness on a lightly floured surface; cut into 3½- x 1-inch strips, using a sharp knife or fluted pastry cutter. Place 1 inch apart on ungreased cookie sheets. Bake strips at 300° for 18 to 22 minutes. Cool 1 minute on cookie sheets; remove to wire racks to cool completely. Yield: 3½ dozen. Judith Polan

Carnegie Hall Cookbook
Carnegie Hall, Inc.
Lewisburg, West Virginia

Pecan Triangles

1 cup unsalted butter, softened
1 cup sugar
1 egg yolk
2 cups all-purpose flour
1½ tablespoons grated lemon rind
1 egg white, beaten
1 cup finely chopped pecans

Beat butter at medium speed with an electric mixer until creamy; add sugar, beating well. Add egg yolk; beat well. Add flour and lemon rind; beat well. Spread dough into a 12- x 9-inch rectangle on a well-greased cookie sheet. Brush with beaten egg white. Sprinkle with pecans, and press lightly into dough. Bake at 275° for 1 hour and 15 minutes or until golden. Immediately cut into 2½-inch squares; cut diagonally into triangles. Cool 1 minute on cookie sheet; remove to wire racks to cool. Yield: 3 dozen.

Bravo! Recipes, Legends & Lore
University Musical Society
Ann Arbor, Michigan

Crème de Menthe Bars

Rich, moist, and luscious layers flavored with chocolate syrup and mint inspired our Test Kitchens staff to give these bars our highest rating.

½ cup butter or margarine, softened
1 cup sugar
4 large eggs
1 teaspoon vanilla extract
1 cup all-purpose flour
½ teaspoon salt
1 (16-ounce) can chocolate syrup
½ cup chopped pecans
½ cup butter or margarine, softened
2 cups sifted powdered sugar
1 to 1½ tablespoons crème de menthe
1 cup (6 ounces) semisweet chocolate morsels
6 tablespoons butter or margarine

Beat ½ cup butter at medium speed with an electric mixer until creamy; add 1 cup sugar, beating well. Add eggs and vanilla; beat well.

Combine flour and salt; add to butter mixture, beating mixture well. Stir in chocolate syrup and pecans. Pour batter into a greased

13- x 9-inch pan. Bake at 350° for 30 minutes. Cool completely in pan on a wire rack.

Beat ½ cup butter at medium speed until creamy; add powdered sugar and crème de menthe, beating until smooth. Spread over cooled brownie layer.

Combine chocolate morsels and 6 tablespoons butter in a small heavy saucepan over low heat, stirring until smooth. Cool 5 minutes, and spread over crème de menthe layer. Cover and chill at least 1 hour. Cut into bars. Yield: 2 dozen. Jodie Gouthier

Favorite Recipes Taste of Tradition
B.A. Ritter Senior Citizen Center
Nederland, Texas

Peanut Butter Swirl Bars

½ cup crunchy peanut butter
⅓ cup butter or margarine, softened
¾ cup firmly packed brown sugar
¾ cup sugar
2 large eggs
2 teaspoons vanilla extract
1 cup all-purpose flour
1 teaspoon baking powder
¼ teaspoon salt
2 cups (12 ounces) semisweet chocolate morsels

Beat first 4 ingredients at medium speed with an electric mixer until creamy. Add eggs and vanilla; beat well.

Combine flour, baking powder, and salt; add to butter mixture, beating well. Spread batter in an ungreased 13- x 9-inch pan. Sprinkle with chocolate morsels. Bake at 350° for 5 minutes. Remove from oven. Run a knife through batter to swirl chocolate. Return to oven, and bake 30 more minutes. Cool completely in pan on a wire rack. Cut into bars. Yield: 2 dozen. Barb Petit

The Cookbook Tour
Good Shepherd Lutheran Church
Plainview, Minnesota

Toffee Cookie Bars

Look for almond brickle chips and English toffee bits on the baking aisle of your grocery store.

½ cup butter or margarine
1½ cups graham cracker crumbs (about 12 rectangle crackers)
1 (14-ounce) can sweetened condensed milk
1¼ cups almond brickle chips
1¼ cups English toffee bits or crushed English toffee candy bars
1 cup (6 ounces) semisweet chocolate morsels
1 cup chopped pecans
½ cup sliced natural almonds

Place butter in a 13- x 9-inch baking dish; bake at 325° for 4 minutes or until butter melts.

Layer graham cracker crumbs and remaining 6 ingredients in baking dish with melted butter. Firmly press mixture in dish.

Bake at 325° for 25 minutes or until edges are lightly browned. Cool completely in dish on a wire rack. Cut into bars. Yield: 2 dozen.

Tropical Toffee Bars

Substitute 1 cup chopped dried pineapple combined with 2 tablespoons almond liqueur, ¾ cup flaked coconut, and 1 (3.5-ounce) jar macadamia nuts, chopped, for the toffee bits, pecans, and almonds.

Picnics, Potlucks & Prizewinners
Indiana 4-H Foundation, Inc.
Indianapolis, Indiana

Ultimate Blondies

These blond beauties filled with peanut butter and chocolate morsels, walnuts, and cinnamon are the ultimate treat. They're so full of goodies that they won't test done with a wooden pick, so look for the edges to become lightly browned.

1 cup butter or margarine, softened
⅔ cup sugar
⅔ cup firmly packed brown sugar
2 large eggs
⅔ cup half-and-half
2 teaspoons vanilla extract
2½ cups all-purpose flour
1 teaspoon baking powder
½ teaspoon salt
1½ teaspoons ground cinnamon
1 cup (6 ounces) semisweet chocolate morsels
1 cup (6 ounces) peanut butter morsels
¾ cup coarsely chopped walnuts, toasted

Beat butter at medium speed with an electric mixer until creamy. Gradually add sugars, beating until light and fluffy. Add eggs, 1 at a time, beating well after each addition. Add half-and-half and vanilla; beat until smooth.

Combine flour and next 3 ingredients; gradually add to butter mixture, beating at low speed after each addition until blended. Add morsels and nuts; beat at low speed until blended.

Spread batter into a greased 13- x 9-inch pan. Bake at 350° for 25 to 30 minutes or until lightly browned. Cool completely in pan on a wire rack. Cut into bars. Yield: 2 dozen. Kimberely Buzzell

Cooking with Pride
Madison Park/Camelview PTO
Phoenix, Arizona

Meringue Brownies

Here's a brownie that boasts a cookie dough on the bottom and a crispy meringue topping. They're a textural delight.

½ cup butter or margarine, softened
½ cup sugar
½ cup firmly packed brown sugar
2 egg yolks
1 tablespoon cold water
1 teaspoon vanilla extract
2 cups all-purpose flour
1 teaspoon baking powder
¼ teaspoon baking soda
¼ teaspoon salt
1½ cups (9 ounces) semisweet chocolate morsels
2 egg whites
½ cup sugar
½ cup chopped pecans, toasted (optional)

Beat butter at medium speed with an electric mixer until creamy; gradually add ½ cup sugar and brown sugar, beating until light and fluffy. Add egg yolks, beating well. Add water and vanilla, beating mixture well.

Combine flour and next 3 ingredients; gradually add to butter mixture, beating at low speed until blended after each addition. (Dough will be crumbly.) Press dough into a buttered 13- x 9-inch pan. Sprinkle with chocolate morsels.

Beat egg whites at high speed with an electric mixer until foamy; gradually add ½ cup sugar, 1 tablespoon at a time, beating until glossy and consistency of marshmallow cream (stiff peaks will not form). Carefully spread egg white mixture over chocolate morsels. (Batter will be thin in pan.) Sprinkle with pecans, if desired. Bake at 375° for 23 minutes or until lightly browned. Cool completely in pan on a wire rack. Cut into squares. Yield: 2½ dozen. Betty Pawlowski

Our Saviour's Lutheran Church 75th Anniversary Cookbook
Our Saviour's Lutheran Church
Casper, Wyoming

Mint Julep Brownies

For a truly sinful dessert experience, serve these bourbon-spiked brownies warm topped with a dainty scoop or two of mint chocolate chip ice cream.

1 cup butter or margarine
4 (1-ounce) unsweetened chocolate squares
4 large eggs
2 cups sugar
1½ cups all-purpose flour
½ teaspoon salt
2 tablespoons bourbon
1 teaspoon peppermint extract
1 tablespoon powdered sugar

Melt butter and chocolate in a heavy saucepan over low heat, stirring until smooth; cool slightly. Beat eggs at medium speed with an electric mixer 2 minutes. Gradually add 2 cups sugar, beating well. Add chocolate mixture, flour, and next 3 ingredients; beat well. Pour batter into a greased and floured 13- x 9-inch pan.

Bake at 350° for 25 to 30 minutes. Cool completely in pan on a wire rack. Cut into bars, and sprinkle brownies with powdered sugar. Yield: 2 dozen.

Muffie Ellis

All We Need Is Love
Columbus-Lowndes Humane Society
Columbus, Mississippi

Cranberry Squares

2 cups all-purpose flour
1½ teaspoons baking powder
½ teaspoon baking soda
1 teaspoon salt
1 cup sugar
¾ cup orange juice
2 tablespoons shortening
1 large egg, lightly beaten
1½ cups fresh or frozen cranberries, chopped
½ cup chopped pecans
¼ cup all-purpose flour
⅓ cup sugar
¾ teaspoon ground cinnamon
2 tablespoons butter or margarine

Combine first 5 ingredients in a large mixing bowl. Add orange juice, shortening, and egg; beat at medium speed with an electric mixer until blended. Fold in cranberries and pecans. Pour into a greased 13- x 9-inch pan.

Combine ¼ cup flour, ⅓ cup sugar, and cinnamon. Cut in butter with a pastry blender until mixture is crumbly; sprinkle over batter.

Bake at 350° for 30 to 35 minutes or until a wooden pick inserted in center comes out clean. Cut into squares. Serve warm. Yield: 15 squares.

The Cookbook of the Museum of Science, Boston
The Volunteer Service League of the Museum of Science, Boston
Boston, Massachusetts

Pumpkin Cheesecake Squares

Pumpkin and spice make these squares perfect holiday fare while a pound cake mix makes them a snap to prepare.

1 (16-ounce) package pound cake mix (we tested with Betty Crocker)
4 teaspoons pumpkin pie spice, divided
3 large eggs, divided
2 tablespoons butter, melted
1 (8-ounce) package cream cheese, softened
1 (15-ounce) can pumpkin
1 (14-ounce) can sweetened condensed milk
½ teaspoon salt
1 cup chopped pecans

Combine cake mix, 2 teaspoons pumpkin pie spice, 1 egg, and butter in a large mixing bowl; beat at low speed with an electric mixer until crumbly. Press dough into a greased 15- x 10-inch jellyroll pan.

Beat softened cream cheese at medium speed until creamy. Add remaining 2 teaspoons pumpkin pie spice, remaining 2 eggs, pumpkin, condensed milk, and salt; beat until blended. Pour over crust; sprinkle with pecans. Bake at 350° for 30 minutes or until set. Cool completely in pan on a wire rack. Cover and chill. Cut into squares. Yield: 4 dozen

Pam Johnson

Angels in the Kitchen Cookbook
Community Presbyterian Church
Celebration, Florida

Honeycutt Divinity

2⅔ cups sugar
⅔ cup water
⅔ cup light corn syrup
2 egg whites
1 teaspoon baking powder
1 teaspoon vanilla extract
1½ cups chopped walnuts

Combine first 3 ingredients in a 3-quart saucepan; cook over low heat, stirring constantly, until sugar dissolves. Cover and cook over medium heat 2 to 3 minutes to wash down sugar crystals from sides of pan. Uncover and cook over medium heat, without stirring, until candy thermometer registers 260° (hard ball stage). Remove from heat.

Beat egg whites and baking powder in a large mixing bowl at high speed with an electric mixer until stiff peaks form.

Pour hot sugar mixture in a heavy stream over beaten egg whites, beating constantly at high speed. Add vanilla, and continue beating just until mixture holds its shape (about 4 minutes). Stir in walnuts.

Spoon into a greased 11- x 7-inch baking dish. Let cool. Cut into squares. Yield: 2 dozen (2 pounds).

Bill Honeycutt

202's Totally Tempting Treasures
American Legion Auxiliary Green-Pierce Unit 202
Wichita Falls, Texas

Tiger Butter

16 (1-ounce) white chocolate baking squares, finely chopped (we tested with Baker's)
¾ cup creamy peanut butter
2 cups (12 ounces) semisweet chocolate morsels

Combine white chocolate and peanut butter in a glass bowl. Microwave at HIGH 2½ minutes or until melted, stirring twice. Pour into a wax paper-lined 15- x 10-inch jellyroll pan, spreading evenly.

Microwave chocolate morsels in a glass bowl at HIGH 2½ minutes or until melted, stirring twice. Pour over white chocolate mixture; swirl gently with a knife. Chill until firm. Break into pieces. Store in an airtight container in refrigerator. Yield: 2 pounds. Marsha Schewe

Savory Secrets
Runnels School
Baton Rouge, Louisiana

Double-Decker Fudge

1½ cups (10 ounces) peanut butter morsels, divided
½ cup cocoa
¼ cup butter or margarine, softened
1 teaspoon vanilla extract
4½ cups sugar
1 (12-ounce) can evaporated milk
1 (7-ounce) jar marshmallow cream
¼ cup butter or margarine

Line a 13- x 9-inch pan with aluminum foil; lightly grease foil, and set pan aside. Place half of peanut butter morsels in a medium bowl; set aside.

Combine cocoa, ¼ cup butter, and vanilla in a mixing bowl; beat at medium speed with an electric mixer until smooth (mixture will be very thick). Stir in remaining half of peanut butter morsels.

Combine sugar and remaining 3 ingredients in a heavy 4-quart saucepan. Cook over medium heat until mixture comes to a boil, stirring constantly. Increase heat to medium-high, and cook 6 more minutes. Remove from heat. Immediately add half of mixture to reserved peanut butter morsels in bowl. Add remaining half of mixture to cocoa mixture. Stir peanut butter morsel mixture 2 minutes or until morsels are completely melted. Pour mixture into prepared pan.

Beat cocoa mixture with a wooden spoon 3 minutes or until morsels melt and mixture is slightly thickened. Spread cocoa mixture over layer in pan. Cool. Remove fudge from pan. Remove foil, and cut fudge into squares. Yield: 8 dozen (about 4 pounds). Angie Oubre

St. Philomena's Jr. Beta Delicious Recipes of the Future
St. Philomena School's Junior Beta Club
Labadieville, Louisiana

Fudge Balls

1½ pounds milk chocolate, broken into pieces (we tested with Hershey's)
1 cup whipping cream
2 cups ground walnuts

Melt chocolate in a heavy saucepan over low heat, stirring until smooth. Meanwhile, beat whipping cream at medium speed with a heavy-duty mixer until soft peaks form. Gradually add melted chocolate, and beat 15 minutes. Cover and chill 8 hours.

Working with half of chocolate mixture at a time, roll into 1-inch balls. (Keep remaining half of chocolate mixture chilled.) Roll balls in walnuts until completely coated. Repeat procedure with remaining half of chocolate mixture and walnuts. Store in an airtight container in refrigerator. Yield: 4 dozen. Jan Rathsack

Home Furniture's 50th Anniversary 1949-1999: Secret Family Cookbook
Make a Wish Foundation
Appleton, Wisconsin

Chocolate-Orange Truffles

Crushed cookies and ground almonds turn these truffles into a cookielike treat.

1 (4-ounce) sweet chocolate bar
20 cream-filled chocolate sandwich cookies, crushed (about 2 cups crumbs)
1 cup ground almonds, toasted
3 tablespoons whipping cream
2 tablespoons orange liqueur
1 tablespoon finely chopped orange rind
1 tablespoon fresh orange juice
Powdered sugar
Toasted ground almonds
Cocoa

Melt chocolate in a heavy saucepan over low heat, stirring until smooth. Remove from heat; stir in cookie crumbs and next 5 ingredients. Shape mixture into 1-inch balls, washing hands as necessary. Cover and chill 20 minutes.

Roll balls in powdered sugar, ground almonds, or cocoa. Store in an airtight container in refrigerator. Yield: 3 dozen. Pam Johnson

Angels in the Kitchen Cookbook
Community Presbyterian Church
Celebration, Florida

Desserts

Mocha Mud Pie, page 144

Bananas Flambé

This dramatic dessert has been prepared table side by experienced servers in New Orleans for many generations. Be careful to flambé the dish a safe distance from the heat source.

½ cup butter or margarine
4 medium bananas, peeled and sliced
¼ cup sugar
¼ cup banana liqueur
½ teaspoon ground cinnamon
¼ cup brandy
Vanilla ice cream

Melt butter in a large skillet over medium-high heat. Add banana; cook, stirring constantly, 1 minute or until tender. Gently stir in sugar, banana liqueur, and cinnamon.

Pour brandy into a small long-handled saucepan; heat just until warm. Remove from heat. Ignite with a long match, and pour over banana. Baste banana with sauce until flames die down. Serve immediately over ice cream. Yield: 4 to 6 servings. Rosalie Herman

Tasty Treasures
Immanuel Lutheran Church Ladies Aid
Leland, Michigan

Summer Jewel

1 cup chopped Fuji or Golden Delicious apple
1 cup cantaloupe or honeydew melon balls
1 cup seedless green grapes
1 cup chopped fresh peaches or plums
1 cup chopped fresh pear
1 cup pitted fresh Bing cherries
1½ cups sugar, divided
1½ cups orange liqueur, divided
1 cantaloupe or small honeydew melon, peeled
Garnish: fresh mint sprigs

Combine first 6 ingredients in a medium bowl; stir in 1 cup sugar and 1 cup orange liqueur. Cover and chill 2 hours.

Slice whole melon into 8 rings, removing and discarding seeds and membranes. Place rings in a shallow dish, and sprinkle with remaining ½ cup sugar and remaining ½ cup orange liqueur. Cover and chill 2 hours.

To serve, place a melon ring on each dessert plate; spoon fruit mixture into center of each ring. Garnish, if desired. Yield: 8 servings.

Seaboard to Sideboard
The Junior League of Wilmington, North Carolina

Raspberries in Chocolate Ganache

Save this elegant dessert for a special occasion. It's a grand choice for an anniversary celebration or Valentine's Day because it makes a cozy two servings.

1 (4-ounce) semisweet chocolate bar, chopped (we tested with Ghirardelli) or ⅔ cup (4 ounces) semisweet chocolate morsels
⅓ cup heavy whipping cream
2 cups fresh raspberries, divided
2 tablespoons sugar
2 tablespoons fresh orange juice
1 tablespoon raspberry liqueur or orange juice
½ teaspoon fresh lemon juice
Garnish: heavy whipping cream, whipped

Place chocolate in a small bowl. Heat ⅓ cup whipping cream in a small saucepan over medium-high heat just to simmering. Pour over chocolate; let stand 4 minutes. Stir until chocolate melts.

Working quickly, spoon chocolate ganache into 2 individual stemmed glasses (such as 8-ounce martini glasses). Turn glasses to coat sides evenly with ganache; let remaining ganache pool in bottom of glasses. Place glasses in freezer until chocolate is firm.

Process 1 cup raspberries, sugar, and next 3 ingredients in a blender until smooth, stopping once to scrape down sides. Pour mixture through a wire-mesh strainer into a bowl, pressing against sides of strainer with back of a spoon. Discard seeds. Cover and chill raspberry puree.

Place remaining 1 cup raspberries in chocolate-coated glasses; spoon raspberry puree over berries. Garnish, if desired. Yield: 2 servings.

Sounds Delicious: The Flavor of Atlanta in Food & Music
Atlanta Symphony Orchestra
Atlanta, Georgia

Cuban Cheesecake Flan

Caramelized sugar drizzles and drips over wedges of this creamy cross between a cheesecake and flan.

½ cup sugar
1 (14-ounce) can sweetened condensed milk
1 (12-ounce) can evaporated milk
1 (8-ounce) package cream cheese, softened
3 large eggs
1 teaspoon vanilla extract

Sprinkle sugar in a small heavy saucepan. Cook over medium heat, stirring constantly with a wooden spoon, until sugar melts and turns light brown. Quickly pour hot caramelized sugar into a lightly oiled 10-inch deep-dish pieplate, tilting to coat bottom; set aside. (Sugar will harden and crack.)

Process sweetened condensed milk and remaining 4 ingredients in a blender until smooth, stopping once to scrape down sides. Pour custard mixture over sugar in pieplate. Place in a large shallow pan. Add hot water to pan to depth of 1 inch. Bake, uncovered, at 350° for 55 minutes or until a knife inserted near center comes out clean.

Remove pieplate from water; cool flan completely in pieplate on a wire rack. Cover and chill 8 hours. Loosen edges of flan with a spatula, and invert onto a rimmed serving plate, letting melted caramelized sugar drizzle over top. Yield: 8 servings.

Dining by Design: Stylish Recipes, Savory Settings
The Junior League of Pasadena, California

Berry Mousse

Add instant refinement to this smooth strawberry standout by serving it in stemmed wine glasses.

1½ cups fresh strawberries (about 16 small)
1 (8-ounce) package cream cheese, cut into cubes and softened
½ cup sifted powdered sugar
½ (8-ounce) container frozen whipped topping, thawed
Toasted sliced natural almonds

Process first 3 ingredients in a food processor until smooth. Transfer mixture to a large bowl; fold whipped topping into berry mixture.

Spoon berry mixture into 6 (6-ounce) dessert dishes. Chill at least 3 hours or up to 8 hours. Sprinkle evenly with almonds. Yield: 6 servings.

Bobbi Hoffman

Carnegie Hall Cookbook
Carnegie Hall, Inc.
Lewisburg, West Virginia

Best-Ever Date Pudding

1 cup all-purpose flour
1 teaspoon baking powder
¼ teaspoon salt
1 cup sugar
½ cup milk
1 cup whole pitted dates, chopped
½ cup chopped walnuts
2 cups boiling water
1 cup firmly packed brown sugar
1 tablespoon butter or margarine
1 teaspoon grated orange rind
Whipped cream (optional)

Combine first 4 ingredients in a medium bowl; stir in milk. Stir in chopped dates and walnuts. Pour batter into a lightly greased 9-inch square pan.

Combine water and next 3 ingredients in a saucepan; bring to a boil. Reduce heat, and simmer, uncovered, 5 minutes. Pour sugar mixture over batter. Bake, uncovered, at 350° for 30 to 35 minutes or until edges are bubbly. Serve warm with whipped cream, if desired. Yield: 9 servings.

Norm Walthers

Cookin' in the Canyon
Jarbidge Community Hall
Jarbidge, Nevada

Pineapple-Angel Food Trifle

Try this pretty layered concoction the next time you need a quick yet impressive dessert for a crowd. Convenience products and a store-bought angel food cake make preparation a breeze.

1 (20-ounce) can crushed pineapple in juice, undrained
2 (3.4-ounce) packages instant vanilla pudding mix
3 cups milk
1 (8-ounce) container sour cream
1 (20-ounce) round angel food cake
1 (8-ounce) container frozen whipped topping, thawed
Toasted flaked coconut (optional)

Drain pineapple, reserving 1 cup juice.

Combine ½ cup pineapple juice, pudding mix, and milk in a large mixing bowl; beat at low speed with an electric mixer until thickened. Fold in pineapple and sour cream.

Cut cake into 3 horizontal layers; cut each cake layer into cubes. Place one-third of cake cubes in a 12-cup trifle dish or large glass bowl. Drizzle cake cubes with one-third of remaining ½ cup pineapple juice. Spoon one-third of pudding mixture over cake cubes. Repeat layers twice. Spread whipped topping over trifle. Sprinkle with coconut, if desired. Cover and chill at least 3 hours. Yield: 12 to 14 servings.

Katie Gardner Jordan

Walking with Christ
First Baptist Church
Mount Airy, North Carolina

Serious Chocolate Freezer Soufflés

Those who are serious about their fondness for chocolate are sure to endorse these pretty chocolate puffs. Their make-ahead, freeze and bake nature adds to their appeal.

½ cup all-purpose flour
¾ cup cocoa
1 cup sugar, divided
¼ teaspoon salt
2 cups milk
6 egg yolks, lightly beaten
2 tablespoons butter or margarine
1 teaspoon vanilla extract
8 egg whites
¼ teaspoon cream of tartar
Hot fudge sauce

Butter bottom and sides of 8 (6-ounce) custard cups or soufflé dishes, and sprinkle lightly with sugar. Set aside.

Combine flour, cocoa, ¾ cup sugar, and salt in a medium saucepan. Gradually whisk in milk. Cook over medium heat, stirring constantly, until thick and bubbly. Remove from heat.

Beat egg yolks until thick and pale. Gradually stir 2 tablespoons hot mixture into yolks; add to remaining hot mixture, stirring constantly. Stir in butter and vanilla.

Beat egg whites and cream of tartar at high speed with an electric mixer until foamy. Add remaining ¼ cup sugar, 1 tablespoon at a time, beating until stiff peaks form and sugar dissolves (2 to 4 minutes). Fold into chocolate mixture. Spoon into prepared cups. Cover and freeze until firm.

When ready to bake, uncover and place 1 inch apart on rack in cold oven. Set oven temperature to 350°. Bake 45 minutes or until tops are puffed. Cut a slit in top of each soufflé, and place 1 teaspoon fudge sauce into each slit. Serve immediately with additional fudge sauce. Yield: 8 servings.

A Thyme to Remember
Dallas County Medical Society Alliance
Dallas, Texas

Apple Burritos

Cap these simple, warm apple wraps with a scoop of creamy vanilla ice cream or frozen yogurt.

1 (21-ounce) can apple pie filling
8 (6-inch) flour tortillas
1½ cups apple cider
¾ cup sugar
¾ cup butter or margarine

Spoon about ⅓ cup pie filling onto each tortilla; roll up tortillas, and place seam side down in a lightly greased 11- x 7-inch baking dish.

Combine apple cider, sugar, and butter in a medium saucepan; bring to a boil. Reserve ½ cup sauce; pour remaining sauce over tortillas. Cover and bake at 350° for 30 minutes. Uncover and bake 18 more minutes or until tortillas are lightly browned. Serve warm with reserved sauce. Yield: 8 servings. Hazel Gee-Allegre

Recipes from the Kitchens of Family & Friends
Gresham Women of Elks
Gresham, Oregon

French Crêpes with Sweet Cherry Sauce

1 cup all-purpose flour
1 teaspoon baking powder
½ teaspoon salt
½ teaspoon sugar
1 cup milk
3 large eggs
1 tablespoon butter or margarine, melted
2 (8-ounce) packages cream cheese, softened
3 tablespoons sugar
1 teaspoon grated lemon rind
½ teaspoon vanilla extract
Sweet Cherry Sauce

Whisk together first 5 ingredients until smooth. Whisk in eggs and butter. Chill batter at least 2 hours.

Stir together cream cheese and next 3 ingredients. Cover and chill.

Coat bottom of a 6-inch crêpe pan or heavy skillet with cooking spray; place over medium heat until hot.

Pour 2 tablespoons batter into pan; quickly tilt pan in all directions so batter covers bottom of pan. Cook 1 minute or until crêpe can be shaken loose from pan. Turn crêpe over, and cook about 30 seconds. Place crêpe on a dish towel to cool. Repeat with remaining batter.

Place about 2½ tablespoons cheese mixture in center of each of 12 crêpes. Roll up loosely. Place crêpes, seam side down, in a 15- x 10-inch jellyroll pan. Cover with aluminum foil. Bake at 400° for 15 minutes or until thoroughly heated. Serve with warm Sweet Cherry Sauce.

Stack the remaining 6 crêpes between sheets of wax paper, and place in an airtight container. Chill up to 2 days, or freeze up to 3 months. Fill as desired with fruit or ice cream. Yield: 12 servings.

Sweet Cherry Sauce

⅓ cup sugar
2 teaspoons cornstarch
½ cup water
2 cups fresh sweet cherries, pitted
½ teaspoon grated lemon rind
1 tablespoon fresh lemon juice

Combine sugar and cornstarch in a medium saucepan. Stir in water. Cook over medium heat, stirring constantly, until mixture thickens and boils. Boil 1 minute, stirring constantly. Stir in cherries, and simmer 4 more minutes. Remove from heat; stir in lemon rind and lemon juice. Yield: 1½ cups.

Sarah Lee McGee

Walking with Christ
First Baptist Church
Mount Airy, North Carolina

Most Wonderful Winter Crisp

3 Granny Smith apples, peeled and sliced
2 cups fresh cranberries
1 (8-ounce) can crushed pineapple in juice, undrained
½ cup sugar
1 cup firmly packed brown sugar
¼ cup all-purpose flour
½ cup butter or margarine
1 cup uncooked regular oats
1 cup chopped pecans
Sweetened whipped cream or vanilla ice cream

Layer first 3 ingredients in a lightly greased 13- x 9-inch baking dish; sprinkle with ½ cup sugar.

Combine brown sugar and flour; cut in butter with a pastry blender until mixture is crumbly. Stir in oats and pecans. Sprinkle oat mixture evenly over fruit mixture. Bake, uncovered, at 375° for 30 minutes or until bubbly and thoroughly heated. Serve with whipped cream or ice cream. Yield: 8 servings.

Note: To make this crisp ahead, cover and chill overnight before baking. Let stand at room temperature 20 minutes before baking as directed.

Tested by Time
Porter Gaud Parents Guild
Charleston, South Carolina

Irish Coffee Meringue Puffs

You'll discover a double dose of rich coffee flavor hidden within these crispy meringue puffs.

½ cup plus 1 tablespoon sugar, divided
¼ cup firmly packed brown sugar, divided
2 teaspoons instant coffee granules
3 egg whites
Filling
½ cup whipping cream
Garnish: chocolate curls or chocolate-covered coffee beans

Line 2 baking sheets with parchment paper. Trace 8 (3-inch) circles on each sheet. Turn paper over, and place on baking sheets.

Combine ¼ cup sugar, 2 tablespoons brown sugar, and instant coffee granules.

Beat egg whites at high speed with an electric mixer until foamy. Gradually add remaining 5 tablespoons sugar and remaining 2 tablespoons brown sugar, 1 tablespoon at a time, beating until stiff peaks form and sugar dissolves (2 to 4 minutes). Fold in coffee mixture. Drop meringues by rounded tablespoonfuls onto parchment circles. Spread meringues with a knife to fill in traced areas. Bake at 250° for 1 hour or until meringues are dry. Gently remove parchment.

Place 1 meringue on each of 4 individual serving plates; top each meringue with about ½ cup filling. Place another meringue on top of filling, and gently press until filling spreads to edges.

Beat whipping cream until stiff peaks form. Top meringues with a dollop of whipped cream. Garnish, if desired. Yield: 8 servings.

Filling

1½ cups whipping cream
3 tablespoons sugar
3 tablespoons Irish whiskey
1 tablespoon instant coffee granules

Beat whipping cream at high speed with an electric mixer until foamy. Add sugar, whiskey, and coffee granules; beat until stiff peaks form. Yield: 4 cups.

Ambrosia
The Junior Auxiliary of Vicksburg, Mississippi

The Raspberry Meringue

This raspberry meringue is actually eight individual meringues that are filled with a lemon mixture and topped with raspberry sauce, whipped cream, and fresh raspberries. Save the extra raspberry sauce to serve over ice cream.

4 large eggs, separated
½ teaspoon cream of tartar
1½ cups sugar, divided
1 tablespoon grated lemon rind
3 tablespoons fresh lemon juice
¼ teaspoon salt
1 cup whipping cream, whipped
1 (12-ounce) package frozen unsweetened raspberries, thawed
2 tablespoons créme de framboise
2 tablespoons sugar
1 teaspoon cornstarch
1 tablespoon water
1 cup whipping cream, whipped
1 pint fresh raspberries

Beat egg whites and cream of tartar at high speed with an electric mixer until foamy. Add 1 cup sugar, 1 tablespoon at a time, beating until stiff peaks form.

Line baking sheets with unglazed brown paper or parchment paper. (Do not use recycled paper.) Drop mixture by rounded teaspoonfuls 2 inches apart onto paper, making 8 mounds. Make an indentation in center of each with back of a spoon.

Bake at 275° for 1 hour. Turn oven off, and cool in oven 2 to 8 hours (do not open oven door). Carefully remove meringues from paper; store in an airtight container up to 1 week.

Beat egg yolks, lemon rind, and lemon juice with a wire whisk 1 to 2 minutes or until frothy. Stir in ½ cup sugar and salt. Cook over medium heat, stirring constantly, until mixture thickens and boils. Remove from heat, and cool completely. Fold in 1 cup whipped cream. Spoon mixture equally into meringue shells. Cover and chill at least 6 hours.

Process thawed raspberries and liqueur in a blender or food processor 10 seconds or until pureed, stopping once to scrape down sides. Pour mixture through a wire-mesh strainer into a saucepan; press with back of spoon against sides of strainer to squeeze out juice, discarding solids. Add 2 tablespoons sugar, stirring until dissolved. Combine cornstarch and water, stirring until smooth. Stir into raspberry mixture. Cook over medium heat, stirring constantly, until mixture thickens and boils. Remove from heat, and cool completely.

Spoon 2 tablespoons raspberry sauce over lemon-filled meringues. Top with whipped cream, and serve with fresh raspberries. Yield: 8 servings.

Southern . . . On Occasion
The Junior League of Cobb-Marietta
Marietta, Georgia

Chocolate Dessert Waffles

Waffles aren't just for breakfast anymore. Make these chocolate goodies a finale to your meal, and top them with ice cream and caramel sauce.

½ cup vegetable oil
2 large eggs
1 teaspoon vanilla extract
¾ cup water
1¼ cups all-purpose flour
1 teaspoon baking soda
½ teaspoon salt
¾ cup sugar
6 tablespoons cocoa
½ teaspoon ground cinnamon
Vanilla ice cream (optional)
Caramel sauce (optional)

Combine first 3 ingredients in a large mixing bowl; beat at medium speed with an electric mixer until foamy (about 2 minutes). Add water, beating well.

Combine flour and next 5 ingredients; gradually add to egg mixture, beating at low speed until blended.

Spread 1 cup batter onto a preheated, oiled waffle iron; spread batter to edges. Bake until waffle iron stops steaming. Repeat procedure with remaining batter. If desired, serve with vanilla ice cream and caramel sauce. Yield: 12 (4-inch) waffles.

Hearthside: A Country Community Cookbook
Christ Community Church
Weare, New Hampshire

German Blitz Torte

½ cup butter or margarine, softened
½ cup sugar
4 large eggs, separated
1 teaspoon vanilla extract
½ teaspoon almond extract
1 cup sifted cake flour
1 teaspoon baking powder
3 tablespoons milk
1 cup sugar
1 tablespoon sugar
¼ teaspoon ground cinnamon
½ cup sliced natural almonds
1 cup whipping cream
2 teaspoons sugar
½ teaspoon vanilla extract

Beat butter at medium speed with an electric mixer until creamy; gradually add ½ cup sugar, beating well. Add egg yolks, 1 at a time, beating after each addition. Stir in 1 teaspoon vanilla extract and almond extract.

Combine flour and baking powder; add to butter mixture alternately with milk, beginning and ending with flour mixture. Mix at low speed until blended after each addition.

Pour batter into 2 greased and floured 9-inch round cakepans, spreading to cover bottom of pans (layers will be thin).

Beat egg whites at high speed until foamy; gradually add 1 cup sugar, 1 tablespoon at a time, beating until stiff peaks form and sugar dissolves (2 to 4 minutes). Spread meringue over batter, spreading to edge of pans.

Combine 1 tablespoon sugar and cinnamon. Sprinkle cinnamon-sugar mixture and almonds over meringue.

Bake at 350° for 30 minutes. Cool completely in pans on wire racks.

Beat whipping cream at high speed until foamy; gradually add 2 teaspoons sugar and ½ teaspoon vanilla, beating until stiff peaks form.

Place 1 cake layer on a serving plate. Spread half of whipped cream over layer. Repeat procedure with remaining cake layer and whipped cream. Cover and chill until ready to serve. Yield: 10 to 12 servings.

Symphony of Flavors
The Associates of the Redlands Bowl
Redlands, California

Old-Fashioned Ice Cream Roll

¾ cup all-purpose flour
¾ teaspoon baking powder
¼ teaspoon salt
4 large eggs
¾ cup sugar
1 teaspoon vanilla extract
¼ cup powdered sugar
½ gallon vanilla ice cream, softened
1 cup firmly packed brown sugar
½ cup sugar
¼ teaspoon salt
½ cup light corn syrup
1 cup whipping cream
Chopped pecans (optional)

Grease a 15- x 10-inch jellyroll pan; line with wax paper, and grease wax paper. Set pan aside.

Combine flour, baking powder, and ¼ teaspoon salt. Beat eggs and ¾ cup sugar at medium speed with an electric mixer 10 minutes or until thick and pale and tripled in volume. Sift flour mixture over batter, and gently fold in flour mixture and vanilla. Spread batter evenly into prepared pan.

Bake at 375° for 10 minutes or just until cake springs back when lightly touched. (Do not overbake.)

Sift powdered sugar in a 15- x 10-inch rectangle on a cloth towel. When cake is done, immediately loosen from sides of pan, and turn out onto sugared towel. Carefully peel off wax paper.

Starting at narrow end, roll up cake and towel together, and cool completely on a wire rack, seam side down. Unroll cake; spread with ice cream, and carefully reroll cake without towel. Freeze 4 hours or until firm.

Combine brown sugar, ½ cup sugar, ¼ teaspoon salt, and corn syrup in a saucepan. Cook over low heat until sugar dissolves. Stir in cream. Serve warm over ice cream roll slices. Sprinkle with chopped pecans, if desired. Yield: 8 to 10 servings. Dorothy Waggener

Scent from P.E.O. Sisterhood
Philanthropic Educational Organization, Chapter AG
Newcastle, Wyoming

Mocha Mud Pie

1 cup hot fudge sauce, divided
1 (13¾-ounce) package macaroon cookies, crumbled
1 quart chocolate fudge ice cream, slightly softened
1 quart coffee ice cream, slightly softened
Crushed toffee bars (optional)

Microwave ½ cup fudge sauce in a glass bowl at HIGH 20 seconds. Press half of crumbled cookies in a greased 9-inch springform pan. Spread chocolate ice cream over cookie crumbs. Drizzle warm fudge sauce over ice cream. Sprinkle with remaining cookie crumbs. Cover and freeze at least 1 hour.

Microwave remaining ½ cup fudge sauce in glass bowl at HIGH 20 seconds. Spread coffee ice cream over cookie crumb layer. Drizzle with sauce. Sprinkle with crushed toffee bars, if desired. Cover and freeze 4 hours or until firm. Yield: 8 servings. Ginny de Steiger

Great Expectations
The Assistance League of Southeastern Michigan
Rochester Hills, Michigan

Ruby Grapefruit and Lemon Granita

A splash of red food coloring adds a flattering blush to this double citrus fruit delight.

2 cups sugar
4 cups water
2 tablespoons grated lemon rind
1 cup fresh lemon juice
1 tablespoon grated grapefruit rind
1 cup fresh ruby red grapefruit juice
1 drop of red liquid food coloring

Combine sugar and water in a medium saucepan; bring to a boil, stirring until sugar dissolves. Boil 5 minutes. Remove from heat, and cool completely. Stir in lemon rind and remaining ingredients.

Pour mixture into a 13- x 9-inch pan; freeze until almost firm, stirring occasionally. Break frozen mixture into chunks. Process in a food processor until smooth. Return mixture to pan; cover and freeze until firm. Let stand at room temperature 20 minutes before serving. Scrape and shave granita with a fork until fluffy. Serve immediately. Yield: 6 cups.

Simple Pleasures: From Our Table to Yours
Arab Mothers' Club
Arab, Alabama

Lemon and Sauternes Ice Cream (Gelato de Limone e Sauternes)

Gelato is Italian for ice cream; it's typically denser than American brands that contain more air. You won't even need an ice cream maker to freeze this frosty refresher that teases your palate with a creamy yet icy texture. It was a real favorite with our staff.

1 cup sugar
1 cup water
2 cups Sauternes or other sweet white wine
½ cup fresh orange juice
½ cup fresh lemon juice
½ cup whipping cream

Combine sugar and water in a saucepan; bring to a boil. Boil 5 minutes, stirring constantly. Remove from heat, and cool completely. Stir in wine, orange juice, and lemon juice. Pour into an 8-inch square pan; freeze 1½ hours or until slushy. Stir well; freeze 1 hour or until ice begins to form again.

Beat whipping cream at medium speed with an electric mixer until stiff peaks form; fold whipped cream into wine mixture. Cover and freeze at least 8 hours before serving. Yield: 4 cups.

Classic Italian Cooking
Italian American Society of San Marco Island
Marco Island, Florida

Gingered Litchi Sorbet

⅓ cup sugar
¾ cup water
1 tablespoon grated fresh ginger
4 (11-ounce) cans peeled litchis in syrup, undrained
½ cup Muscat Canelli or other sweet white wine

Combine first 3 ingredients in a small saucepan, and cook over medium-low heat until sugar melts, stirring occasionally. Reduce heat, and simmer 5 minutes. Remove from heat, and cool completely.

Drain litchis, reserving ½ cup syrup. Process litchis and reserved syrup in a blender or food processor until smooth. Pour mixture through a wire mesh strainer into a bowl, discarding pulp.

Combine pureed litchis, ginger syrup, and wine. Pour mixture into freezer container of a 2-quart or 1-gallon hand-turned or electric freezer. Freeze according to manufacturer's instructions, stopping after 30 minutes. (Electric freezer will not stop on its own.)

Serve immediately, or transfer sorbet to a 9- x 5-inch loafpan. Cover and freeze until firm. Yield: 3½ cups.

Symphony of Flavors
The Associates of the Redlands Bowl
Redlands, California

Fresh Mango Sorbet

To ensure that this sorbet is top-notch, look for unblemished mangoes with yellow skin and a pretty reddish blush. Ripe ones will hold for a couple of days in a plastic bag in the refrigerator.

2 large ripe mangoes, chopped
1 cup mango nectar
¾ cup sugar
1 tablespoon grated lime rind
½ cup fresh lime juice

Process all ingredients in a food processor until smooth. Pour mixture into freezer container of a 2-quart hand-turned or electric freezer. Freeze according to manufacturer's instructions. Yield: 4 cups.

Gracious Gator Cooks
The Junior League of Gainesville, Florida

Eggs & Cheese

Eggs Diablo, page 148

Eggs Diablo

A dash of green chiles and picante sauce adds magic to these stuffed eggs. Use Monterey Jack cheese with peppers for even more sorcery.

6 hard-cooked eggs, peeled
2 tablespoons finely shredded Monterey Jack cheese
2 tablespoons finely chopped green onions
2 tablespoons canned chopped green chiles, undrained
2 tablespoons mayonnaise
2 tablespoons picante sauce
¼ teaspoon salt
¼ teaspoon pepper
Garnish: roasted sweet red pepper strips

Cut eggs in half lengthwise, and carefully remove yolks. Mash yolks; stir in cheese and next 6 ingredients. Spoon into egg whites. Garnish, if desired. Yield: 12 servings.

Savoring the Southwest Again
Roswell Symphony Guild
Roswell, New Mexico

Salsa Eggs

6 large eggs, lightly beaten
1 (4.5-ounce) can chopped green chiles, drained
1 jalapeño pepper, seeded and minced
¼ teaspoon salt
Dash of ground red pepper
2 tablespoons butter
½ cup finely chopped red bell pepper
Salsa
Sour cream

Stir together first 5 ingredients in a bowl. Melt butter in a large skillet over medium-high heat, tilting pan to coat bottom. Add bell pepper; cook, stirring constantly, 3 minutes or until tender. Reduce heat to medium-low. Add egg mixture; cook, without stirring, until mixture begins to set on bottom. Draw a spatula across bottom of pan to form large curds. Continue cooking until eggs are thickened and firm, but still moist. Serve with salsa and sour cream. Yield: 3 servings.

Pick of the Crop, Two
North Sunflower PTA
Drew, Mississippi

Southwestern Eggs Benedict

Spicy sausage, crispy corn tortillas, fresh cilantro, and salsa transform traditional eggs Benedict into a southwestern fiesta of flavors. Try tortilla chips instead of corn tortillas for a simple change of pace.

⅓ cup sour cream
3 tablespoons whipping cream
2 tablespoons chopped fresh cilantro
½ teaspoon salt
¼ teaspoon pepper
4 (6-inch) corn tortillas
Vegetable cooking spray
1½ pounds ground hot pork sausage
4 garlic cloves, chopped
2 tablespoons chopped fresh chives
1 tablespoon chopped fresh parsley
1 tablespoon chopped fresh thyme
½ teaspoon pepper
2 tablespoons olive oil
¼ cup white vinegar
8 large eggs
Salsa

Stir together first 5 ingredients in a small bowl; cover and chill.

Lightly coat tortillas with cooking spray; place on a baking sheet. Bake at 350° for 8 minutes or until golden, turning once; set aside.

Stir together sausage and next 5 ingredients in a medium bowl. Shape mixture into 8 (½-inch-thick) patties. Place olive oil in a large skillet over medium heat until hot. Add patties, and cook 7 minutes on each side or until done. Set aside.

Lightly grease a large saucepan. Add water to depth of 2 inches; add vinegar. Bring to a boil; reduce heat, and maintain at a light simmer. Break eggs, 1 at a time, into a measuring cup or saucer; slip eggs, 1 at a time, into water mixture, holding cup as close as possible to surface of water. Simmer 5 minutes or until done. Remove eggs with a slotted spoon. Trim edges, if desired.

To serve, place a tortilla on individual serving plates. Top each tortilla with 2 sausage patties and 2 poached eggs. Top with sour cream mixture. Serve with salsa. Yield: 4 servings.

Perennial Palette
Southborough Gardeners
Southborough, Massachusetts

Miniature Mexican Frittatas

Cottage cheeses may differ in liquid content. If your brand of cottage cheese seems too wet, drain it in a colander to remove excess water.

1 (10-ounce) package frozen chopped spinach, thawed
1 cup small-curd cottage cheese
½ cup grated Parmesan cheese
½ cup (2 ounces) shredded Cheddar cheese
4 large eggs
¼ cup milk
1 teaspoon ground cumin
¼ teaspoon pepper
2 tablespoons chopped fresh cilantro or parsley
Warm salsa
Sour cream

Place spinach between paper towels, and squeeze until barely moist. Combine spinach, cottage cheese, Parmesan cheese, and Cheddar cheese in a medium bowl.

Whisk together eggs and next 3 ingredients in a medium bowl. Add to spinach mixture; stir in cilantro.

Spoon mixture into greased muffin pans, filling three-fourths full. Bake at 375° for 20 to 25 minutes or until egg is set. Let stand 5 minutes; remove from pans. Serve warm with warm salsa and sour cream. Yield: 1 dozen.

Irene Holdren

Past to Present: A Pictorial Cookbook
Washington School Restoration Committee
Oakland, Oregon

Three-Pepper Frittata

A colorful trio of bell pepper strips peeks out from beneath a warm blanket of egg-soaked bread cubes, tender garden vegetables, and creamy cheeses.

8 white bread slices, cubed and divided
1 large purple onion, thinly sliced (about 2¼ cups)
1 red bell pepper, cut into thin strips (about 1 cup)
1 yellow bell pepper, cut into thin strips (about 1 cup)
1 orange bell pepper, cut into thin strips (about 1 cup)
3 garlic cloves, minced
¼ cup olive oil, divided
2 yellow squash, thinly sliced (about 2⅓ cups)
2 zucchini, thinly sliced (about 3 cups)
1 (8-ounce) package fresh mushrooms, sliced
6 large eggs
¼ cup whipping cream
2½ teaspoons salt
2 teaspoons freshly ground pepper
2 cups (8 ounces) shredded Swiss cheese
1 (8-ounce) package cream cheese, cubed and softened

Press half of bread cubes in a lightly greased 10-inch springform pan. Wrap bottom and sides of pan with aluminum foil; set aside.

Sauté onion and next 4 ingredients in 2 tablespoons oil in a large skillet over medium-high heat 5 minutes or until tender; drain and set aside.

Sauté yellow squash and zucchini in 1 tablespoon oil in skillet over medium-high heat 7 minutes or until tender; drain and set aside.

Sauté mushrooms in remaining 1 tablespoon oil in skillet over medium-high heat 4 minutes or until tender; drain and set aside.

Whisk together eggs and next 3 ingredients in a large bowl. Stir in sautéed vegetables. Stir in remaining half of bread cubes, Swiss cheese, and cream cheese. Spoon mixture into prepared pan; place pan on a baking sheet.

Bake, uncovered, at 325° for 1 hour and 15 minutes or until set. Let stand 15 minutes. Carefully remove foil and sides of pan. Serve warm. Yield: 8 servings.

A Sunsational Encore
The Junior League of Greater Orlando, Florida

Zippy Artichoke Oven Omelet

¾ cup medium or hot salsa
1 (14-ounce) can artichoke hearts, drained and chopped
1 cup (4 ounces) shredded Monterey Jack cheese
1 cup (4 ounces) shredded sharp Cheddar cheese
¼ cup grated Parmesan cheese
6 large eggs
1 (8-ounce) container sour cream
Garnishes: tomato wedges, fresh parsley sprigs

Spread salsa in a greased 10-inch quiche dish. Arrange artichoke over salsa; sprinkle with cheeses.

Process eggs in a blender until smooth. Add sour cream, and process until smooth, stopping once to scrape down sides. Pour egg mixture over cheeses.

Bake, uncovered, at 350° for 35 minutes or until omelet is set. Let stand 5 minutes before serving. Garnish, if desired. Yield: 4 to 6 servings.

Gator Championship Recipes
Florida Goal-Liners
McIntosh, Florida

Broccoli, Pepper, and Mozzarella Omelet

1 cup broccoli flowerets
1 garlic clove, sliced
¼ cup olive oil, divided
1 cup thinly sliced onion
½ cup julienne-sliced red bell pepper
6 large eggs
⅓ cup heavy whipping cream
1 teaspoon grated lemon rind
¼ teaspoon salt
¼ teaspoon pepper
¼ teaspoon dried oregano
¼ teaspoon dried rosemary
1 cup (4 ounces) shredded mozzarella cheese

Cook broccoli in boiling water 3 minutes or until crisp-tender; drain. Plunge into ice water to stop the cooking process; drain. Pat dry, and set aside.

Sauté garlic in 2 tablespoons olive oil in a large skillet over medium-high heat until golden. Discard garlic, reserving oil in skillet. Add onion and red bell pepper; cover and cook over low heat 10 minutes, stirring occasionally. Cool slightly.

Whisk together eggs and whipping cream in a medium bowl. Stir in broccoli, onion mixture, lemon rind, and next 4 ingredients.

Heat a 10-inch omelet pan or oven-safe nonstick skillet over medium heat until hot. Add remaining 2 tablespoons olive oil, and tilt pan to coat bottom. Pour egg mixture into pan. As mixture starts to cook, gently lift edges of omelet with a spatula, and tilt pan so uncooked portion flows underneath. Cook 5 minutes or until center is almost set. Broil 5½ inches from heat 2 minutes or until set. Sprinkle with cheese, and broil 3 more minutes or until golden. Serve immediately. Yield: 4 servings. Valerie Pritchard

Exclusively Broccoli Cookbook
Coventry Historical Society
Coventry, Connecticut

Superman Omelet

This hearty meat and potato omelet is guaranteed to satisfy supersized appetites.

1½ tablespoons vegetable oil
1½ cups frozen shredded hash brown potatoes
1 tablespoon finely chopped onion
2 large eggs, beaten
½ cup diced ham
½ cup (2 ounces) shredded colby, mozzarella, or Monterey Jack cheese

Heat oil in a large skillet over medium-high heat until hot. Arrange potato in a circle in center of skillet, leaving about 2 inches around edges; cook until edges of potato are golden. Turn potato; reduce heat to medium. Sprinkle onion around potato along edge of pan; pour egg over onion. Cook until egg begins to set. Sprinkle ham over egg and potato; cook until egg is set. Sprinkle cheese over egg and potato; fold omelet in half. Cook just until cheese melts. Serve immediately. Yield: 1 to 2 servings. Larry Thompson

Feeding the Flock
St. Philips Episcopal Church
Topeka, Kansas

Baked Scrambled Eggs

Our special stratalike brunch casserole boasts a blend of smoked ham, dried tomatoes, and diced Gouda cheese.

8 large eggs, beaten
1½ cups milk
6 ounces Gouda cheese, diced
6 ounces smoked ham, diced
¼ cup chopped green onions
¼ cup dried tomatoes in oil, drained and chopped
¼ teaspoon pepper
½ cup (2 ounces) shredded Cheddar cheese, divided
12 ounces Italian bread, cubed (about 9 cups)

Stir together first 7 ingredients in a large bowl. Stir in ¼ cup Cheddar cheese. Add bread cubes; toss well. Let stand 5 minutes.

Pour mixture into a greased 13- x 9-inch baking dish. Sprinkle with remaining ¼ cup Cheddar cheese. Bake, uncovered, at 350° for 35 minutes or until set. Let stand 5 minutes before serving. Yield: 9 servings.

Loretta Gomez

Heaven's Bounty
Long Beach Catholic School Parents' Club
Long Beach, New York

Busy Morning Breakfast Bake

If you're not a morning person, this make-ahead breakfast casserole is for you. Just stick it in the oven when you wake up!

1 pound hot or mild ground pork sausage
½ (16-ounce) package frozen shredded hash brown potatoes (about 3 cups)
1 cup (4 ounces) shredded sharp Cheddar cheese
6 large eggs, beaten
¾ cup milk
¾ teaspoon dry mustard
½ teaspoon salt
Dash of pepper

Brown sausage in a large skillet, stirring until it crumbles and is no longer pink; drain. Layer potato, sausage, and cheese in a greased 13- x 9-inch baking dish. Combine egg and remaining 4 ingredients; pour over sausage mixture. Cover and chill 8 hours.

Cover and bake at 350° for 30 minutes; uncover and bake 5 more minutes or until set. Let stand 10 minutes before serving. Yield: 6 servings.

Carol Dennison

Cookbook Seasoned with Love
Upsala Community Presbyterian Church
Sanford, Florida

Country Breakfast Casserole

All your breakfast favorites–sausage, eggs, and grits–are cooked in one dish. Add hot biscuits and juice, and you'll be ready to tackle the day ahead.

1 pound ground mild pork sausage
3½ cups water
1 teaspoon salt
1 cup uncooked quick-cooking grits
1½ cups (6 ounces) shredded Cheddar cheese, divided
4 large eggs, lightly beaten
¾ cup milk
¼ cup butter or margarine, melted
¼ teaspoon pepper

Brown sausage in a large skillet, stirring until it crumbles and is no longer pink; drain.

Bring water and salt to a boil in a medium saucepan; stir in grits. Return to a boil; cover, reduce heat, and simmer 5 minutes, stirring occasionally. Remove from heat; add 1 cup cheese, stirring until cheese melts. Stir in sausage, eggs, and remaining 3 ingredients.

Pour mixture into a greased 11- x 7-inch baking dish; sprinkle with remaining ½ cup cheese. Bake, uncovered, at 350° for 45 minutes or until set. Let stand 5 minutes before serving. Yield: 6 servings.

Secrets of Amelia
McArthur Family Branch YMCA
Fernandina Beach, Florida

Artichoke and Smoked Ham Strata

Sourdough bread imparts its distinctive tanginess to this baked egg dish layered with smoked ham, marinated artichoke hearts, and three cheeses. Note that a one-pound loaf of sourdough bread with crust removed will give you just the right amount of bread cubes.

2 cups milk
¼ cup olive oil
8 cups 1-inch sourdough bread cubes
1½ cups whipping cream
5 large eggs
3 garlic cloves, minced
1½ teaspoons salt
¾ teaspoon ground white pepper
½ teaspoon ground nutmeg
3 (4-ounce) packages goat cheese, crumbled
2 tablespoons chopped fresh sage
1 tablespoon chopped fresh thyme
1½ teaspoons herbes de Provence
¾ pound smoked ham, chopped
3 (6½-ounce) jars marinated artichoke hearts, drained
1 cup (4 ounces) shredded fontina cheese
1½ cups grated Parmesan cheese

Combine milk and oil in a large bowl; add bread cubes. Let stand 10 minutes.

Whisk together whipping cream and next 5 ingredients in a large bowl. Stir in goat cheese.

Combine sage, thyme, and herbes de Provence in a small bowl.

Place half of bread mixture in a greased 13- x 9-inch baking dish. Top with half each of ham, artichoke hearts, herb mixture, and cheeses. Pour half of cream mixture over cheeses. Repeat layers, ending with cream mixture. Cover and chill at least 8 hours.

Let stand at room temperature 30 minutes. Bake, uncovered, at 350° for 55 minutes or until set and lightly browned. Yield: 8 servings.

Dining by Design: Stylish Recipes, Savory Settings
The Junior League of Pasadena, California

Breakfast Tortilla Torta

If you like to get an early start, prepare the potato and sausage mixtures for this egg and cheese dish the night before.

1 tablespoon olive oil
1 pound new potatoes, thinly sliced
1 cup sliced green onions, divided (about 8)
1 teaspoon chili powder
½ teaspoon salt, divided
6 large eggs
1 cup canned whole kernel corn, drained
½ teaspoon pepper
1 pound ground hot pork sausage
1 red bell pepper, finely chopped
1¼ cups salsa, divided
5 (10-inch) flour tortillas
½ cup (2 ounces) shredded Cheddar cheese
Salsa
Sour cream

Heat oil in a large skillet over medium heat until hot; add potato, and cook 12 minutes or until tender, stirring occasionally. Add ⅓ cup green onions, chili powder, and ¼ teaspoon salt; cook 2 more minutes. Pour into a bowl; set aside.

Whisk together eggs, corn, remaining ¼ teaspoon salt, and pepper. Pour mixture into a lightly greased skillet, and cook over medium heat 2 to 3 minutes, stirring often (mixture will be slightly runny). Pour into a bowl; set aside.

Brown sausage, red bell pepper, and remaining ⅔ cup green onions in skillet, stirring until sausage crumbles and is no longer pink. Drain and pat dry with paper towels. Wipe drippings from skillet with a paper towel. Stir in ¼ cup salsa.

Lightly grease a 10-inch springform pan. Place a tortilla in pan. Spread potato mixture over tortilla. Top with a tortilla, pressing flat. Spread half of sausage mixture over tortilla. Top with another tortilla, egg mixture, tortilla, remaining half of sausage mixture, and remaining tortilla. Spread remaining 1 cup salsa over last tortilla. Sprinkle with cheese. Bake, uncovered, at 400° for 40 minutes or until set, shielding with aluminum foil after 20 minutes to prevent excessive browning. Let stand 10 minutes before serving. Serve with additional salsa and sour cream. Yield: 10 to 12 servings. Eva Ann McLean

Southern Elegance: A Second Course
The Junior League of Gaston County
Gastonia, North Carolina

Fighter Pilot Quiche

1 unbaked 9-inch frozen deep-dish pastry shell
1 (10-ounce) package frozen chopped spinach, partially thawed
1 cup chopped cooked ham
1½ cups (6 ounces) shredded sharp Cheddar cheese
4 large eggs
1 (8-ounce) container sour cream
½ cup chopped almonds, toasted
½ to 1 (2.8-ounce) can French fried onions
1 teaspoon dried thyme
½ teaspoon salt
½ teaspoon dry mustard
¼ teaspoon pepper
⅛ teaspoon ground mace
¾ cup grated Parmesan cheese

Prick bottom and sides of pastry shell with a fork. Bake at 400° for 3 minutes; remove from oven, and gently prick again with a fork. Bake pastry shell 5 more minutes.

Combine spinach and next 11 ingredients. Pour mixture into prepared crust, and sprinkle with Parmesan cheese. Bake, uncovered, at 350° for 50 minutes or until set. Let stand 10 minutes before serving. Yield: 6 servings.

Nancy Whitaker

All We Need Is Love
Columbus-Lowndes Humane Society
Columbus, Mississippi

Mexican Quiches

½ cup butter or margarine, softened
1 (3-ounce) package cream cheese, softened
1 cup all-purpose flour
1 cup (4 ounces) shredded Monterey Jack cheese
1 (4.5-ounce) can chopped green chiles, undrained
2 large eggs
½ cup whipping cream
¼ teaspoon salt
⅛ teaspoon pepper

Beat butter and cream cheese at medium speed with an electric mixer until smooth. Add flour, and beat well. Shape dough into a ball; cover and chill 20 minutes. Shape dough into 36 (¾-inch) balls. Place in ungreased miniature (1¾-inch) muffin pans, and shape each ball into a shell. Divide shredded cheese and green chiles evenly among shells.

Whisk together eggs and remaining 3 ingredients. Spoon mixture evenly into shells. Bake at 350° for 35 minutes or until set. Serve warm. Yield: 3 dozen.
Toni Smith

Angels in the Kitchen
Grace Episcopal Church
Anderson, South Carolina

Frozen Cheese Soufflé

3 tablespoons butter or margarine
¼ cup all-purpose flour
1 cup milk
¼ to ½ teaspoon salt
⅛ teaspoon ground red pepper
1½ cups (6 ounces) shredded sharp Cheddar cheese
4 large eggs, separated
¼ teaspoon cream of tartar

Melt butter in a heavy saucepan over low heat; whisk in flour until smooth. Cook 1 minute, whisking constantly. Gradually whisk in milk; cook over medium heat, whisking constantly, until mixture is thickened and bubbly. Stir in salt and pepper. Add cheese, stirring until cheese melts.

Beat egg yolks until thick and pale. Gradually stir about one-fourth of hot cheese mixture into yolks; add to remaining hot mixture, stirring constantly. Remove from heat, and cool slightly.

Beat egg whites and cream of tartar at high speed with an electric mixer until soft peaks form. Fold into cheese mixture. Pour cheese mixture into an ungreased 1½-quart soufflé dish. Cover and freeze.

When ready to bake, uncover and place in cold oven. Set oven temperature to 300°. Bake 1 hour and 12 to 14 minutes or until puffed and golden. Serve immediately. Yield: 4 servings.

Pick of the Crop, Two
North Sunflower PTA
Drew, Mississippi

Cinnamon-Raisin Breakfast Pudding

Thick slices of raisin bread are doused with a sweetly spiced custard to create this breakfast indulgence. Be sure to buy an unsliced loaf of cinnamon-raisin bread from your local bakery. Presliced bread won't be thick enough to soak up all the sweetness.

1 (¾-pound) unsliced loaf cinnamon-raisin bread
5 large eggs
3 egg yolks
1 cup half-and-half
¾ cup milk
1 tablespoon vanilla extract
1 teaspoon ground cinnamon
½ teaspoon ground nutmeg
½ cup butter or margarine, melted
Powdered sugar

Trim crust from bread, and cut into 4 (2-inch-thick) slices. Arrange slices in a well-greased 9-inch square pan.

Whisk together eggs and next 6 ingredients in a large bowl. Spoon egg mixture over bread slices. Cover and chill 8 hours.

Drizzle melted butter over egg mixture. Bake, uncovered, at 350° for 55 to 60 minutes or until set. Sprinkle with powdered sugar. Serve warm. Yield: 4 to 6 servings.

What Can I Bring?
The Junior League of Northern Virginia
McLean, Virginia

French Toast

3 large eggs
¼ cup half-and-half
1 tablespoon sugar
½ teaspoon ground cinnamon
2 tablespoons orange juice concentrate, thawed
2 tablespoons orange liqueur
1 (1-pound) loaf cinnamon, raisin, or cinnamon-raisin bread, cut into 1-inch-thick slices (about 9 slices)
3 tablespoons butter or margarine, divided
Warm maple syrup
Grated orange rind
Powdered sugar

Whisk together first 6 ingredients in a medium bowl; pour into a shallow dish. Arrange 3 slices of bread in egg mixture; let stand 1 minute.

Melt 1 tablespoon butter in a large skillet over medium heat; add egg-soaked bread, and cook 4 minutes on each side or until lightly browned. Transfer to a serving platter; keep warm. Repeat procedure with remaining egg mixture, bread slices, and butter.

Combine maple syrup and orange rind; pour over French toast. Sprinkle with powdered sugar. Yield: 4 servings.

Past to Present: A Pictorial Cookbook
Washington School Restoration Committee
Oakland, Oregon

Breakfast Sausage Bread

2 (1-pound) loaves frozen bread dough, thawed (we tested with Rich's)
Vegetable cooking spray
½ pound ground mild pork sausage
½ pound ground hot pork sausage
1½ cups diced fresh mushrooms
½ cup chopped onion
2 large eggs, lightly beaten
2½ cups (10 ounces) shredded mozzarella cheese
1 teaspoon garlic powder
1 teaspoon dried basil
1 teaspoon dried parsley flakes
1 teaspoon dried rosemary
1 large egg, lightly beaten

Place dough on a greased baking sheet; coat dough with cooking spray. Cover and let rise in a warm place (85°), free from drafts, 1 hour or until doubled in bulk.

Meanwhile, brown sausage in a large skillet, stirring until it crumbles and is no longer pink; drain. Add mushrooms and onion; cook 5 minutes or until vegetables are tender. Remove from heat; stir in 2 eggs and next 5 ingredients.

Roll 1 loaf into a 16- x 12-inch rectangle. Spread half of sausage mixture over loaf, leaving a 1-inch margin. Roll up dough, starting at short side, pressing firmly to eliminate air pockets; pinch ends to seal. Place dough, seam side down, on greased baking sheet. Repeat procedure with remaining portion of dough and sausage mixture. Bake at 350° for 25 minutes. Brush with 1 beaten egg. Bake 10 more minutes or until golden. Serve warm. Yield: 16 servings. Garth E. Stickle

From the Kitchens of Lake Wynonah
Civic Association of Lake Wynonah
Auburn, Pennsylvania

Fish & Shellfish

Tequila-Lime Shrimp, page 182

Catfish Classique

1 large egg
½ cup milk
2 cups all-purpose flour
1¼ teaspoons salt, divided
2½ teaspoons ground red pepper, divided
4 (6-ounce) catfish fillets (½ inch thick)
Vegetable oil
1 tablespoon butter or margarine
12 unpeeled, large fresh shrimp
2 teaspoons minced garlic (about 2 cloves)
¼ cup dry vermouth
2 cups whipping cream
¼ cup chopped green onions, divided
2 teaspoons fresh lemon juice
Garnish: lemon wedges

Combine egg and milk, stirring until blended. Combine flour, 1 teaspoon salt, and 1 teaspoon red pepper in a shallow dish. Dredge catfish fillets in flour mixture, dip in milk mixture, and dredge again in flour mixture.

Pour oil to depth of 2 inches into a Dutch oven; heat to 375°. Fry fillets, 2 at a time, 6 minutes or until golden; drain on paper towels. Set aside, and keep warm.

Melt butter in a large skillet over medium heat. Add shrimp and garlic; sauté 4 minutes or until shrimp turn pink. Remove shrimp from skillet, reserving drippings in pan. Set shrimp aside; keep warm.

Add vermouth to skillet; bring to a boil, and cook 1 minute, stirring constantly. Add whipping cream, half of green onions, lemon juice, remaining ¼ teaspoon salt, and remaining 1½ teaspoons red pepper; cook sauce 15 minutes or until thickened, stirring often.

To serve, place catfish on a serving platter, and drizzle with sauce. Top with shrimp, and sprinkle with remaining green onions. Garnish, if desired. Yield: 4 servings.

Linen Napkins to Paper Plates
The Junior Auxiliary of Clarksville, Tennessee

Flounder with Crab Stuffing

2 tablespoons butter or margarine
1 medium onion, finely chopped
2 tablespoons chopped celery
2 tablespoons chopped green bell pepper
1 garlic clove, minced
¾ cup fine, dry breadcrumbs (store-bought)
1 large egg, lightly beaten
1 tablespoon chopped fresh parsley
1 teaspoon salt
½ teaspoon pepper
⅛ teaspoon dried thyme
1 cup fresh lump crabmeat, drained
4 (¾-pound) whole flounder, dressed (head and fins removed)
¼ cup butter or margarine, melted
½ teaspoon salt
Garnish: lemon wedges

Melt 2 tablespoons butter in a large skillet over medium heat; add onion and next 3 ingredients, and sauté 8 minutes or until tender.

Combine breadcrumbs and next 5 ingredients in a large bowl. Stir in onion mixture and crabmeat.

Cut a deep pocket down the center of each flounder; place each flounder on a baking sheet. Brush with ¼ cup melted butter; sprinkle with ½ teaspoon salt. Fill each pocket with one-fourth of crabmeat mixture (about ¾ cup). Cover and bake at 375° for 30 minutes; uncover and bake 10 more minutes or until fish flakes with a fork. Garnish, if desired. Yield: 4 servings.

Virginia Anderson

St. Andrew's Cooks Again
Presbyterian Women of St. Andrew
Beaumont, Texas

Grouper Mediterranean

This recipe uses a little sambuca, a not-too-sweet, anise-flavored Italian liqueur. If you don't have any on hand, simply use a dry white wine in its place.

½ cup chopped onion
1 tablespoon minced garlic (about 3 cloves)
2 tablespoons olive oil
1 (28-ounce) can crushed tomatoes, undrained
½ cup dry white wine
½ cup chopped fresh parsley
¼ cup drained capers
½ teaspoon dried rosemary
½ teaspoon dried oregano
¼ teaspoon dried crushed red pepper
1 tablespoon olive oil
3 pounds grouper fillets (about ¾ inch thick)
2 tablespoons sambuca or dry white wine
1 (8-ounce) package feta cheese, crumbled

Sauté onion and garlic in 2 tablespoons hot oil in a large skillet over medium-high heat 2 minutes.

Add tomatoes and next 6 ingredients to skillet. Bring to a boil; reduce heat, and simmer, uncovered, 10 minutes.

Pour 1 tablespoon oil into a 15- x 10-inch jellyroll pan; tilt to coat bottom. Cut grouper into 6 portions, and arrange in a single layer in prepared pan. Pour tomato mixture over grouper.

Bake, uncovered, at 450° for 15 minutes. Drizzle with sambuca, and sprinkle with feta cheese. Broil 5½ inches from heat 4 minutes or until cheese is lightly browned. Yield: 6 servings. Doris Harvey

Victorian Secrets
The Chiselers, Inc.
Tampa, Florida

Orange Roughy with Star Fruit Salsa

Star fruit, named for its striking shape, is at its showy best when purchased at its peak from summer's end to mid-winter.

1 cup sliced fresh strawberries
2 medium star fruit (carambola), thinly sliced
½ cup minced onion
1 tablespoon chopped jalapeño pepper
1 tablespoon minced fresh cilantro
1 teaspoon grated lime rind
1 tablespoon fresh lime juice
¼ teaspoon ground coriander
⅛ teaspoon ground red pepper
2 tablespoons fresh lime juice
2 teaspoons butter or margarine, melted
6 (4-ounce) orange roughy fillets
Garnish: fresh cilantro sprigs

Combine first 9 ingredients in a medium bowl to make salsa. Cover and chill 2 hours.

Combine 2 tablespoons lime juice and butter in a small bowl. Place fillets on a lightly greased rack in a broiler pan. Brush with butter mixture. Broil 5½ inches from heat 5 minutes or until fish flakes with a fork. Serve with salsa. Garnish, if desired. Yield: 6 servings.

Simply Divine
Second-Ponce de Leon Baptist Church
Atlanta, Georgia

Dijon Grilled Salmon

6 (5-ounce) salmon steaks (¾ inch thick)
¾ cup olive oil
3 tablespoons minced shallots
3 tablespoons Dijon mustard
3 tablespoons lemon juice
½ teaspoon salt
¼ teaspoon pepper

Place salmon in a shallow dish. Combine olive oil, minced shallots, mustard, and lemon juice in a small bowl; pour over salmon. Cover and chill 1½ hours, turning once. Remove salmon from marinade, discarding marinade.

Coat grill basket with cooking spray; arrange salmon in basket, and sprinkle with salt and pepper. Place grill basket on food rack, and grill, covered with grill lid, over medium-high heat (350° to 400°) about 5 minutes on each side or until fish flakes with a fork. Yield: 6 servings.

Regina Charlton

Alaska's Best
Alaska Telephone Pioneers
Anchorage, Alaska

Salmon in Pastry Crust

Spinach- and Parmesan-topped salmon fillets are enclosed in golden puff pastry to create this elegant entrée.

1 (10-ounce) package frozen chopped spinach, thawed
1 (17¼-ounce) package frozen puff pastry sheets, thawed
1 (1¾-pound) salmon fillet (2 inches thick), skinned
½ cup grated Parmesan cheese
½ cup mayonnaise
½ teaspoon salt
½ teaspoon pepper
1 large egg, lightly beaten
1 tablespoon water

Press spinach between layers of paper towels to remove excess moisture; set aside.

Roll each pastry sheet into a 16- x 10-inch rectangle on a lightly floured surface. Place salmon in the center of 1 pastry sheet.

Combine spinach, cheese, mayonnaise, ¼ teaspoon salt, and ¼ teaspoon pepper. Sprinkle remaining ¼ teaspoon salt and remaining ¼ teaspoon pepper over salmon. Spread spinach mixture on top of salmon.

Place remaining pastry sheet over salmon and spinach. Moisten edges of pastry with water, and seal pastry around salmon; trim off excess pastry. Gently press pastry edges to seal with a fork. Cut leaves out of excess pastry, if desired, and use to decorate top of pastry around salmon. Place on an ungreased baking sheet.

Combine egg and water. Brush egg mixture over pastry; poke holes in pastry to vent. Bake, uncovered, at 350° for 45 minutes or until golden. Yield: 6 to 8 servings.

Dining by Design: Stylish Recipes, Savory Settings
The Junior League of Pasadena, California

Psari Plaki (Greek Baked Fish)

This traditional Greek dish is served on Palm Sunday.

2 pounds red snapper, haddock, or bluefish fillets (1¼ inches thick)
¾ cup chopped green onions
2 garlic cloves, minced
½ cup olive oil
2 cups peeled, seeded, and chopped tomato (about 2 tomatoes)
1 cup chopped fresh parsley
1 cup dry white wine
1 teaspoon dried oregano
½ teaspoon salt
½ teaspoon freshly ground pepper
1 medium onion, thinly sliced and separated into rings

Place fish fillets in a greased 13- x 9-inch baking dish.

Sauté green onions and garlic in hot oil in a large skillet over medium heat 5 minutes or until lightly browned. Add tomato and next 5 ingredients; bring to a boil. Cover, reduce heat, and simmer 10 minutes. Pour sauce over fish; top with onion rings.

Bake, uncovered, at 400° for 20 minutes or until fish flakes with a fork. Yield: 4 servings.

The Albany Collection: Treasures and Treasured Recipes
Women's Council of the Albany Institute of History & Art
Albany, New York

Yellowtail Snapper with Onions

5 large purple onions
2 tablespoons olive oil
½ cup firmly packed brown sugar
⅓ cup balsamic vinegar
3 tablespoons butter or margarine
2 teaspoons salt, divided
1½ teaspoons freshly ground pepper, divided
¼ cup butter or margarine
1 large shallot, minced
¼ cup Madeira
1 tablespoon lemon juice
¾ cup whipping cream
4 (6- to 8-ounce) yellowtail snapper fillets
2 tablespoons olive oil

Cut onions into ¼-inch-thick slices, and separate into rings. Sauté onion in 2 tablespoons hot oil in a large heavy skillet or Dutch oven over medium heat 25 minutes or until onion is dark brown. Add brown sugar and vinegar; cook until most of the liquid has evaporated. Add 3 tablespoons butter, ½ teaspoon salt, and ½ teaspoon pepper; stir until butter melts. Set aside, and keep warm.

Melt ¼ cup butter in a small saucepan over medium heat; add shallot, and sauté until tender. Stir in Madeira and lemon juice; cook over medium-high heat until mixture is reduced by half. Add cream, ½ teaspoon salt, and ½ teaspoon pepper; bring to a boil. Reduce heat to medium-low, and simmer, uncovered, 30 minutes or until thickened, stirring occasionally.

Sprinkle fillets with remaining 1 teaspoon salt and remaining ½ teaspoon pepper. Heat 2 tablespoons olive oil in a large ovenproof skillet over medium-high heat. Place 2 fillets, skin side up, in skillet, and cook 3 minutes or until lightly browned; turn fillets, and place skillet in a 400° oven. Bake 8 to 10 minutes or until fish flakes with a fork. Remove fillets, reserving drippings in pan. Set fillets aside, and keep warm. Repeat procedure with remaining fillets. Spoon Madeira sauce onto individual serving plates, and top with fillets and onion. Yield: 4 servings.

Made in the Shade
The Junior League of Greater Fort Lauderdale, Florida

New England Stuffed Sole

3 white bread slices, toasted
½ cup butter or margarine, melted and divided
½ medium onion, grated
2 tablespoons chopped fresh parsley
1 tablespoon fresh lemon juice
1 teaspoon soy sauce
¼ teaspoon salt
¼ teaspoon pepper
¼ teaspoon ground sage
8 (6-ounce) sole or flounder fillets
Garnishes: lemon wedges, fresh parsley sprigs

Process toasted bread in a food processor until crumbs are fine. Combine crumbs, 6 tablespoons melted butter, onion, and next 6 ingredients in a small bowl.

Spoon 2 tablespoons breadcrumb mixture onto each fillet; roll up fillets. Place fillets, seam side down, in an ungreased 13- x 9-inch baking dish; drizzle evenly with remaining 2 tablespoons butter.

Bake, uncovered, at 350° for 30 minutes or until fish flakes with a fork. Garnish, if desired. Yield: 8 servings.

Out of the Ordinary
The Hingham Historical Society
Hingham, Massachusetts

Caribbean Swordfish with Thai Banana Salsa

Mellow bananas are paired with the traditional Thai cuisine flavors of fish sauce, chili sauce, and ginger in this unique, delicious salsa.

3 tablespoons reduced-sodium soy sauce
3 tablespoons dry sherry or rice wine
2 tablespoons oyster sauce
2 tablespoons vegetable oil
1 tablespoon honey
4 (1-inch-thick) swordfish steaks (about 1¾ pounds)
Thai Banana Salsa

Combine first 5 ingredients in a large heavy-duty, zip-top plastic bag; add swordfish. Seal and chill 1 hour, turning occasionally.

Remove swordfish from marinade, discarding marinade.

Coat food rack with cooking spray; place on grill over medium-high heat (350° to 400°). Place swordfish on rack, and grill, covered with grill lid, about 6 minutes on each side or until fish flakes with a fork. Serve with Thai Banana Salsa. Yield: 4 servings.

Thai Banana Salsa

2 medium-firm bananas (bananas should be slightly green), chopped
1 red bell pepper, chopped
¼ cup chopped fresh cilantro
2 tablespoons brown sugar
2 tablespoons minced fresh ginger
2 tablespoons fresh orange juice
2 tablespoons fresh lime juice
2 tablespoons fish sauce
2 teaspoons Thai chili paste

Combine all ingredients in a small bowl, and stir gently. Serve salsa within 2 hours of preparation. Yield: 2¼ cups.

Dining by Design: Stylish Recipes, Savory Settings
The Junior League of Pasadena, California

Swordfish Steaks with Pineapple Salsa

1 pineapple, peeled, quartered, and cored
¼ cup vegetable oil
1 red bell pepper, seeded and diced
1 green bell pepper, seeded and diced
1 small purple onion, chopped
3 tablespoons chopped fresh cilantro
2 tablespoons chopped fresh chives
2 tablespoons chopped fresh parsley
2 tablespoons fresh lime juice
1 jalapeño pepper, seeded and minced
1 teaspoon salt, divided
1 teaspoon pepper, divided
4 (7-ounce) swordfish steaks (1 inch thick)
1 tablespoon vegetable oil

Broil pineapple 3 inches from heat 5 minutes on each side or until lightly browned. Chop pineapple.

Combine pineapple, ¼ cup vegetable oil, and next 8 ingredients in a bowl. Stir in ½ teaspoon salt and ½ teaspoon pepper. Cover and chill salsa 2 hours.

Brush swordfish with 1 tablespoon oil. Sprinkle with remaining ½ teaspoon salt and ½ teaspoon pepper.

Coat food rack with cooking spray; place on grill over medium-high heat (350° to 400°). Place swordfish on rack, and grill, covered with grill lid, about 5 minutes on each side or until fish flakes with a fork. Serve with Pineapple Salsa. Yield: 4 servings. Donna Wilkes

Tried and True from Riverview
Riverview Hospital Auxiliary
Wisconsin Rapids, Wisconsin

Grilled Trout

Lemon slices are stuffed into each trout during grilling, adding a tangy citrus flavor to the fish and to the sauce that's drizzled over each fillet.

3 (1-pound) whole trout, dressed (heads and fins removed)
3 tablespoons butter or margarine, melted
2 medium lemons, thinly sliced
3 tablespoons butter or margarine
2 tablespoons fresh lemon juice
¼ teaspoon pepper
Garnishes: fresh parsley sprigs, lemon slices

Brush cavity of fish with 3 tablespoons melted butter; stuff each fish with lemon slices.

Coat grill basket with cooking spray; arrange fish in basket. Place grill basket on food rack, and grill, covered with grill lid, over medium-high heat (350° to 400°) about 3 to 4 minutes on each side or until fish flakes with a fork.

Melt 3 tablespoons butter in a small saucepan over medium heat; cook 3 minutes or until golden. Stir in lemon juice and pepper.

Separate each trout into 2 fillets; discard lemon slices. Place trout, skin side down, on a serving platter. Drizzle butter sauce evenly over fillets. Garnish, if desired. Yield: 6 servings. Sue Lowe

Favorite Recipes
Friends of Memorial Hospital
Weiser, Idaho

Tuna Steaks Niçoise

6 (8-ounce) tuna steaks (1 inch thick)
¼ cup fresh lemon juice
¼ cup dry vermouth
2½ tablespoons olive oil, divided
1 tablespoon minced fresh ginger
¼ teaspoon sugar
¼ teaspoon freshly ground pepper, divided
2 cups finely chopped onion
1 tablespoon minced garlic (about 3 cloves)
1 (8-ounce) can tomato sauce
2 medium tomatoes, peeled, seeded, and chopped
¼ cup chopped pimiento-stuffed olives
3 tablespoons brandy
1 tablespoon minced fresh basil
⅛ teaspoon dried crushed red pepper
6 pimiento-stuffed olives, sliced

Place tuna in a shallow dish. Combine lemon juice, vermouth, 1 tablespoon oil, ginger, sugar, and ⅛ teaspoon pepper in a small bowl; pour over tuna. Cover and chill 2 hours, turning once.

Sauté onion and garlic in 1 tablespoon hot oil in a medium saucepan over medium-high heat until tender. Add remaining ⅛ teaspoon pepper, tomato sauce, and next 5 ingredients. Bring to a boil; cover, reduce heat, and simmer 20 minutes. Set aside, and keep warm.

Remove tuna from marinade, reserving marinade.

Heat remaining ½ tablespoon oil in a large skillet over medium-high heat. Add tuna, and cook 2 minutes on each side. Place tuna in an ungreased 11- x 7-inch baking dish. Pour reserved marinade over tuna. Bake, uncovered, at 400° for 9 minutes or until fish flakes with a fork.

To serve, spoon tomato sauce evenly onto 6 plates; top each with a tuna steak and sliced olives. Yield: 6 servings.

Shalom on the Range
Shalom Park
Aurora, Colorado

Grilled Tuna Steaks

Italian dressing mix and soy sauce boost the flavor of these easy grilled tuna steaks.

1 cup water
1 cup soy sauce
½ cup vegetable oil
1 (0.7-ounce) envelope Italian dressing mix
4 (1-inch-thick) tuna steaks (about 2½ pounds)

Combine first 4 ingredients in a large heavy-duty, zip-top plastic bag; add tuna. Seal and chill 1 hour, turning occasionally.

Remove tuna from marinade, discarding marinade.

Coat food rack with cooking spray; place on grill over medium-high heat (350° to 400°). Place tuna on rack; grill, covered with grill lid, about 5 minutes on each side or until fish flakes with a fork. Yield: 4 servings.
Cindy Tanner

The Art of Cooking
The Muscle Shoals District Service League
Sheffield, Alabama

Stuffed Clams

To make the clams easier to shuck, bake them at 400° for 5 to 10 minutes or just until the clams begin to open.

9 pounds cherrystone clams, scrubbed
½ cup soft breadcrumbs (homemade)
¼ cup (1 ounce) shredded Swiss cheese
2 slices bacon, cooked and crumbled
2 tablespoons dry white wine
1 tablespoon minced fresh parsley
1 tablespoon butter or margarine, melted
1 teaspoon Worcestershire sauce
¼ teaspoon pepper

Shuck clams; release meat from bottom shells, reserving 16 shells. Arrange shells on an ungreased baking sheet; set aside.

Chop clam meat (about 1½ cups); drain. Combine clam meat, breadcrumbs, and remaining 7 ingredients in a bowl. Fill each clam shell with 1 heaping tablespoon clam mixture. Bake, uncovered, at 375° for 20 minutes. Serve immediately. Yield: 4 servings. Pat Sowinski

A Perfect Measurement of Love
Little Flower Children's Services of New York
Wading River, New York

Panfried Crab Cakes

⅓ cup sour cream
1 large egg, lightly beaten
¼ cup milk
2 garlic cloves, minced
1 teaspoon ground white pepper
1 teaspoon curry powder
1 teaspoon chili powder
½ teaspoon salt
1 pound fresh lump crabmeat, drained
1¼ cups fine, dry breadcrumbs (store-bought)
¾ cup chopped green onions
⅓ cup olive oil

Combine first 8 ingredients in a large bowl. Add crabmeat, 1 cup breadcrumbs, and green onions. Shape mixture into 12 (2½-inch) patties; dredge in remaining ¼ cup breadcrumbs. Cover and chill at least 1 hour.

Fry 6 patties in 3 tablespoons hot olive oil in a large nonstick skillet over medium-high heat 2 minutes on each side or until golden; drain. Repeat procedure with remaining patties and oil. Yield: 3 to 4 servings. Ryan Family

Heaven's Bounty
Long Beach Catholic School Parents' Club
Long Beach, New York

Crab Monza

2 (10-ounce) packages frozen puff pastry shells, thawed (12 shells)
¼ cup butter or margarine, melted
2 (8-ounce) packages sliced fresh mushrooms
1 pound fresh lump crabmeat, drained
1 cup heavy whipping cream
¼ cup dry sherry
1 teaspoon Worcestershire sauce
2 shallots, minced
3 tablespoons all-purpose flour
1 teaspoon salt
½ teaspoon freshly ground pepper
½ cup freshly grated Parmesan cheese
¼ teaspoon paprika

Bake pastry shells according to package directions; cool.

Melt butter in a Dutch oven over medium-high heat; add mushrooms, and sauté until tender. Add crabmeat and next 7 ingredients; cook 2 minutes.

Heap crab mixture into pastry shells. Sprinkle with cheese and paprika. Bake, uncovered, at 350° for 10 to 12 minutes or until golden. Yield: 6 servings.

A Century of Serving
The Junior Board of Christiana Care, Inc.
Wilmington, Delaware

Fried Soft-Shell Crabs with Rémoulade Sauce

If you're unfamiliar with how to handle soft-shell crabs, you can ask for the crabs to be cleaned at the seafood counter.

8 fresh soft-shell crabs (about 2 pounds)
1 large egg, lightly beaten
½ cup milk
⅔ cup cornmeal
½ teaspoon kosher salt
½ teaspoon freshly ground pepper
⅓ cup vegetable oil
Rémoulade Sauce

To clean crabs, remove spongy gills that lie under the tapering points on either side of back shell. Place crabs on back, and remove the small piece at lower part of shell that terminates in a point (the apron). Wash crabs thoroughly; drain well.

Combine egg and milk in a large shallow dish. Combine cornmeal, salt, and pepper. Add crabs to egg mixture, turning to coat. Remove crabs from egg mixture, and dredge in cornmeal mixture.

Pour oil into a large heavy skillet. Fry crabs, in batches, in hot oil over medium-high heat 3 minutes on each side or until browned; drain. Serve with Rémoulade Sauce. Yield: 4 servings.

Rémoulade Sauce

½ cup mayonnaise
½ cup chili sauce
3 tablespoons Dijon mustard
2 tablespoons minced green onions
2 tablespoons chopped, drained capers
2 tablespoons fresh lemon juice
1 tablespoon prepared horseradish
⅛ teaspoon freshly ground pepper
⅛ teaspoon hot sauce

Combine all ingredients. Cover and chill. Yield: 1½ cups.

Bay Tables
The Junior League of Mobile, Alabama

Baked Scallops

Enjoy these delicate fennel seed-encrusted scallops with a crisp green salad and crusty bread.

1½ pounds sea scallops (about 24)
1 large egg, lightly beaten
1 tablespoon water
½ cup fine, dry breadcrumbs (store-bought)
¼ teaspoon salt
¼ teaspoon freshly ground pepper
¼ teaspoon fennel seeds, crushed
2 tablespoons butter or margarine, melted
1 tablespoon lemon juice

Drain scallops; pat dry.

Combine egg and water in a bowl. Combine breadcrumbs and next 3 ingredients. Dip each scallop into egg mixture; dredge in breadcrumb mixture.

Place scallops in a lightly greased 15- x 10-inch jellyroll pan. Drizzle scallops with melted butter and lemon juice. Bake, uncovered, at 450° for 15 to 20 minutes or until scallops are done and lightly browned. Yield: 4 servings.

MaryDae Fisher

Cookin' in the Canyon
Jarbidge Community Hall
Jarbidge, Nevada

Sautéed Scallops with Vermouth and Cream

12 ounces uncooked dried angel hair pasta
¼ cup all-purpose flour
¾ teaspoon salt, divided
½ teaspoon freshly ground pepper, divided
2 pounds bay scallops
¼ cup butter or margarine, melted
¾ cup whipping cream
⅓ cup vermouth
¼ cup chopped fresh parsley
3 tablespoons fresh lemon juice

Cook pasta according to package directions; drain and keep warm.

Meanwhile, combine flour, ½ teaspoon salt, and ¼ teaspoon pepper in a large heavy-duty, zip-top plastic bag; seal and shake well.

Drain scallops; pat dry. Place in bag; seal and shake to coat scallops completely. Remove scallops, shaking off excess flour.

Sauté scallops in melted butter in a large skillet over medium-high heat 4 minutes. Add remaining ¼ teaspoon salt, remaining ¼ teaspoon pepper, whipping cream, and remaining 3 ingredients. Bring to a boil; reduce heat, and simmer, uncovered, 1 minute. Serve over pasta. Yield: 6 servings. Trish Bridge

Notable Feasts
Friends of the Cape Cod Symphony Orchestra
Yarmouth Port, Massachusetts

Cooper River Shrimp Creole

Golden raisins nicely sweeten this spicy Creole dish.

5 pounds unpeeled, medium-size fresh shrimp
2 large onions, chopped
2 medium-size green bell peppers, chopped
4 celery ribs, chopped
½ cup olive oil
1 cup golden raisins
1 cup chili sauce
1 cup dry white wine
2 teaspoons salt
1 teaspoon sugar
1 teaspoon curry powder
2 (14-ounce) cans crushed tomatoes, undrained
3 bay leaves
Hot cooked rice

Peel shrimp, and devein, if desired; set aside.

Sauté onion, green pepper, and celery in hot oil in a Dutch oven over medium-high heat until tender. Add raisins and next 7 ingredients. Bring to a boil; cover, reduce heat, and simmer 30 minutes, stirring occasionally. Add shrimp; cook 5 more minutes or until shrimp turn pink. Discard bay leaves. Serve over rice. Yield: 6 to 8 servings.

Tested by Time
Porter Gaud Parents Guild
Charleston, South Carolina

Shrimp and Grits

Ask the seafood department to steam the fresh shrimp if you'd like to omit the first step of this recipe.

7¼ cups water, divided
2 pounds unpeeled, medium-size fresh shrimp
2 large onions, chopped
1 large green bell pepper, chopped
6 tablespoons bacon drippings
¼ cup all-purpose flour
¼ cup chili sauce
1 tablespoon Worcestershire sauce
1 teaspoon salt
½ teaspoon pepper
4 cups hot cooked grits

Bring 6 cups water to a boil; add shrimp, and cook 3 to 5 minutes or until shrimp turn pink. Drain and rinse with cold water. Chill. Peel shrimp, and devein, if desired.

Sauté onion and green pepper in hot bacon drippings in a large skillet over medium heat until tender. Add shrimp and 1 cup water; simmer 3 minutes. Combine remaining ¼ cup water and flour, stirring until smooth. Add flour mixture to shrimp mixture; cook until thickened, stirring constantly. Stir in chili sauce and next 3 ingredients; simmer, stirring constantly, 3 minutes.

To serve, spoon grits into individual serving bowls. Spoon shrimp mixture over grits. Yield: 4 servings.

Seaboard to Sideboard
The Junior League of Wilmington, North Carolina

Tequila-Lime Shrimp

2½ pounds unpeeled, large fresh shrimp
½ cup olive oil
¼ cup fresh lime juice
¼ cup tequila
2 shallots, chopped
2 garlic cloves, minced
1 teaspoon salt
1 teaspoon ground cumin
½ teaspoon pepper

Peel shrimp, leaving tails intact; devein, if desired. Combine oil and remaining 7 ingredients in a bowl; stir in shrimp. Cover; chill 1 hour.

Remove shrimp from marinade, discarding marinade. Thread 9 shrimp on each of 6 (12-inch) metal skewers. (Thread tail and neck of each shrimp onto skewers so shrimp will lie flat.)

Coat food rack with cooking spray; place on grill over medium-high heat (350° to 400°). Place skewers on rack; grill, without grill lid, about 3 to 4 minutes on each side or until shrimp turn pink. Yield: 6 servings.

Note: Shrimp can be baked in an oven. Remove shrimp from marinade, discarding marinade. Place shrimp in an ungreased 15- x 10-inch jellyroll pan. Bake, uncovered, at 400° for 10 to 12 minutes or until shrimp turn pink.

A Sunsational Encore
The Junior League of Greater Orlando, Florida

Grilled Seafood Brochettes

8 unpeeled, large fresh shrimp
½ cup olive oil
2 tablespoons fresh lemon juice
1 garlic clove, minced
1 teaspoon ground ginger
¼ teaspoon salt
¼ teaspoon pepper
8 sea scallops
½ pound fresh tuna fillets, cut into 8 pieces
½ large green bell pepper, cut into ½-inch pieces
8 cherry tomatoes
2 small onions, cut into 8 wedges each
Garnish: lemon wedges

Peel shrimp, and devein, if desired.

Combine oil and next 5 ingredients in a shallow dish. Add shrimp, scallops, and next 4 ingredients. Cover and chill 1 hour.

Remove seafood and vegetables from marinade, discarding marinade. Thread seafood and vegetables evenly onto 8 (10-inch) metal skewers.

Coat food rack with cooking spray; place on grill over medium-high heat (350° to 400°). Place skewers on rack; grill, covered with grill lid, about 3 minutes on each side or until shrimp turn pink, scallops are done, and fish flakes with a fork. Garnish, if desired. Yield: 4 servings.

Flavors of Hawaii
Child and Family Service Guild
Honolulu, Hawaii

Seafood Gruyère

This extravagantly rich soup showcases its fabulous mix of fresh seafood when served immediately.

1 pound unpeeled, medium-size fresh shrimp
3 (8-ounce) frozen lobster tails, thawed
3 tablespoons butter or margarine, melted
12 ounces sliced fresh mushrooms
1 cup butter or margarine
1 cup all-purpose flour
4 cups milk
2 cups chicken broth
1½ tablespoons lemon juice
1 tablespoon tomato paste
¼ teaspoon garlic powder
¼ teaspoon dry mustard
¼ teaspoon pepper
1½ pounds whitefish fillets, cut into 2-inch slices
1½ pounds bay scallops
1 pound fresh lump crabmeat
4 cups (16 ounces) shredded Gruyère cheese
3 cups hot cooked rice (optional)
¼ cup chopped walnuts (optional)
¼ cup chopped green bell pepper (optional)

Peel shrimp, and devein, if desired. Set aside.

Split lobster tails lengthwise. Remove meat, and slice. Set aside.

Melt 3 tablespoons butter in a large skillet over medium heat; add mushrooms, and sauté 5 minutes. Set aside.

Melt 1 cup butter in a large heavy Dutch oven over low heat; whisk in flour until smooth. Cook 1 minute, whisking constantly. Gradually whisk in milk and chicken broth. Whisk in lemon juice and next 4 ingredients. Cook over medium heat, whisking constantly, until mixture is thickened and bubbly (about 10 minutes). Stir in shrimp, lobster, mushrooms, fish, scallops, and crabmeat. Cook, stirring constantly, 10 to 15 minutes or until fish flakes with a fork. (Soup will be thick at first but will thin as seafood cooks.) Remove soup from heat; stir in cheese. If desired, combine rice, walnuts, and green pepper in a large bowl. Serve soup immediately over rice mixture, if desired. Yield: 22 cups.

Marie Souza

Homemade with Love
Swanton-Missisquoi Valley Lions Club
Highgate Center, Vermont

Meats

Lamb Sauté, page 196

Eye-of-Round with Horseradish Cream

Yes, the 20-minute cook time is correct for this recipe. By baking at the high temperature and keeping the oven door closed 2 hours, this roast cooks up extra tender and flavorful.

1 cup dry red wine
½ cup butter or margarine, melted
1 (4-pound) eye-of-round roast
1 tablespoon salt
1 teaspoon pepper
Horseradish Cream

Combine wine and butter in a large heavy-duty, zip-top plastic bag; add roast. Seal and chill at least 8 hours or up to 24 hours, turning occasionally.

Remove roast from marinade, discarding marinade. Place roast in a 13- x 9-inch pan lined with heavy-duty aluminum foil. Combine salt and pepper, and rub over surface of roast.

Bake, uncovered, at 500° for 20 minutes. Turn oven off. Do not open oven door for 2 hours. Meat thermometer should register 145°(medium rare) or 160° (medium). Thinly slice meat, reserving pan juices. Serve meat with pan juices and Horseradish Cream. Yield: 8 servings.

Horseradish Cream

1 (8-ounce) package cream cheese, softened
1½ tablespoons prepared horseradish
2 teaspoons Dijon mustard

Combine all ingredients, stirring until smooth. Cover and chill at least 2 hours. Yield: about 1 cup.

Linen Napkins to Paper Plates
The Junior Auxiliary of Clarksville, Tennessee

Rosemary-Roasted Prime Rib

Fragrant rosemary leaves permeate this roast with their distinctive lemony-pine flavor magic.

1 (6-pound) boneless rib roast, trimmed
¼ cup olive oil
15 garlic cloves, chopped (about ½ cup)
½ cup fresh rosemary leaves
½ teaspoon salt
½ teaspoon pepper

Rub roast with 2 tablespoons olive oil. Combine garlic, rosemary, salt, and pepper; sprinkle mixture over roast, covering completely. Drizzle with remaining 2 tablespoons oil. Place roast on a lightly greased rack in a roasting pan. Insert a meat thermometer into thickest part of roast.

Bake, uncovered, at 350° for 2 hours or until thermometer registers 145° (medium-rare). Cover roast with aluminum foil to prevent excessive browning, if necessary. Let stand 15 minutes before slicing. Yield: 8 servings.

Sounds Delicious: The Flavor of Atlanta in Food & Music
Atlanta Symphony Orchestra
Atlanta, Georgia

Standing Rib Roast au Jus and Yorkshire Pudding

1 (8-pound) fully trimmed 3-rib roast
5 garlic cloves
½ teaspoon salt
½ teaspoon freshly ground pepper
Yorkshire Pudding
Jus

Place roast, rib side down, in a lightly greased shallow roasting pan. Cut small slits in meat, and insert whole garlic cloves. Rub salt and pepper into fat across top of roast. Tie roast with heavy string at 2-inch intervals. Insert a meat thermometer into roast, making sure it does not touch fat or bone.

Bake, uncovered, at 325° for 3 hours or until thermometer registers 145° (medium rare). Remove from oven; cover roast with aluminum foil, and let stand 20 minutes before slicing. (This allows juices to retreat back into the meat; the temperature of roast will rise slightly.) Pour off pan drippings, reserving ½ cup drippings for Yorkshire Pudding. Leave browned bits in pan for Jus. Serve roast with Yorkshire Pudding and Jus. Yield: 12 servings.

Yorkshire Pudding

1½ cups all-purpose flour
¾ cup water
¾ cup milk
3 large eggs, beaten
¾ teaspoon salt
½ cup pan drippings from rib roast

Process first 5 ingredients in a food processor 3 minutes or until smooth. Cover and chill 30 minutes. Add ½ cup pan drippings to a 13- x 9-inch pan. Heat pan in oven at 425° for 5 minutes. Quickly pour cold flour mixture into hot pan; do not stir. Bake at 425° for 18 minutes; reduce oven temperature to 350°, and bake 18 more minutes. Yield: 12 servings.

Jus

½ cup dry red wine
1½ cups water
4 teaspoons liquid beef concentrate
¼ teaspoon salt
¼ teaspoon pepper
2 teaspoons cornstarch
1 tablespoon water

Add wine to roasting pan with browned bits; cook over high heat 2 minutes, stirring to loosen particles from bottom of pan. Add water and liquid beef concentrate; boil 3 minutes. Stir in salt and pepper. Combine cornstarch and water, stirring until smooth; stir into sauce. Cook, stirring constantly, until mixture is thickened and bubbly. Yield: 1¼ cups.

Yuletide on Hilton Head: A Heritage of Island Flavors
United Way of Beaufort County
Hilton Head Island, South Carolina

Grilled Beef Tenderloin Diablo

This tenderloin grills up extra juicy with a marinade of sherry and fresh herbs and a coating of kosher salt that seals in the juices.

1½ cups dry sherry
⅔ cup dark sesame oil
½ cup orange juice
1 small onion, minced
3 garlic cloves, pressed
2 bay leaves
2 tablespoons chopped green onions
1 tablespoon chopped fresh basil
1 tablespoon chopped fresh chives
1 tablespoon chopped fresh oregano
1 tablespoon Worcestershire sauce
1 tablespoon soy sauce
1 teaspoon salt
1 teaspoon pepper
1½ teaspoons hot sauce
1 (4- to 5-pound) beef tenderloin, trimmed
1 cup kosher salt

Combine first 15 ingredients in a large heavy-duty, zip-top plastic bag. Add tenderloin; seal and chill 8 hours, turning occasionally.

Remove tenderloin from marinade, discarding marinade. Roll tenderloin in kosher salt until meat is coated.

Grill, covered with grill lid, over medium-high heat (350° to 400°) about 30 to 40 minutes or until a meat thermometer inserted into thickest part of tenderloin registers 145° (medium rare) or 160° (medium). Yield: 8 to 10 servings.

Seaboard to Sideboard
The Junior League of Wilmington, North Carolina

Italian Stuffed Flank Steak

A fresh spinach stuffing, thin slices of salty prosciutto, and roasted red peppers nestle within tender rolls of flank steak.

1 (10-ounce) package fresh spinach, trimmed
½ cup soft breadcrumbs (homemade), toasted
½ cup freshly grated Parmesan cheese
¼ cup olive oil
2 garlic cloves
1 (1½-pound) flank steak
¾ teaspoon salt, divided
¾ teaspoon freshly ground pepper, divided
4 ounces thinly sliced prosciutto
1 (15-ounce) jar roasted sweet red peppers, drained and cut into ½-inch strips (we tested with Mezzeta)
1 fresh hot cherry pepper, seeded and minced (optional)
1 tablespoon olive oil

Heat a large skillet over medium heat; add spinach. Cover and cook 5 minutes or until wilted, stirring occasionally. Drain spinach in a colander, pressing with paper towels to remove excess moisture. Process spinach, breadcrumbs, and next 3 ingredients in a food processor until smooth, stopping once to scrape down sides.

Trim fat from steak. Butterfly steak by making a lengthwise cut down center of 1 flat side, cutting to within ½ inch of other side. From bottom of cut, slice horizontally to ½ inch from left side; repeat procedure to right side. Open steak, and season with ½ teaspoon salt and ½ teaspoon pepper. Place prosciutto over steak, leaving a 1-inch border; top with red pepper strips. Spread spinach mixture over pepper strips. Sprinkle with minced cherry pepper, if desired. Roll up, jellyroll fashion, starting with long side. Tie with heavy string at 2-inch intervals. Brush with 1 tablespoon olive oil; sprinkle with remaining ¼ teaspoon salt and remaining ¼ teaspoon pepper. Place in a greased 13- x 9-inch pan.

Bake, uncovered, at 350° for 1 hour or until a meat thermometer inserted into center of roll registers 145° (medium rare). Let stand 10 minutes before slicing. Yield: 6 servings. Pam D'Alessandro

The Heart of Pittsburgh
Sacred Heart Elementary School PTG
Pittsburgh, Pennsylvania

Philly Burgers

Crispy french fried onions cook inside these burgers and crown a cheese and mushroom mixture slathered on top after grilling. Sandwich the bounty in kaiser rolls for burgers your family won't soon forget.

1 pound ground chuck
2 tablespoons Worcestershire sauce, divided
4 teaspoons prepared mustard, divided
1 (2.8-ounce) can French fried onions, divided
1 (3-ounce) package cream cheese, softened
1 (2.5-ounce) jar sliced mushrooms, drained
1 teaspoon dried parsley flakes
4 kaiser rolls

Combine ground chuck, 1 tablespoon Worcestershire sauce, 3 teaspoons mustard, and half of onions. Shape mixture into 4 patties. Grill, without grill lid, over medium heat (300° to 350°) about 15 minutes or until a meat thermometer inserted into thickest part of 1 patty registers 160°, turning once.

Meanwhile, combine cream cheese, remaining 1 tablespoon Worcestershire sauce, remaining 1 teaspoon mustard, mushrooms, and parsley. Spread mixture on cooked patties. Top with remaining half of onions. Broil 3 inches from heat 1 minute. Serve on rolls. Yield: 4 servings.

Karen Pett

Taste Buds–A Collection of Treasured Recipes
Alliance of the Illinois State Dental Society
Springfield, Illinois

Sicilian Meat Roll

2 pounds ground chuck
¾ cup soft breadcrumbs (homemade)
½ cup tomato juice
2 large eggs, lightly beaten
1 medium onion, finely chopped
⅓ cup chopped fresh parsley or 2 tablespoons dried parsley flakes
1½ teaspoons chopped fresh oregano or ½ teaspoon dried oregano
1 teaspoon garlic salt
¼ teaspoon pepper
5 thin slices cooked ham (about 3 ounces)
1 cup (4 ounces) shredded mozzarella cheese
3 slices mozzarella cheese, cut in half diagonally

Combine first 9 ingredients in a large bowl. Shape meat mixture into a 10- x 12-inch rectangle on a sheet of aluminum foil. Arrange ham slices evenly over meat mixture; sprinkle with shredded mozzarella. Roll up, jellyroll fashion, starting at short side, using foil to lift. Press edges and ends to seal.

Place meat roll, seam side down, in an ungreased 13- x 9-inch pan. Bake, uncovered, at 350° for 1 hour and 15 minutes or until a meat thermometer inserted in center of roll registers 160°. Arrange mozzarella slices on top of roll; bake 5 more minutes or until cheese melts. Yield: 8 servings.

Marilyn Bonaguro

Taste Buds–A Collection of Treasured Recipes
Alliance of the Illinois State Dental Society
Springfield, Illinois

Spinach Enchilada

This outstanding make-ahead, take-along casserole is made with a base of butter-dipped corn tortillas and beef; then packed to the brim with a spicy mix of chiles and cheese.

1 (10-ounce) package frozen chopped spinach, thawed
2 pounds ground chuck
1 medium onion, chopped
1 (10-ounce) can diced tomatoes and green chiles, undrained (we tested with Ro-Tel)
½ teaspoon salt
½ teaspoon ground cumin
¼ teaspoon garlic powder
¼ teaspoon pepper
1 (10¾-ounce) can cream of mushroom soup
1 (10¾-ounce) can golden mushroom soup
1 (8-ounce) container sour cream
⅓ cup milk
12 (6-inch) corn tortillas
¼ cup butter or margarine, melted
1 (4.5-ounce) can chopped green chiles, undrained
2 cups (8 ounces) shredded sharp Cheddar cheese, divided

Drain spinach in a colander, pressing with paper towels to remove excess moisture; set aside.

Cook ground chuck and onion in a large skillet, stirring until beef crumbles and is no longer pink; drain and return to skillet. Stir in reserved spinach, diced tomatoes and green chiles, and next 4 ingredients; set aside.

Stir together soups, sour cream, and milk; set aside.

Dip tortillas in melted butter. Layer half of tortillas in a greased 13- x 9-inch baking dish. Top with meat mixture; sprinkle with chopped green chiles. Sprinkle 1½ cups cheese over chopped green chiles. Top with remaining half of tortillas dipped in butter; spread soup mixture over tortillas. Cover and chill 8 hours.

Uncover and sprinkle with remaining ½ cup cheese; let stand at room temperature 20 minutes. Bake, uncovered, at 350° for 45 minutes or until bubbly. Let stand 10 minutes before serving. Yield: 8 to 10 servings.

Betty Gray McFarland

Of Books and Cooks
Woman's Book Club
Harrison, Arkansas

Veal Parmesan

1 pound veal cutlets
1 cup soft breadcrumbs (homemade)
½ cup grated Parmesan cheese, divided
¼ cup chopped fresh parsley
½ teaspoon salt
¼ teaspoon pepper
2 large eggs, lightly beaten
¼ cup olive oil
2½ cups chunky garlic and herb tomato sauce
¾ pound mozzarella cheese, cut into 8 slices

Place cutlets between 2 sheets of heavy-duty plastic wrap, and flatten to ⅛-inch thickness, using a meat mallet or rolling pin. Combine breadcrumbs, ¼ cup Parmesan cheese, parsley, salt, and pepper. Dip cutlets into beaten egg, and dredge in breadcrumb mixture, coating both sides.

Sauté cutlets in hot oil in a large skillet over high heat 1 minute on each side. Spread ½ cup tomato sauce in an ungreased 11- x 7-inch baking dish. Arrange cutlets over sauce in dish; top with remaining sauce. Sprinkle with remaining ¼ cup Parmesan cheese. Bake, uncovered, at 350° for 20 minutes. Remove from oven, and top with mozzarella cheese. Bake 5 more minutes or until cheese melts. Yield: 4 servings.

Anita Aleo

Generations of Good Food
Jeannette Public Library
Jeannette, Pennsylvania

Stuffed Veal Pillows

Tender veal cutlets are stuffed with cheese and prosciutto, and then smothered in a buttery Sauterne-laced sauce.

12 veal cutlets (about 1½ pounds)
12 thin slices prosciutto or cooked ham
12 thin slices mozzarella cheese
2 tablespoons butter or margarine
2 tablespoons olive oil
½ cup Sauterne or other sweet white wine
1 teaspoon butter or margarine
¼ teaspoon salt
¼ teaspoon pepper

Place meat between 2 sheets of heavy-duty plastic wrap, and flatten to ¼-inch thickness, using a meat mallet or rolling pin. Place 1 slice prosciutto and 1 slice cheese on each cutlet. Roll up cutlets, jellyroll fashion, and secure with wooden picks.

Combine 2 tablespoons butter and olive oil in a large skillet; place over medium-high heat until hot. Add veal rolls; cook 5 minutes or until fully cooked and browned on all sides, turning occasionally. Transfer veal rolls to a serving platter, reserving drippings in pan; keep veal rolls warm.

Add wine to skillet; cook over high heat 30 seconds, stirring to loosen particles from bottom of skillet. Remove from heat; stir in 1 teaspoon butter, salt, and pepper. Serve over veal. Yield: 6 servings.

Tutto Bene
Salvatore Mancini Lodge #2440
North Providence, Rhode Island

Lamb Sauté

1 pound fresh spinach
1½ pounds lean boneless lamb
½ teaspoon salt, divided
½ teaspoon pepper, divided
2 tablespoons olive oil, divided
1 medium onion, sliced
1 red bell pepper, cut into thin strips
1 yellow bell pepper, cut into thin strips
1 teaspoon minced garlic (about 1 clove)
½ teaspoon dried crushed red pepper
Hot cooked rice

Remove stems from spinach; wash leaves thoroughly, and tear into large pieces. Set aside.

Slice lamb diagonally across grain into thin strips. Sprinkle lamb with ¼ teaspoon salt and ¼ teaspoon pepper. Sauté in 1 tablespoon hot oil in a large skillet over medium-high heat 3 minutes. Remove lamb; set aside.

Sauté onion in remaining 1 tablespoon hot oil in skillet over medium-high heat 1 minute. Add bell peppers and garlic, and sauté 3 minutes. Add spinach, and cook over medium heat 1 minute or until spinach wilts. Add lamb, remaining ¼ teaspoon salt, remaining ¼ teaspoon pepper, and crushed red pepper; cook 3 minutes or until thoroughly heated. Serve over rice. Yield: 4 servings.

Back to the Table
Episcopal Church Women—Christ Church
Raleigh, North Carolina

Apricot-Pecan Stuffed Pork Loin with Bourbon Sauce

The bourbon sauce for this roast requires "flaming" on the cooktop to burn off the alcohol and to prevent the sauce from flaming in the oven.

1½ cups dried apricot halves
½ cup chopped pecans
1 garlic clove
¾ teaspoon salt, divided
¼ teaspoon pepper
2 tablespoons dried thyme, divided
¼ cup molasses, divided
¼ cup peanut oil, divided
1 (5-pound) rolled boneless pork loin roast
1 cup bourbon
1 cup chicken broth
¼ cup whipping cream

Process apricot halves, pecans, garlic, ½ teaspoon salt, and pepper in a food processor until coarsely chopped. Add 1 tablespoon thyme, 1 tablespoon molasses, and 2 tablespoons oil; process until finely chopped but not smooth. Set aside.

Remove strings from roast. Trim excess fat. Butterfly roast by making a lengthwise cut down center of each piece, cutting to within ½ inch of other side. From bottom of cut, slice horizontally to ½ inch from left side; repeat procedure on right side. Open roast, and repeat with other loin half.

Place between 2 sheets of heavy-duty plastic wrap; flatten to ½-inch thickness, using a meat mallet or rolling pin. Repeat procedure with remaining loin half.

Spread apricot mixture on pork loin halves. Roll up each loin half, jellyroll fashion, starting with long side. Secure at 2-inch intervals with heavy string; place pork rolls, seam side down, in a shallow roasting pan. Brush with remaining 2 tablespoons oil; sprinkle with remaining 1 tablespoon thyme.

Combine bourbon, chicken broth, and remaining 3 tablespoons molasses in a large saucepan; bring to a boil. Remove from heat; carefully ignite bourbon mixture with a long match. When flames die, pour over pork rolls.

Bake, uncovered, at 350° for 1 to 1½ hours or until meat thermometer inserted into thickest part registers 160°. Remove from pan, reserving drippings in pan; keep pork warm.

Add cream and remaining ¼ teaspoon salt to pan drippings; cook over medium-high heat, stirring constantly, until slightly thickened. Serve pork with sauce. Yield: 10 servings. Paula Bucher

We're Cooking Up Something New:
50 Years of Music, History, and Food
Wichita Falls Symphony League
Wichita Falls, Texas

Cumin Pork Roast with Wild Mushroom Sauce

Natural juices and browned bits left in the roasting pan form the base of the triple mushroom sauce that accompanies this cumin-scented roast.

1 (3½-pound) boneless center-cut pork loin roast
1 tablespoon ground cumin
1½ teaspoons salt, divided
1¼ teaspoons pepper, divided
2 tablespoons butter or margarine
1 (8-ounce) package sliced fresh mushrooms
¼ pound sliced fresh oyster mushrooms
¼ pound sliced fresh shiitake mushrooms
½ cup chopped shallot
1 garlic clove, minced
1 tablespoon seeded and minced jalapeño pepper, divided
2 tablespoons chopped fresh cilantro
2 tablespoons chopped fresh oregano
1 teaspoon ground cumin
2 tablespoons all-purpose flour
¼ cup dry sherry
1 (14½-ounce) can chicken broth
1 tablespoon butter or margarine
Garnish: fresh cilantro sprigs

Place roast, fat side up, on a rack in a shallow roasting pan. Cut small slits in roast at ½-inch intervals. Combine 1 tablespoon cumin, 1 teaspoon salt, and 1 teaspoon pepper; gently rub seasoning mixture over entire surface of roast.

Bake, uncovered, at 375° for 50 minutes or until a meat thermometer inserted into thickest part registers 160°. Let stand 10 to 15 minutes before slicing. Reserve drippings.

Meanwhile, melt 2 tablespoons butter in a large skillet over medium heat. Add mushrooms, shallot, garlic, and 1 teaspoon jalapeño pepper; sauté 15 minutes or until mushrooms are very tender and beginning to brown. Remove from heat. Stir chopped cilantro, oregano, 1 teaspoon ground cumin, remaining ½ teaspoon salt, and remaining ¼ teaspoon pepper into mushroom mixture. Set aside.

Combine flour and sherry in a small bowl, whisking until smooth. Pour reserved drippings into a large skillet. Add chicken broth; bring to a boil, and reduce heat to medium. Gradually whisk flour mixture into broth mixture; cook over medium heat until thickened, stirring constantly. Add 1 tablespoon butter and remaining 2 teaspoons jalapeño pepper; cook, stirring constantly, 1 minute. Stir in reserved mushroom mixture, and cook, stirring occasionally, 5 more minutes. Serve roast with sauce. Garnish, if desired. Yield: 8 servings.

Always in Season
The Junior League of Salt Lake City, Utah

Indonesian Pork Roast

Serve the tender shreds of pork with mashed potatoes or rice to soak up the vinegary garlic- and soy-infused pan juices.

3 pounds boneless pork loin roast
1 tablespoon vegetable oil
½ cup soy sauce
⅓ cup white vinegar
¼ cup water
1 garlic clove, minced
1 chicken bouillon cube

Cook pork roast in hot oil in a large skillet over medium-high heat until browned on all sides. Drain roast, discarding pan drippings. Return roast to skillet.

Combine soy sauce and remaining 4 ingredients; pour over roast. Bring to a boil; cover, reduce heat, and simmer 3 hours or until roast is tender. Shred roast with a fork before serving. Serve roast with pan juices. Yield: 8 servings.

Leatrice Chee

The Tastes and Tales of Moiliili
Moiliili Community Center
Honolulu, Hawaii

Herbed Pork Pinwheels

Colorful bits of bell pepper, onion, and celery cartwheel along the layers of rolled pork.

3 small red bell peppers, chopped
¾ cup chopped onion
¾ cup chopped celery
1½ teaspoons dried thyme
¾ teaspoon garlic salt
¾ teaspoon ground red pepper
¾ teaspoon paprika
3 tablespoons vegetable oil
3 (¾-pound) pork tenderloins
1 tablespoon lemon pepper, divided
1½ tablespoons fennel seeds, crushed

Sauté first 7 ingredients in hot oil in a large skillet over medium-high heat 8 to 10 minutes or until vegetables are tender; set aside.

Cut each pork tenderloin lengthwise down center of flat side, cutting to within ½ inch of other side. Place each between 2 sheets of heavy-duty plastic wrap, and flatten to a 12- x 8-inch rectangle of even thickness, using a meat mallet or rolling pin. Sprinkle 1½ teaspoons lemon pepper evenly over pork tenderloins.

Spoon one-third of bell pepper mixture onto each tenderloin, spreading to within ½ inch of sides; roll up tenderloins, jellyroll fashion, starting with long side. Tie with heavy string at 1½-inch intervals. Rub remaining 1½ teaspoons lemon pepper and fennel seeds evenly on top and sides of tenderloins.

Place tenderloin rolls, seam side down, on a lightly greased baking sheet. Bake, uncovered, at 325° for 50 to 60 minutes or until a meat thermometer inserted into thickest part registers 160°. Let stand 10 minutes; remove strings, and slice tenderloins. Yield: 8 to 10 servings.

Pick of the Crop, Two
North Sunflower PTA
Drew, Mississippi

Oriental Pork and Rice

Shreds of crispy iceberg lettuce tossed in just before serving add unexpected texture to this simple pork pleaser.

1 (1-pound) pork tenderloin, cut into chunks
1 tablespoon vegetable oil
½ cup diced onion
2 cups water
1½ cups uncooked instant rice (we tested with Minute Rice)
3 tablespoons soy sauce
½ teaspoon garlic salt
2 cups shredded iceberg lettuce
Soy sauce (optional)

Cook pork in hot oil in a large skillet over medium-high heat 4 minutes or until browned. Add onion; cook, stirring constantly, 3 minutes or until tender. Add water and next 3 ingredients; bring mixture to a boil. Remove from heat; cover and let stand 5 minutes. Stir in lettuce just before serving. Serve with additional soy sauce, if desired. Yield: 4 servings.

Shirley Spildie

Our Heritage Cookbook
First Baptist Church
Billings, Montana

Stuffed Pork Chops

¼ pound ground pork sausage
1 cup (4 ounces) shredded Muenster cheese, divided
½ cup chopped fresh mushrooms
2 tablespoons chopped onion
½ teaspoon seasoned salt
4 (1½-inch-thick) boneless pork loin chops (about 1¾ pounds), trimmed and cut with pockets
4 slices bacon
½ teaspoon freshly ground pepper
½ cup milk
1 tablespoon all-purpose flour
2 tablespoons dry white wine
¼ teaspoon garlic salt

Brown sausage in a small skillet, stirring until it crumbles and is no longer pink; drain.

Combine sausage, ½ cup cheese, mushrooms, onion, and seasoned salt. Stuff about 2 tablespoons sausage mixture into each pork chop pocket. Wrap 1 slice bacon around edge of each chop, and secure with wooden picks. Sprinkle pepper evenly over chops.

Grill, covered with grill lid, over medium-high heat (350° to 400°) about 18 minutes or until done, turning once; keep warm.

Combine milk and remaining 3 ingredients in a saucepan; cook over medium heat 3 minutes, stirring constantly. Add remaining ½ cup Muenster cheese, stirring until cheese melts. Serve pork chops with cheese sauce. Yield: 4 servings. Michelle Wildenradt

Cook Bookery
The University of Illinois College of Medicine at Peoria, Illinois

Harvest Ham

One of the trademarks of country ham is its saltiness. To remove some of the salt and to restore moisture to the ham, soak the ham at least 24 hours or up to 3 days, changing the water every 12 hours.

1 (15-pound) uncooked country ham
2 tablespoons whole cloves
½ cup firmly packed dark brown sugar
½ cup honey mustard
½ cup honey
1 teaspoon ground ginger
2 cups apple juice
1 cup pineapple juice
1 cup Madeira
2 cups dried apricot halves
1 cup golden raisins

Place ham in a very large container; cover with water, and soak at least 24 hours. Pour off water. Scrub ham with warm water, using a stiff brush, and rinse well.

Remove skin, leaving a ¼-inch layer of fat. Score fat in a diamond design, using a sharp knife. Stud with whole cloves. Place ham in a large roasting pan.

Combine brown sugar, mustard, honey, and ginger. Coat exposed portion of ham evenly with mustard mixture. Pour apple juice and pineapple juice into roasting pan. Cover and bake at 350° for 2 hours. Add Madeira, apricot halves, and raisins to pan. Cover and bake 1½ more hours or until a meat thermometer inserted into thickest part of ham registers 142°. To serve, slice ham across grain into very thin slices. Yield: 26 servings. Stacy Taylor Layton

Beyond Cotton Country
The Junior League of Morgan County
Decatur, Alabama

French Club Sandwiches

Tailgating takes a tasty turn when this winning cream cheese club sandwich is served.

2 (8-ounce) packages cream cheese, softened
¼ cup mayonnaise
¾ cup finely chopped celery
½ cup (2 ounces) shredded Cheddar cheese
⅓ cup chopped fresh parsley
2 tablespoons finely chopped onion
1 tablespoon lemon juice
1 tablespoon Worcestershire sauce
¼ teaspoon seasoned salt
2 (1-pound) French baguettes
2 pounds thinly sliced cooked ham
6 dill pickles, thinly sliced lengthwise

Combine cream cheese and mayonnaise; beat at medium speed with an electric mixer until mixture is creamy. Stir in celery and next 6 ingredients.

Cut baguettes horizontally in half lengthwise; spread cream cheese mixture evenly over cut sides of bread. Place ham evenly on bottom halves of baguettes; top ham with pickle. Cover with tops of baguettes. Cut each baguette into 6 portions. Yield: 12 servings.

Down by the Water
The Junior League of Columbia, South Carolina

Polish Sausage Platter

6 slices bacon
1½ pounds kielbasa, cut into 4-inch pieces
1 large onion, sliced
1 (12-ounce) can beer
1 large cabbage, thickly sliced (about 2 pounds)
1½ teaspoons salt
1 teaspoon sugar
⅛ teaspoon pepper
Quartered red potatoes (optional)
Quartered carrots (optional)

Cook bacon in a Dutch oven until crisp; remove bacon, and drain on paper towels, reserving 2 tablespoons drippings in pan. Crumble bacon, and set aside.

Sauté sausage and onion in hot pan drippings until onion is tender. Add beer, and bring to a boil. Reduce heat, and simmer, uncovered,

10 minutes. Add cabbage and next 3 ingredients; stir in reserved bacon. If desired, add potato and carrot. Bring to a boil; cover, reduce heat, and simmer 25 minutes. Serve with a slotted spoon. Yield: 4 to 6 servings.
Kay Maris

Of Books and Cooks
Woman's Book Club
Harrison, Arkansas

Sausage Ratatouille

2 large eggplants, cut into 1-inch pieces
¾ teaspoon salt, divided
1 pound hot Italian sausage
2 tablespoons olive oil
1 medium onion, thinly sliced
2 green bell peppers, thinly sliced
2 tomatoes, seeded and cut into 1-inch pieces
⅔ cup chopped fresh basil
½ teaspoon freshly ground pepper

Place eggplant in a colander; sprinkle with ¼ teaspoon salt. Set aside, and let drain.

Cut sausage diagonally into 1-inch-thick slices. Cook sausage in a large skillet in hot oil over medium-high heat until browned; remove sausage, reserving 3 tablespoons drippings in pan.

Sauté eggplant, onion, and bell pepper in reserved pan drippings over medium-high heat 8 minutes. Add sausage and tomato; cover, reduce heat, and simmer 12 minutes or until vegetables are tender. Stir in basil, remaining ½ teaspoon salt, and ground pepper. Serve immediately. Yield: 4 to 6 servings.

Perennial Palette
Southborough Gardeners
Southborough, Massachusetts

Grilled Venison Roast

1 (5-pound) venison chuck roast, trimmed
2 large garlic cloves, halved
½ cup Worcestershire sauce
2 tablespoons soy sauce
2 teaspoons garlic powder
2 teaspoons lemon pepper
Hickory chips
4 (14½-ounce) cans chicken broth
1 (10-ounce) jar red currant jelly
½ cup bourbon
2 tablespoons black peppercorns
1 tablespoon gin
¼ teaspoon dried thyme

Make 4 small slits in top of roast. Insert a garlic half into each slit. Combine Worcestershire sauce and next 3 ingredients. Place in a large shallow dish or a large heavy-duty, zip-top plastic bag; add roast. Cover or seal, and chill 2 hours, turning occasionally. Remove roast from marinade, discarding marinade.

Soak hickory chips in water at least 1 hour. Prepare charcoal fire by piling charcoal on each side of grill, leaving center empty. Place a drip pan between coals and fill with water. Prepare fire; let burn 15 to 20 minutes. Drain chips, and place on hot coals.

Coat food rack with cooking spray, and place on grill over coals. Arrange roast on rack over drip pan; grill, covered with grill lid, 3 hours or until a meat thermometer inserted into thickest part of meat registers 160°. Refill water pan, and add charcoal as needed. Transfer roast to a serving platter, reserving 2 tablespoons pan drippings. Cover roast with aluminum foil, and let stand 10 to 15 minutes before slicing.

Combine chicken broth and remaining 5 ingredients in a large saucepan. Bring to a boil; reduce heat, and simmer, uncovered, 1 hour or until liquid is reduced to 4 cups. Stir in reserved pan drippings. Serve venison with sauce. Yield: 15 to 18 servings.

Pick of the Crop, Two
North Sunflower PTA
Drew, Mississippi

Pasta, Rice & Grains

Red Pepper and Olive Pasta, page 216

Baked Pasta with Shiitake Mushrooms and Prosciutto

To save a bit of time, put on a big pot of water and bring it to a boil for the pasta while you prepare this delectable three-cheese and shiitake mushroom sauce.

1 pound fresh shiitake mushrooms
2 cups finely chopped onion
2 large garlic cloves, minced
1 teaspoon dried basil
1 teaspoon dried oregano
¼ teaspoon dried crushed red pepper
2 tablespoons olive oil, divided
¼ cup unsalted butter, divided
3 tablespoons all-purpose flour
2 cups milk
2 (28-ounce) cans diced tomatoes, drained
¼ pound thinly sliced prosciutto, cut into strips
1½ cups freshly grated Parmesan cheese, divided
1 cup (4 ounces) shredded fontina cheese
1 cup (4 ounces) crumbled Gorgonzola cheese
1 cup chopped fresh parsley, divided
16 ounces uncooked dried farfalle (bow tie pasta)
½ teaspoon salt
¼ teaspoon black pepper

Remove stems from mushrooms; reserve for other uses. Slice mushroom caps, and set aside.

Sauté onion and next 4 ingredients in 1 tablespoon oil in a large skillet over medium-high heat until onion is tender. Transfer onion mixture to a large bowl.

Heat remaining 1 tablespoon oil in skillet over medium-high heat until hot. Add mushrooms, and cook 5 minutes or until mushrooms begin to brown, stirring often. Transfer to bowl with onion mixture.

Melt 3 tablespoons butter in skillet over low heat. Add flour, stirring until smooth. Cook 1 minute, stirring constantly. Gradually add milk; cook over medium heat, stirring constantly, until mixture is thickened and bubbly. Pour sauce over vegetable mixture; stir in tomatoes, prosciutto, 1¼ cups Parmesan cheese, fontina cheese, Gorgonzola cheese, and ⅔ cup chopped parsley.

Cook pasta according to package directions. Drain and add to mushroom mixture; stir in salt and pepper.

Transfer pasta mixture to a greased 15- x 10-inch baking dish. Sprinkle with remaining ¼ cup Parmesan cheese; dot with remaining 1 tablespoon butter. Cover and bake at 400° for 25 minutes; uncover and bake 10 more minutes or until golden. Let stand 15 minutes before serving. Sprinkle with remaining ⅓ cup parsley. Yield: 10 servings.

A Century of Serving
The Junior Board of Christiana Care, Inc.
Wilmington, Delaware

Pasta with Country Ham, Snow Peas, and Asparagus

1 (2-ounce) package pine nuts
1½ pounds fresh asparagus spears
8 ounces fresh snow pea pods, cut diagonally into thirds
16 ounces uncooked dried farfalle (bow tie pasta)
6 ounces country ham, cut into thin strips
1 tablespoon butter or margarine, melted
1 cup whipping cream
1½ teaspoons dried tarragon
1 cup freshly grated Parmesan cheese
2 tablespoons minced fresh parsley
Steamed mussels (optional)

Bake pine nuts in a shallow pan at 350° for 5 minutes or until toasted, stirring occasionally; set aside.

Snap off tough ends of asparagus; cut asparagus into ¾-inch pieces. Cook, uncovered, in boiling water in a large skillet 6 minutes or until crisp-tender. Plunge asparagus into ice water to stop the cooking process. Add snow peas to boiling water in skillet. Cook 1 minute or until crisp-tender. Add snow peas to asparagus in ice water; set aside.

Cook pasta in a large Dutch oven according to package directions.

Meanwhile, cook ham in melted butter in skillet over medium-high heat 1 to 2 minutes. Sir in whipping cream and tarragon, and cook 1 minute. Drain pasta, and return to pan. Drain vegetables. Add vegetables, cream mixture, Parmesan cheese, and parsley to pasta; toss well. Sprinkle with reserved pine nuts. Serve with mussels, if desired. Yield: 6 servings.

Seaboard to Sideboard
The Junior League of Wilmington, North Carolina

Fettuccine with Cream, Basil, and Romano

Crumbled bacon, freshly grated Romano cheese, and fresh sprigs of basil mingle in the hot cooked fettuccine, creating a meal-in-one dish for two.

8 ounces uncooked dried fettuccine
4 slices bacon
4 green onions, chopped (about ½ cup)
½ cup whipping cream
½ cup freshly grated Romano cheese
⅓ cup chopped fresh basil
Freshly ground pepper
Freshly grated Romano cheese
Freshly grated Parmesan cheese (optional)

Cook fettuccine according to package directions. Drain and place in a large bowl.

Meanwhile, cook bacon in a large skillet until crisp; remove bacon, and drain on paper towels, reserving drippings in skillet. Crumble bacon, and set aside. Add green onions to drippings, and cook, stirring constantly, 1 minute. Add cream; bring to a boil. Reduce heat, and simmer, uncovered, 1 minute or until slightly thickened. Stir in ½ cup Romano cheese and basil.

Pour sauce over pasta; add crumbled bacon, and toss well. Sprinkle pasta with pepper, additional Romano cheese, and Parmesan cheese, if desired. Yield: 2 servings. Danny Scalzitti

Generations of Good Food
Jeannette Public Library
Jeannette, Pennsylvania

Fettuccine with Prosciutto and Smoked Salmon

½ cup chopped onion
2 tablespoons unsalted butter, melted
¼ cup dry white wine
1 tablespoon chopped fresh parsley
4 ounces smoked salmon, thinly sliced
4 ounces prosciutto, thinly sliced
1 cup whipping cream
3 large eggs, lightly beaten
½ cup freshly grated Parmesan cheese
¼ teaspoon ground white pepper
1 (10-ounce) package refrigerated fettuccine

Sauté onion in melted butter in a large skillet over medium-high heat 5 minutes or until tender. Add wine and parsley; stir well. Reduce heat, and simmer, uncovered, until liquid is reduced by half. Add salmon and prosciutto. Remove from heat, and stir well.

Bring whipping cream just to a simmer. Gradually stir about one-fourth of hot whipping cream into beaten egg; add egg mixture to remaining hot whipping cream, stirring constantly. Add Parmesan cheese and pepper; stir well. Cook, stirring constantly, over low heat until thickened.

Cook fettuccine according to package directions; drain well. Combine salmon mixture with cooked fettuccine. Pour whipping cream mixture over hot fettuccine mixture; toss well. Serve immediately. Yield: 4 servings.

Down by the Water
The Junior League of Columbia, South Carolina

Mexican Lasagna

Head south of the border with this lasagna by replacing traditional Italian-style ingredients with refried beans, ground cumin, picante sauce, and Monterey Jack cheese. The lasagna stirs together quickly because you don't have to cook the noodles separately.

1 pound ground round
1 (16-ounce) can refried beans
2 teaspoons dried oregano
1 teaspoon ground cumin
¾ teaspoon garlic powder
12 uncooked dried lasagna noodles
2½ cups picante sauce
2¼ cups water
1 (16-ounce) container sour cream
¾ cup thinly sliced green onions
1 (2¼-ounce) can sliced ripe olives, drained
1 cup (4 ounces) shredded Monterey Jack cheese

Cook ground beef in a large skillet, stirring until it crumbles and is no longer pink; drain. Stir together beef, refried beans, and next 3 ingredients in a large bowl. Place 4 uncooked lasagna noodles in a lightly greased 13- x 9-inch baking dish. Spread half of beef mixture over noodles. Top with 4 noodles and remaining beef mixture. Place remaining 4 lasagna noodles on top of beef mixture.

Stir together picante sauce and water. Pour over noodles. Cover and bake at 350° for 1 hour and 30 minutes. Combine sour cream, green onions, and olives; spoon over noodles. Top with cheese. Bake, uncovered, 5 more minutes or until cheese melts. Yield: 9 servings.

The Albany Collection: Treasures and Treasured Recipes
Women's Council of the Albany Institute of History & Art
Albany, New York

New Pasta with Lemon Chicken

A crisp green salad and crunchy breadsticks are the perfect partners for this fresh lemon- and oregano-flavored chicken and pasta entrée.

8 ounces uncooked dried linguine
2 garlic cloves, minced
1 tablespoon extra-virgin olive oil
1 pound skinned and boned chicken breast halves, cut into ½-inch strips
1 (8-ounce) package sliced fresh mushrooms
1 tablespoon butter or margarine, melted
¼ cup fresh lemon juice
½ teaspoon dried oregano
¼ teaspoon freshly ground pepper
2 tablespoons cornstarch
1 (14½-ounce) can chicken broth
2 tablespoons chopped fresh parsley

Cook pasta according to package directions; drain and keep warm.

Sauté garlic in hot oil in a large skillet over medium heat 30 seconds or until golden. Add chicken, and cook 5 minutes, stirring constantly. Remove chicken from skillet; set aside.

Cook mushrooms in melted butter in skillet over medium heat until tender; stir in reserved chicken, lemon juice, oregano, and pepper.

Combine cornstarch and chicken broth in a small bowl, whisking until smooth. Pour over chicken mixture; cook, stirring constantly, 2 minutes or until sauce thickens. Serve sauce over pasta, and sprinkle pasta with parsley. Yield: 3 servings.

Café Weller . . . Tastes to Remember
Apple Corps of the Weller Health Education Center
Easton, Pennsylvania

Seaside Pasta

This Italian-inspired dish is very versatile; prepare it sans shrimp, and serve it as a side dish.

½ pound unpeeled, medium-size fresh shrimp
1½ ounces dried tomatoes
½ cup boiling water
10 fresh asparagus spears
¼ cup olive oil
1 small bunch green onions, chopped and divided
¼ cup sliced ripe olives
2 tablespoons pine nuts
2 tablespoons chopped fresh basil
4 ounces dried linguine, cooked
¼ cup freshly grated Parmesan cheese
¼ teaspoon salt
⅛ teaspoon pepper

Peel shrimp, and devein, if desired. Set aside.

Soak tomatoes in boiling water 10 minutes; drain and chop.

Snap off tough ends of asparagus. Cut asparagus into 1½-inch pieces. Cook shrimp in hot oil in a large skillet over medium-high heat 2 minutes, stirring constantly. Add reserved tomatoes, asparagus, half of green onions, olives, pine nuts, and basil. Cook 2 minutes, stirring often.

Combine linguine, shrimp mixture, 2 tablespoons cheese, salt, and pepper; sprinkle with remaining half of green onions and remaining 2 tablespoons cheese. Yield: 2 to 3 servings.

Apron Strings: Ties to the Southern Tradition of Cooking
The Junior League of Little Rock, Arkansas

Manicotti

8 ounces uncooked manicotti shells
1 pound ground chuck
¾ cup chopped onion
1 cup small-curd cottage cheese
½ cup mayonnaise
½ teaspoon salt
½ teaspoon pepper
1 (48-ounce) jar pasta sauce (we tested with Prego traditional sauce)
2½ cups (10 ounces) shredded mozzarella cheese

Cook manicotti shells according to package directions; drain and set aside.

Meanwhile, cook ground beef and onion in a large skillet, stirring until meat crumbles and is no longer pink; drain. Return beef mixture to skillet. Stir in cottage cheese and next 3 ingredients; cool slightly.

Stuff meat mixture into manicotti shells. Place stuffed shells into a lightly greased 13- x 9-inch baking dish. Spread pasta sauce over stuffed shells. Sprinkle with mozzarella cheese. Bake, uncovered, at 350° for 45 minutes. Let stand 10 minutes before serving. Yield: 7 servings.

Mary Jean Dzurisin

Cook Bookery
The University of Illinois College of Medicine at Peoria
Peoria, Illinois

Creamy Tomato-Sausage Sauce with Shells

Pungent bits of fresh rosemary and grated Parmigiano-Reggiano cheese give this creamy pasta pleaser personality.

1 pound mild Italian sausage
8 ounces uncooked medium pasta shells
1 tablespoon butter or margarine, melted
1½ pounds plum tomatoes, coarsely chopped
3 tablespoons water
1 teaspoon finely chopped fresh rosemary
½ teaspoon salt
¼ teaspoon dried crushed red pepper
¾ cup heavy whipping cream
½ cup freshly grated Parmigiano-Reggiano or Parmesan cheese

Cook sausage in boiling water to cover 3 minutes. Drain; let cool, and thinly slice.

Cook pasta according to package directions, including salt. Drain and keep warm. Meanwhile, cook sausage in butter in a large skillet until browned. Stir in tomato and next 4 ingredients. Bring to a boil; cook, uncovered, 10 minutes or until tomato is soft, stirring often. Add whipping cream; cook until mixture is reduced by half, stirring often.

Pour sauce over pasta; add cheese, and toss well. Yield: 4 to 6 servings.

What Can I Bring?
The Junior League of Northern Virginia
McLean, Virginia

Red Pepper and Olive Pasta

½ cup pine nuts
2 large red bell peppers
16 ounces uncooked dried penne
2 tablespoons olive oil
4 green onions, sliced
2 garlic cloves, minced
⅔ cup chopped ripe Greek or Moroccan olives
⅔ cup chopped green Sicilian or Italian olives
½ to 1 teaspoon ground red pepper
½ cup dried tomatoes in oil, drained and chopped
Freshly grated Parmesan cheese (optional)
Freshly ground black pepper (optional)

Bake pine nuts in a shallow pan at 350° for 5 minutes or until nuts are toasted, stirring occasionally. Set aside.

Broil peppers on an aluminum foil-lined baking sheet 5½ inches from heat about 5 minutes on each side or until peppers look blistered. Place peppers in a heavy-duty, zip-top plastic bag; seal and let stand 10 minutes to loosen skins. Peel peppers; remove and discard seeds. Cut peppers into thin strips; set aside.

Cook pasta according to package directions; drain and place in a serving bowl. Meanwhile, heat oil in a large skillet over medium heat. Add green onions and garlic; cook 3 minutes or until green onions are tender, stirring often. Add pepper strips, olives, and ground red pepper; cook 5 minutes, stirring often. Add olive mixture to pasta; toss. Add reserved pine nuts and dried tomatoes; toss well. If desired, serve with Parmesan cheese and black pepper. Yield: 6 servings.

International Home Cooking
The United Nations International School Parents' Association
New York, New York

Spaghetti Pie

8 ounces uncooked dried spaghetti
2 large eggs
½ cup grated Parmesan cheese
2 tablespoons butter or margarine, melted
1 cup ricotta cheese
1 (14-ounce) jar spaghetti sauce
1 cup (4 ounces) shredded mozzarella cheese

Cook spaghetti according to package directions; drain.

Stir together eggs, Parmesan cheese, and butter in a large bowl. Add spaghetti, and toss. Spoon spaghetti mixture into a greased 10-inch pieplate. Spread ricotta over spaghetti. Top with spaghetti sauce, and sprinkle with mozzarella cheese. Cover and bake at 350° for 1 hour. Uncover and bake 7 more minutes. Let stand 5 minutes before serving. Yield: 6 servings.

Lisa O'Neill

From the Kitchens of Lake Wynonah
Civic Association of Lake Wynonah
Auburn, Pennsylvania

Shrimp and Feta Cheese Vermicelli

This fresh shrimp and tender pasta dish benefits from lots of tangy, salty crumbles of rich feta cheese.

8 ounces uncooked dried vermicelli
1 pound unpeeled, medium-size fresh shrimp
¼ teaspoon dried crushed red pepper
¼ cup olive oil, divided
⅔ cup crumbled feta cheese
1 (14½-ounce) can diced tomatoes, undrained
¼ cup dry white wine
¾ teaspoon dried basil
½ teaspoon minced garlic
½ teaspoon dried oregano
¼ teaspoon salt
¼ teaspoon black pepper

Cook pasta according to package directions; drain and keep warm.

Peel shrimp, and devein, if desired. Sauté shrimp and red pepper in 2 tablespoons hot oil in a large skillet over medium-high heat 1 minute. Place shrimp in a greased 11- x 7-inch baking dish. Sprinkle with feta cheese.

Heat remaining 2 tablespoons oil in skillet over medium heat. Add tomatoes and remaining 6 ingredients; bring to boil. Reduce heat, and simmer, uncovered, 10 minutes, stirring occasionally. Spoon tomato mixture over shrimp. Bake, uncovered, at 400° for 10 minutes. Serve over pasta. Yield: 3 servings.

Southern Elegance: A Second Course
The Junior League of Gaston County
Gastonia, North Carolina

Nutty Raisin Couscous

¼ cup pine nuts
1½ cups chicken broth
1½ cups water
½ cup raisins
2 tablespoons butter or olive oil
¼ teaspoon salt
¼ teaspoon pepper
1½ cups uncooked couscous

Bake pine nuts in a shallow pan at 350° for 5 minutes or until toasted, stirring occasionally. Set aside.

Stir together chicken broth and next 5 ingredients in a saucepan; bring to a boil, stirring occasionally.

Stir in couscous; cover, remove from heat, and let stand 5 minutes or until liquid is absorbed. Fluff with a fork, and sprinkle with reserved pine nuts. Serve immediately. Yield: 6 to 8 servings.

It's a Snap
The Haven of Grace
St. Louis, Missouri

Bayou Rice

Rice and ground chuck get a spicy bayou kick courtesy of hot sauce, chili powder, jalapeño pepper, and green chiles.

1 pound ground chuck
1 medium onion, chopped
1 medium-size green bell pepper, chopped
1 garlic clove, minced
2 cups hot cooked rice
1 (10-ounce) can diced tomatoes and green chiles
1 cup grated Parmesan cheese
1 cup water
1 (4.5-ounce) can chopped green chiles, undrained
1 tablespoon Worcestershire sauce
1 large jalapeño pepper, seeded and chopped
1 teaspoon chopped fresh cilantro
1 teaspoon chili powder
1 teaspoon hot sauce
½ teaspoon salt
½ teaspoon freshly ground pepper
1 (8-ounce) container sour cream
1 medium tomato, chopped

Cook ground beef in a Dutch oven, stirring until it crumbles and is no longer pink; drain. Add onion, green bell pepper, and garlic; cook over medium heat 5 minutes. Stir in rice and next 11 ingredients. Reduce heat, and simmer, uncovered, 5 minutes. Stir in sour cream and tomato. Yield: 6 servings. Jane Hickman

Down Home Dining in Mississippi
Mississippi Homemaker Volunteers, Inc.
Water Valley, Mississippi

Korean-Style Fried Rice

1 garlic clove, minced
1½ tablespoons soy sauce
¼ teaspoon sugar
¼ teaspoon dark sesame oil
¼ pound boneless pork loin chops, cut into thin strips
2 tablespoons canola oil
¾ pound fresh bean sprouts
3 cups cold cooked rice
1 cup sliced green onions
3 tablespoons soy sauce

Stir together first 4 ingredients in a bowl. Add pork, and toss well. Cover and chill 15 minutes.

Heat canola oil in a large nonstick skillet or wok over medium-high heat 1 to 2 minutes. Add pork mixture; stir-fry 2 minutes or until lightly browned. Add bean sprouts and rice, and stir-fry 2 minutes or until rice is thoroughly heated. Add green onions and soy sauce; toss well. Serve immediately. Yield: 4 servings.

The Tastes and Tales of Moiliili
Moiliili Community Center
Honolulu, Hawaii

Sweet Indian Curried Rice

1½ cups uncooked converted rice
1½ teaspoons curry powder
3 tablespoons butter or margarine, melted and divided
3 cups chicken broth
½ cup chopped green bell pepper
½ cup chopped celery
1 cup raisins
½ cup sliced green onions
½ teaspoon seasoned salt
3 tablespoons pine nuts, toasted
3 tablespoons diced pimiento, drained
1½ tablespoons brown sugar
1½ tablespoons chutney
1½ tablespoons white vinegar

Cook rice and curry powder in 1½ tablespoons melted butter in a medium saucepan over low heat 3 minutes, stirring constantly. Stir in chicken broth. Bring to a boil; cover, reduce heat, and simmer 20 minutes or until broth is absorbed and rice is tender.

Cook bell pepper and celery in remaining 1½ tablespoons melted butter in a large skillet, stirring constantly, until tender. Stir in raisins, green onions, and seasoned salt; cook 2 minutes, stirring constantly.

Stir together pine nuts, pimiento, and remaining 3 ingredients in a small bowl. To serve, mound rice mixture on a serving platter, and top with raisin mixture; drizzle with chutney mixture. Yield: 6 servings.

Allison Wright

The Monarch's Feast
Mary Munford PTA
Richmond, Virginia

Baked Red Wine Risotto

While this is not the traditional method for preparing risotto, it results in a very special rice dish starring radicchio and golden raisins.

3 cups dry red wine
1 (32-ounce) carton chicken broth
1 cup coarsely chopped radicchio
½ cup golden raisins
1 garlic clove, minced
2 tablespoons olive oil
¼ teaspoon salt
⅛ teaspoon pepper
1 medium onion, finely chopped (about 1¼ cups)
3 tablespoons butter or margarine, melted
2 cups uncooked Arborio rice
2 tablespoons tomato paste
1½ cups grated Parmesan cheese, divided
¼ teaspoon salt
2 tablespoons chopped fresh chives (optional)

Bring wine to a boil in a 3-quart saucepan; boil 10 minutes or until reduced to 2 cups. Combine 1½ cups reduced wine and chicken broth; set aside, and keep warm. Set remaining ½ cup wine aside, and keep warm.

Cook radicchio, raisins, and garlic in hot olive oil in a large skillet over medium-high heat, stirring constantly, 2 minutes or until radicchio wilts. Add ¼ teaspoon salt and pepper. Set aside; keep warm.

Cook onion in butter in a large skillet over medium-high heat, stirring constantly, until tender. Stir in rice and tomato paste. Spoon into a greased 13- x 9-inch casserole. Pour chicken broth mixture over rice mixture. Add ¾ cup cheese and ¼ teaspoon salt.

Cover and bake at 375° for 10 minutes. Remove from oven; uncover and stir in radicchio mixture and reserved ½ cup reduced wine. Cover and bake 35 minutes or until liquid is absorbed and rice is tender. Remove from oven, and sprinkle with remaining ¾ cup cheese and chives, if desired. Yield: 8 servings.

Bravo! Recipes, Legends & Lore
University Musical Society
Ann Arbor, Michigan

Chinese Risotto with Shiitake Mushrooms

4 cups chicken broth
1 cup water
1 tablespoon dark sesame oil
2 teaspoons minced serrano chile
2 teaspoons minced garlic
1½ tablespoons soy sauce
1 tablespoon rice wine vinegar
⅛ teaspoon sugar
3 tablespoons vegetable oil
½ cup chopped shallot (about 5 large)
5 ounces fresh shiitake mushrooms, stems removed
1 cup chopped smoked chicken or pork
1 cup uncooked Arborio rice
1 cup chopped fresh turnip or mustard greens
1 cup chopped fresh cilantro

Combine broth and water in a medium saucepan; bring to a boil. Reduce heat to medium-low, and keep hot.

Heat sesame oil in a large saucepan over medium heat. Add chile; cook 1 minute, stirring often. Stir in garlic; cook 1 minute. Remove from heat; stir in soy sauce, vinegar, and sugar. Transfer soy sauce mixture to a small bowl; set aside.

Add vegetable oil to pan; place over medium-high heat until hot. Add shallot; sauté 2 minutes. Add mushrooms and chicken; sauté 1 minute. Stir in rice; reduce heat to medium, and cook, stirring constantly, 2 minutes. Add ½ cup hot broth mixture, stirring constantly, until liquid is absorbed. Repeat procedure with remaining broth mixture, ½ cup at a time. (Total cooking time is about 40 minutes.)

Stir in turnip greens and cilantro; cook, stirring constantly, 1 minute. Stir in reserved soy sauce mixture. Yield: 4 servings.

A Thyme to Remember
Dallas County Medical Society Alliance
Dallas, Texas

Grits Fiesta Pie

Tamale and taco fans will cheer for this winning cheesy grits pie.

1 cup water
¼ teaspoon garlic powder
½ cup uncooked quick-cooking grits
½ cup (2 ounces) shredded Cheddar cheese
¼ cup all-purpose flour
1 large egg, lightly beaten
¾ pound ground chuck or sirloin
1 (1¼-ounce) envelope taco seasoning mix
1 cup (4 ounces) shredded Monterey Jack cheese, divided
⅓ cup chopped tomato
¼ cup sliced ripe olives
3 tablespoons chopped green bell pepper
2 large eggs, lightly beaten
2 tablespoons milk

Bring water and garlic powder to a boil in a 3-quart saucepan; add grits. Return to a boil; reduce heat, and cook, uncovered, stirring constantly, 4 minutes. Remove from heat.

Combine Cheddar cheese and flour; stir into grits mixture. Add 1 beaten egg, and stir until blended. Spoon mixture into a lightly greased 9-inch pieplate; press with back of a spoon in bottom and up sides to form a shell.

Cook ground beef in a large skillet, stirring until it crumbles and is no longer pink; drain. Stir in taco seasoning mix, and spread into pieplate. Top with ¾ cup Monterey Jack cheese, tomato, olives, and green pepper. Combine 2 beaten eggs and milk. Pour over pie.

Bake, uncovered, at 375° for 25 minutes. Remove from oven; sprinkle with remaining ¼ cup Monterey Jack cheese. Let stand 5 minutes before serving. Yield: 4 to 6 servings. William Stoneman

Designer's Recipes for Living
East Tennessee Interior Design Society
Knoxville, Tennessee

Quinoa Pilaf

Quinoa (pronounced KEEN-wah) is a tiny bead-shaped grain that cooks like regular rice. Look for it in health food stores or in large supermarkets.

⅓ cup pumpkin kernels
¾ cup uncooked quinoa
1½ cups water
1 cup peeled, diced jícama
1 cup chopped purple onion
1 cup frozen whole kernel corn, thawed
½ cup chopped green bell pepper
½ cup chopped red bell pepper
2 teaspoons seeded, minced jalapeño pepper
2 teaspoons olive oil
1 cup chopped tomato
½ cup sliced green onions
3 tablespoons fresh lime juice
2 tablespoons chopped walnuts
½ teaspoon salt

Bake pumpkin kernels in a shallow pan at 350° for 3 minutes or until toasted, stirring occasionally. Set aside.

Place quinoa in a small bowl; cover with warm water, and rub quinoa between hands (water will be cloudy). Drain and repeat procedure until water is clear; drain quinoa well.

Bring 1½ cups water to a boil in a large saucepan; add quinoa. Return to a boil; cover, reduce heat, and simmer 20 minutes. Fluff with a fork.

Sauté jícama and next 5 ingredients in hot oil in a large skillet 5 minutes or until tender. Add quinoa, pumpkin kernels, tomato, and remaining ingredients; cook until thoroughly heated. Yield: 12 servings.

Sybil Miller

A Taste of Tradition
Temple Emanu-El
Providence, Rhode Island

Pies & Pastries

Pear Tart, page 240

China Clipper Apple Pie

Generous slices of this double-crust delight are brimming with juicy, sweetly tart apple slices infused with brewed tea, ginger, and cinnamon.

1 (15-ounce) package refrigerated piecrusts
1 cup sugar
2 tablespoons all-purpose flour
¼ teaspoon salt
1 teaspoon ground cinnamon
½ teaspoon ground ginger
3 tablespoons strongly brewed tea
1 tablespoon lemon juice
4 cups peeled, sliced Granny Smith apple (3 to 4 apples)
2 tablespoons butter or margarine

Fit 1 piecrust into a 9-inch pieplate according to package directions.

Stir together sugar and next 6 ingredients. Alternate layers of apple and sugar mixture in piecrust, heaping apple slightly in center. Dot with butter.

Roll remaining piecrust to press out fold lines. Place piecrust over filling; trim off excess pastry along edges. Fold edges under, and crimp. Cut slits in top of pastry to allow steam to escape.

Bake at 450° for 15 minutes. Reduce oven temperature to 350°. Shield pie with aluminum foil to prevent excessive browning, and bake 50 more minutes. Cool pie completely on a wire rack. Yield: 1 (9-inch) pie.

Mary E. Guggisberg

Recipes and Remembrances
Otsego County Historical Society
Gaylord, Michigan

Triberry Cobbler Pie

This triple berry pie is thick and juicy like a cobbler, but boasts a double piecrust.

2 (16½-ounce) cans blackberries, undrained
1 cup fresh or frozen blueberries
¼ cup fresh or frozen cranberries, chopped
6 tablespoons all-purpose flour, divided
1 (15-ounce) package refrigerated piecrusts
1 cup sugar
⅛ teaspoon salt
½ teaspoon ground cinnamon
⅛ teaspoon grated lemon rind
1 tablespoon fresh lemon juice
1 tablespoon butter or margarine

Drain blackberries, reserving ½ cup liquid. Stir together blackberries, blueberries, and cranberries in a large bowl. Sprinkle berries with 2 teaspoons flour; stir gently, and set aside.

Fit 1 piecrust into a 9-inch deep-dish pieplate according to package directions.

Combine remaining ⅓ cup flour, sugar, and next 3 ingredients in a medium saucepan. Gradually add reserved blackberry juice, stirring until smooth. Cook over medium heat, stirring constantly, until thickened. Remove from heat, and stir in lemon juice. Pour sauce over berries; stir gently. Pour berries into prepared piecrust. Dot with butter.

Roll remaining piecrust to press out fold lines. Place piecrust over filling; trim off excess pastry along edges. Fold edges under, and crimp. Cut slits in top of pastry to allow steam to escape.

Bake at 425° for 40 minutes. Shield pie with aluminum foil to prevent excessive browning, if necessary. Cool on a wire rack. Yield: 1 (9-inch) pie.

Mary Lyall

Alaska's Best
Alaska Telephone Pioneers
Anchorage, Alaska

Pear Pie

This fruit pie is exceptionally delicious with shredded sharp Cheddar cheese in the crust and a brown sugar mixture crumbled over fresh Bartlett pears.

1 cup all-purpose flour
¼ teaspoon salt
⅓ cup shortening
½ cup (2 ounces) shredded sharp Cheddar cheese
3 to 4 tablespoons ice water
5½ cups peeled and sliced Bartlett pear (about 3 pounds)
2 teaspoons lemon juice
½ cup sugar
¼ cup all-purpose flour
¼ teaspoon ground cinnamon
¾ cup firmly packed light brown sugar
½ cup all-purpose flour
⅓ cup butter or margarine

Combine 1 cup flour and salt; cut in shortening with pastry blender until mixture is crumbly. Add cheese; sprinkle ice water, 1 tablespoon at a time, evenly over surface; stir with a fork until dry ingredients are moistened. Shape into a ball.

Roll pastry to ⅛-inch thickness on a lightly floured surface. Place in a 10-inch pieplate; trim off excess pastry along edges. Fold edges under, and crimp. Set aside.

Stir together pear and next 4 ingredients in a large bowl. Spoon into pastry shell.

Combine brown sugar and ½ cup flour; cut in butter with pastry blender until mixture is crumbly. Sprinkle topping over pear filling. Bake at 375° for 1 hour or until golden. Cool completely on a wire rack. Yield: 1 (10-inch) pie.

Sounds Delicious: The Flavor of Atlanta in Food & Music
Atlanta Symphony Orchestra
Atlanta, Georgia

Orange-Pecan Pie

3 large eggs, lightly beaten
¾ cup sugar
1 cup light corn syrup
2 tablespoons grated orange rind
¼ cup fresh orange juice
2 tablespoons butter or margarine, melted
1 cup coarsely chopped pecans
1 unbaked 9-inch pastry shell
Whipped cream

Stir together first 6 ingredients in a large bowl. Arrange pecans in pastry shell; pour filling over pecans. Bake at 325° for 50 minutes or until set. Cool on a wire rack. Serve with whipped cream. Yield: 1 (9-inch) pie.

Barbara Anderson

The Monarch's Feast
Mary Munford PTA
Richmond, Virginia

Triple Crown Pie

¾ cup sugar
6 tablespoons butter or margarine, melted
¾ cup light corn syrup
3 large eggs
1 teaspoon vanilla extract
1 cup coarsely chopped pecans
½ cup semisweet chocolate mini-morsels
1 unbaked 9-inch pastry shell

Whisk together sugar and butter in a large bowl. Add corn syrup, eggs, and vanilla. Stir in pecans and chocolate mini-morsels; pour into pastry shell.

Bake at 350° for 45 to 50 minutes or until set and lightly browned. Shield edges of pastry with aluminum foil during the last 10 minutes of baking to prevent excessive browning, if necessary. Cool on a wire rack. Yield: 1 (9-inch) pie.

Linda Bonacorso

Fruits of Our Labor
St. Joseph Parish
Lincoln, Nebraska

Mixed Berry Meringue Pie

2 egg whites
¼ teaspoon cream of tartar
½ cup sugar
1 (8-ounce) container sour cream
¾ cup sifted powdered sugar
½ (8-ounce) package cream cheese, softened
1 teaspoon grated orange rind
1 teaspoon fresh orange juice
2 cups fresh strawberries
1 cup fresh blueberries
¼ cup apple jelly, melted

Grease bottom of a 9-inch pieplate; set aside.

Beat egg whites and cream of tartar at high speed with an electric mixer until foamy. Gradually add ½ cup sugar, 1 tablespoon at a time, beating until stiff peaks form and sugar dissolves (2 to 4 minutes).

Spoon meringue into prepared pieplate. Spread meringue on bottom and up sides of pieplate, using back of a spoon. Bake at 275° for 1 hour. Turn oven off; leave meringue in oven 45 minutes with door closed. Cool completely on a wire rack.

Combine sour cream and next 4 ingredients in a small mixing bowl. Beat at medium speed 2 to 3 minutes until creamy. Spoon filling into meringue shell. Spread on bottom and up sides. Chill at least 2 hours and up to 5 hours. (Chilling longer may soften crust.)

Place strawberries, stem side down, over filling. Sprinkle blueberries over strawberries. Brush or drizzle apple jelly over berries. Yield: 1 (9-inch) pie.

Sarah Shockley

Designer's Recipes for Living
East Tennessee Interior Design Society
Knoxville, Tennessee

Authentic Bahamian Coconut Cream Pie

Relax and experience the tropical splendor of this coconut milk custard pie. It's enveloped by puffy clouds of sweetened whipped cream.

1 (14-ounce) can coconut milk, divided
3 egg yolks
½ cup sugar
3 tablespoons all-purpose flour
½ teaspoon salt
1 large egg, lightly beaten
3 tablespoons cornstarch
½ cup frozen coconut, thawed
½ teaspoon vanilla extract
1 baked 9-inch pastry shell
1 cup heavy whipping cream
1 tablespoon sugar
¼ cup frozen coconut, thawed and toasted

Pour 1 cup coconut milk into a heavy saucepan, and place over medium heat until hot; set aside.

Meanwhile, beat egg yolks until thick and pale. Add ½ cup sugar and next 3 ingredients; beat well.

Whisk together ¼ cup coconut milk and cornstarch until smooth. Stir in remaining coconut milk. Stir coconut milk mixture into egg yolk mixture.

Gradually stir about one-fourth of reserved hot coconut milk into egg mixture; add to remaining hot coconut milk, stirring constantly. Cook over medium heat, stirring constantly with a wire whisk, until mixture thickens and comes to a boil (mixture will appear curdled; keep whisking until thickened and smooth). Remove from heat; stir in ½ cup coconut and vanilla. Cover with plastic wrap, gently pressing directly onto the custard; chill 2 hours. Spoon chilled coconut mixture into pastry shell; cover and chill 3 hours.

Beat whipping cream until foamy; gradually add 1 tablespoon sugar, beating until soft peaks form. Top pie with whipped cream, and sprinkle with toasted coconut. Yield: 1 (9-inch) pie. Luann Stratton

Chautauqua Porches–A Centennial Cookbook
Colorado Chautauqua Cottagers, Inc.
Boulder, Colorado

Peanut Butter Pie

Who doesn't love the delicious duo of peanut butter and chocolate? It's a winning combination to peanut butter lovers of all ages.

1¼ cups chocolate wafer cookie crumbs (22 cookies)
¼ cup sugar
¼ cup butter or margarine, melted
1 (8-ounce) package cream cheese, softened
1 cup sugar
1 cup creamy peanut butter
1 tablespoon butter or margarine, softened
1 teaspoon vanilla extract
1 cup heavy whipping cream, whipped
Garnish: grated dark chocolate

Stir together first 3 ingredients; reserve ¼ cup crumb mixture. Press remaining crumb mixture in bottom and up sides of a 9-inch pieplate. Bake at 375° for 10 minutes. Cool on a wire rack.

Beat cream cheese and next 4 ingredients at medium speed with an electric mixer until smooth. Gently fold in whipped cream. Gently spoon mixture into prepared crust. Sprinkle with reserved crumb mixture. Cover and chill at least 3 hours. Garnish, if desired. Yield: 1 (9-inch) pie.

Shirley Willenbring

North Country Cooking
51st National Square Dance Convention
St. Paul, Minnesota

Pumpkin Sunday Pie

Homemade butterscotch sauce tops off this frozen delight of ice cream layered with pumpkin.

1¼ cups sugar
1 cup canned mashed pumpkin
1 teaspoon pumpkin pie spice
½ teaspoon salt
1 cup whipping cream, whipped
3 cups vanilla ice cream, softened
1 baked 9-inch pastry shell
Butterscotch Sauce

Stir together first 4 ingredients in a large bowl; fold in whipped cream.

Spoon ice cream into pastry shell, and spread evenly. Spoon pumpkin mixture over ice cream. Cover and freeze at least 3 hours. Serve with warm Butterscotch Sauce. Yield: 1 (9-inch) pie.

Butterscotch Sauce

1 cup firmly packed light brown sugar
½ cup light corn syrup
½ cup water
1 teaspoon vanilla extract

Stir together first 3 ingredients in a medium saucepan; bring to a boil. Cook, uncovered, 5 minutes. Remove from heat; stir in vanilla. Yield: about 1 cup.

Mary Jo Fisk

Our Country Christmas Collection
Skaggs Community Health Center
Branson, Missouri

Espresso Ice Cream Pie with Caramel Sauce and Raspberries

4 cups vanilla ice cream, softened
¼ cup instant espresso granules
1 (6-ounce) chocolate crumb crust
Caramel Sauce
1 cup fresh raspberries

Process ice cream and espresso granules in a food processor until smooth, stopping once to scrape down sides. Spoon mixture into crust; cover and freeze 2 hours.

To serve, spoon about ¼ cup Caramel Sauce onto 6 individual dessert plates; top each with a pie slice. Sprinkle with raspberries. Yield: 1 (9-inch) pie.

Caramel Sauce

1 cup sugar
1 cup water
1 cup whipping cream
⅛ teaspoon salt
1 teaspoon vanilla extract

Stir together sugar and water in a saucepan; place over medium-high heat. Cook, uncovered, 10 to 15 minutes or until mixture turns golden (do not stir). Remove from heat; stir in whipping cream until smooth. (Place over medium-low heat if mixture becomes too firm to blend.) Cool 30 minutes. Stir in salt and vanilla. Cover and chill. Yield: about 1½ cups.

Gracious Gator Cooks
The Junior League of Gainesville, Florida

Apple-Walnut Cobbler

Batter-topped apple slices make this cobbler a memorable one. Serve it warm with scoops of creamy vanilla ice cream for an unbeatable combo.

4 cups peeled, thinly sliced Granny Smith apple (3 to 4 apples)
¾ cup chopped walnuts, divided
½ cup sugar
½ teaspoon ground cinnamon
1 cup all-purpose flour
1 cup sugar
1 teaspoon baking powder
¼ teaspoon salt
1 large egg, lightly beaten
½ cup evaporated milk
⅓ cup butter or margarine, melted

Arrange apple in a greased 10-inch pieplate. Combine ½ cup walnuts, ½ cup sugar, and cinnamon; sprinkle over apple.

Combine flour and next 3 ingredients. Stir together egg, evaporated milk, and butter. Add egg mixture to flour mixture; stirring until blended. Pour batter over apple mixture. Sprinkle with remaining ¼ cup walnuts.

Bake, uncovered, at 325° for 55 minutes. Serve warm with ice cream. Yield: 8 servings.

Roberta Love

Our Heritage Cookbook
First Baptist Church
Billings, Montana

Cherry Cobbler

4 cups pitted fresh sweet cherries (we tested with Bing)
¾ cup sugar
2 tablespoons cornstarch
1½ teaspoons grated lemon rind
1 tablespoon fresh lemon juice
½ teaspoon ground cinnamon
¼ teaspoon ground nutmeg
3 tablespoons butter
½ cup all-purpose flour
¼ cup sugar
1½ teaspoons baking powder
¼ teaspoon salt
2 tablespoons butter
¼ cup whipping cream
1 tablespoon butter, melted
2 tablespoons sugar
Rum Whipped Cream

Stir together first 7 ingredients in a medium bowl. Pour fruit mixture into a greased 8-inch square baking dish. Dot with 3 tablespoons butter; set aside.

Combine flour and next 3 ingredients; cut in 2 tablespoons butter with pastry blender until mixture is crumbly. Sprinkle whipping cream, 1 tablespoon at a time, evenly over surface; stir with a fork until dry ingredients are moistened. Shape into a ball.

Roll pastry into an 8-inch square on a lightly floured surface. Place over cherry mixture. Brush dough with 1 tablespoon melted butter; sprinkle with 2 tablespoons sugar. Bake at 400° for 30 minutes or until golden. Let stand 10 minutes. Serve warm with Rum Whipped Cream. Yield: 4 to 6 servings.

Rum Whipped Cream

1 cup whipping cream
½ cup sour cream
¼ cup firmly packed light brown sugar
2 tablespoons dark rum

Beat all ingredients at high speed with an electric mixer until soft peaks form. Yield: 2½ cups.

Always in Season
The Junior League of Salt Lake City, Utah

Pumpkin Cobbler

2 large eggs, beaten
1 cup evaporated milk
1 (29-ounce) can pumpkin
1 cup sugar
½ cup firmly packed dark brown sugar
1 tablespoon all-purpose flour
1 teaspoon ground cinnamon
½ teaspoon salt
¼ teaspoon ground ginger
¼ teaspoon ground cloves
¼ teaspoon ground nutmeg
½ cup butter or margarine, melted
1 cup all-purpose flour
1 cup sugar
4 teaspoons baking powder
½ teaspoon salt
1 cup milk
1 teaspoon vanilla extract
1 tablespoon butter or margarine
2 tablespoons sugar

Stir together first 3 ingredients in a large bowl. Add 1 cup sugar and next 7 ingredients; stir well, and set pumpkin mixture aside.

Pour melted butter into a 13- x 9-inch baking dish. Stir together 1 cup flour and next 5 ingredients. Pour batter over melted butter in baking dish. Spoon pumpkin mixture over batter (do not stir).

Dot with 1 tablespoon butter, and sprinkle with 2 tablespoons sugar. Bake, uncovered, at 350° for 1 hour. Let stand 20 minutes. Serve warm. Yield: 10 to 12 servings.

A Century of Serving
The Junior Board of Christiana Care, Inc.
Wilmington, Delaware

Taffy Apple Pizza

Treat your family to pizza for dessert! They'll love the sugar cookie crust that's layered with cream cheese and apples. And don't forget to top it off with your favorite caramel sauce.

½ cup water
1 tablespoon lemon juice
5 medium Braeburn or Fuji apples, peeled and thinly sliced
1 (20-ounce) package refrigerated sugar cookie dough
2 (8-ounce) packages cream cheese, softened
1 cup firmly packed brown sugar
1 teaspoon vanilla extract
¼ cup caramel topping

Combine water and lemon juice in a medium bowl; add apple slices.

Press cookie dough evenly onto an ungreased 12-inch pizza pan. Bake at 350° for 15 minutes or until golden. Cool crust in pan on a wire rack.

Beat cream cheese, brown sugar, and vanilla at medium speed with an electric mixer until smooth. Spread over cookie crust.

Drain apple slices; arrange over cream cheese layer. Drizzle with caramel topping. Yield: 16 servings. Amy M. Rappenecker

Iowa: A Taste of Home
Iowa 4-H Foundation
Ames, Iowa

Lemon Macaroon Tarts

2 cups flaked coconut
½ cup sugar
6 tablespoons all-purpose flour
1 teaspoon vanilla extract
2 egg whites
Lemon Filling
Garnishes: whipped cream, toasted flaked coconut

Stir together first 5 ingredients. Divide mixture evenly among 12 lightly greased muffin cups (about 3 tablespoons coconut mixture in each cup). Press mixture onto bottoms and up sides of cups.

Bake at 400° for 10 to 13 minutes or until golden. Cool in pan on a wire rack 2 minutes. Remove from pan; cool completely on wire rack. Fill with Lemon Filling. Garnish, if desired. Yield: 12 tarts.

Lemon Filling

¾ cup sugar
5 teaspoons cornstarch
⅓ cup water
1 tablespoon grated lemon rind
⅓ cup fresh lemon juice
1 large egg, lightly beaten
2 drops of yellow food coloring (optional)

Combine sugar and cornstarch in a small heavy saucepan. Gradually whisk in water, lemon rind, and lemon juice.

Bring to a boil over medium-high heat; cook 1 minute, stirring constantly. Reduce heat to low. Gradually stir about 2 tablespoons hot mixture into beaten egg; add to remaining hot mixture, stirring constantly. Cook, stirring constantly, 3 minutes or until thickened. Transfer to a bowl; stir in food coloring, if desired. Cover with plastic wrap, gently pressing directly onto the filling, and chill. Yield: about 1 cup.

Chautauqua Celebrations
Wythe Arts Council, Ltd.
Wytheville, Virginia

Pear Tart

Make this tart year-round by using Bartlett pears in the summer and Bosc pears in the winter. Both varieties of pears hold their shape well when cooked.

½ (15-ounce) package refrigerated piecrusts
2 tablespoons blackberry jelly
⅓ cup sliced natural almonds, coarsely chopped
4 ripe pears, peeled and cut into ½-inch slices
¼ cup lemon juice
3 tablespoons sugar
1 tablespoon hazelnut liqueur
2 tablespoons butter or margarine
2 tablespoons sliced natural almonds
¼ cup whipping cream, whipped

Fit pastry into a 9-inch tart pan; trim off excess pastry along edges. Prick pastry with a fork. Bake at 375° for 10 to 12 minutes or until golden. Cool completely in pan on a wire rack.

Spread jelly in bottom of tart shell; sprinkle with chopped almonds. Toss pear slices in lemon juice; drain.

Arrange pear slices over chopped almonds in a spoke pattern. Sprinkle with sugar and liqueur; dot with butter. Sprinkle with sliced almonds. Bake at 375° for 35 minutes. Serve warm with whipped cream. Yield: 1 (9-inch) tart.

Joy Ward

We Cook Too
Women's Committee, Wadsworth Atheneum
West Hartford, Connecticut

Apple Strudel with Phyllo

A dollop of custard sauce, ice cream, or whipped cream caps this flaky pastry nicely. Use Golden Delicious or Granny Smith apples for this easy strudel.

⅓ cup sugar
1 teaspoon ground cinnamon
1½ pounds cooking apples, peeled and thinly sliced (about 3 apples)
5 sheets phyllo dough
½ cup butter or margarine, melted

Combine sugar and cinnamon. Stir together one-third of sugar mixture and apple slices.

Place 1 sheet of phyllo dough on a clean towel. Brush with melted butter. Top with another sheet of phyllo, and repeat procedure until all sheets of dough have been brushed with butter.

Arrange apple mixture lengthwise over top one-third of dough. Sprinkle with another one-third of sugar mixture. Starting at long sides, use towel to lift and roll dough over apple, jellyroll fashion. Fold and tuck ends under. Place dough, seam side down, on a lightly greased baking sheet. Brush with remaining melted butter. Sprinkle remaining one-third of sugar mixture over dough.

Bake at 400° for 30 minutes or until golden. Serve warm. Yield: 8 to 10 servings.

Monica Indihar

Recipes & Remembrances
Frank P. Tillman Elementary PTO
Kirkwood, Missouri

Banana Split Cream Puffs

1 cup water
½ cup butter or margarine
1 cup all-purpose flour
¼ teaspoon salt
4 large eggs
1 cup sliced fresh strawberries
1 large banana, peeled and thinly sliced
1 (8-ounce) can pineapple tidbits in juice, drained
½ cup fudge sauce
3 cups vanilla ice cream

Combine water and butter in a medium saucepan; bring to a boil. Add flour and salt, stirring vigorously over medium-high heat until mixture leaves sides of pan and forms a smooth ball. Remove from heat, and cool 4 to 5 minutes.

Add eggs, 1 at a time, beating thoroughly with a wooden spoon until smooth after each addition.

Drop cream puff paste into 12 equal mounds 3 inches apart on an ungreased baking sheet. Bake at 400° for 30 minutes or until golden and puffed. Transfer to a wire rack; cool away from drafts. Cut top off each cream puff; pull out and discard soft dough inside.

Combine fruit; gently toss. Heat fudge sauce according to directions on jar.

Fill each cream puff with ¼ cup ice cream. Spoon fruit over ice cream. Replace tops; drizzle with hot fudge sauce. Serve immediately. Yield: 12 servings.

Note: Cream puffs may be made ahead. A ¼-cup ice cream scoop may be used to make ice cream portions; freeze scoops of ice cream on a baking sheet until needed.

Hearthside: A Country Community Cookbook
Christ Community Church
Weare, New Hampshire

Poultry

Baked Stuffed Chicken with Sweet Pepper Sauce, page 253

Capital City Chicken

Create a sweet and savory meal by marinating chicken quarters in a garlicky blend punctuated with prunes, olives, and capers. If you'd like to make fewer servings, just cut the ingredient amounts in half.

1 garlic bulb
1 cup pitted prunes
¾ cup salad olives
½ cup red wine vinegar
½ cup olive oil
¼ cup dried oregano
¼ cup capers, slightly drained
6 bay leaves
1½ teaspoons coarse-grain sea salt
1½ teaspoons freshly ground pepper
4 (2½-pound) whole chickens, quartered
1 cup firmly packed light brown sugar
1 cup dry white wine
¼ cup minced fresh parsley

Separate and peel garlic cloves; process in a small food processor until pureed, stopping to scrape down sides. Stir together garlic, prunes, and next 8 ingredients in a large bowl; add chicken quarters, turning to coat. Cover and chill 8 hours.

Remove chicken from marinade, reserving marinade.

Arrange chicken in 2 (13- x 9-inch) pans; pour marinade over chicken. Sprinkle with brown sugar; drizzle with wine.

Bake, uncovered, at 350° for 1 hour or until done, basting often with marinade. Discard bay leaves. Sprinkle chicken with parsley. Serve with a slotted spoon. Yield: 12 servings.

Back to the Table
Episcopal Church Women–Christ Church
Raleigh, North Carolina

Chicken in Orange Sauce

1 (2½- to 3-pound) whole chicken, cut up
½ cup butter or margarine, melted
¼ cup all-purpose flour
2 tablespoons light brown sugar
1 teaspoon salt
½ teaspoon ground ginger
⅛ teaspoon pepper
1½ cups orange juice
½ cup water
Hot cooked rice

Cook chicken in melted butter in a large skillet over medium-high heat until browned; remove from pan, and set aside.

Reduce heat to medium-low. Add flour and next 4 ingredients to skillet; cook, stirring constantly with a wire whisk, until thick and bubbly. Gradually stir in orange juice and water; bring to a boil over medium heat. Cook 1 minute.

Return chicken to skillet, and bring sauce to a boil. Cover, reduce heat, and simmer 25 minutes or until chicken is done. Transfer chicken to a serving platter; cook sauce, uncovered, 5 minutes or until slightly thickened. Serve chicken and sauce over rice. Yield: 4 servings.

Ami McMahan

Diamond Delights
Diamond Hill Elementary School
Abbeville, South Carolina

Chicken with Porcini Mushrooms

Browned chicken pieces enjoy the company of a generous amount of crushed tomato, porcini mushrooms, and wine sauce. Serve this rich chicken dish with bread, rice, or egg noodles to soak up the scrumptious sauce.

1 cup dried porcini mushrooms, chopped
2 cups warm water
2 cups all-purpose flour
2¼ teaspoons salt, divided
1¼ teaspoons pepper, divided
2 (2½- to 3-pound) whole chickens, cut up and skinned
⅓ cup olive oil
1½ cups chopped onion
3 garlic cloves, minced
1 (28-ounce) can crushed tomatoes, undrained
½ cup dry white wine
1 bay leaf

Stir together mushrooms and warm water; let stand 20 minutes. Pour mixture through a wire-mesh strainer lined with paper towels into a bowl; reserve mushrooms and 1 cup liquid.

Place flour, 2 teaspoons salt, and 1 teaspoon pepper in a large heavy-duty, zip-top plastic bag. Place chicken pieces in bag, a few at a time; seal bag securely, and shake to coat chicken completely. Remove chicken, and cook, in batches, in hot oil in a large Dutch oven over medium-high heat until browned. Remove chicken from pan, reserving drippings in pan; set chicken aside.

Add onion and garlic to drippings in pan, and cook, stirring constantly, until tender. Return chicken to pan. Add reserved mushrooms, reserved 1 cup liquid, tomatoes, wine, and bay leaf; bring to a boil. Cover, reduce heat, and simmer 1 hour. Discard bay leaf. Stir in remaining ¼ teaspoon salt and remaining ¼ teaspoon pepper. Yield: 6 servings.

International Home Cooking
The United Nations International School Parents' Association
New York, New York

Mexican Chicken Mole

Unsweetened chocolate adds subtle richness to this spicy Mexican specialty. The concoction partners well with jalapeño-flecked rice, warm cornbread, and a crisp green salad.

1 (2½- to 3-pound) whole chicken, cut up, or 2½ pounds chicken pieces
¼ cup olive oil
½ medium onion, minced (about ½ cup)
4 garlic cloves, minced
2 (8-ounce) cans tomato sauce
1 (1-ounce) unsweetened chocolate square
1½ tablespoons creamy peanut butter
1½ teaspoons chili powder
1 teaspoon salt
½ teaspoon pepper
¼ teaspoon ground cinnamon
⅛ teaspoon ground cloves
3 tablespoons sliced natural almonds (optional)
2 tablespoons sesame seeds (optional)

Cook chicken in hot oil in a Dutch oven over medium-high heat until chicken is browned, turning once. Remove chicken, reserving drippings in pan.

Sauté onion in drippings 3 minutes or until tender. Add garlic, and cook 1 minute. Stir in tomato sauce and next 7 ingredients. If desired, stir in almonds and sesame seeds. Add chicken; cover, reduce heat, and simmer 1 hour. Yield: 4 servings.

Black Tie & Boots Optional
Colleyville Woman's Club
Colleyville, Texas

Chutney Chicken

4 pounds chicken thighs
1 teaspoon salt
½ teaspoon pepper
3 tablespoons vegetable oil
1 medium onion, chopped (about 1¼ cups)
1 Granny Smith apple, cut into ½-inch pieces (about 1½ cups)
2 celery ribs, chopped (about ½ cup)
1 large carrot, chopped (about ½ cup)
1 tablespoon all-purpose flour
2 teaspoons curry powder
¾ cup chicken broth
2 tablespoons grated orange rind
½ cup orange juice
⅓ cup mango chutney
1 bay leaf
Hot cooked rice
Chopped peanuts (optional)

Sprinkle chicken with salt and pepper. Brown chicken on both sides in hot oil in a large skillet 8 to 10 minutes. Remove chicken, reserving 1 tablespoon drippings in skillet.

Sauté onion and next 3 ingredients in drippings in skillet over medium-high heat 7 minutes or until tender. Stir in flour and curry powder. Cook, stirring constantly, 1 minute. Gradually add chicken broth and next 4 ingredients. Return chicken to skillet. Bring to a boil; cover, reduce heat, and simmer 30 minutes or until chicken is tender. Discard bay leaf. Serve chicken over rice; sprinkle with peanuts, if desired. Yield: 6 servings. Beverly Roberts Collins

Our Heritage Cookbook
First Baptist Church
Billings, Montana

Aunt Nancy's Chicken "Spareribs"

2 pounds skinned chicken thighs
1 tablespoon vegetable oil
½ cup water
⅓ cup firmly packed brown sugar
⅓ cup soy sauce
¼ cup apple juice
2 tablespoons ketchup
1 tablespoon white vinegar
1 garlic clove, minced
½ teaspoon dried crushed red pepper
¼ teaspoon ground ginger
1 tablespoon cornstarch
1 tablespoon water
Hot cooked rice

Cook chicken in hot oil in a large skillet over medium-high heat 7 minutes or until browned, turning often.

Stir together ½ cup water and next 8 ingredients in a medium bowl; add to chicken in skillet. Bring to a boil; cover, reduce heat, and simmer 20 minutes or until chicken is done.

Combine cornstarch and 1 tablespoon water, stirring until mixture is smooth. Add cornstarch mixture to chicken mixture. Cook, stirring constantly, until mixture is thickened. Serve over rice. Yield: 4 servings. Missy and Carl Benson

The Monarch's Feast
Mary Munford PTA
Richmond, Virginia

Oven-Fried Ranch Drumsticks

Biscuit mix flavored with Ranch-style dressing mix makes this casual family fare easy to prepare.

1 cup biscuit mix
1 (1-ounce) envelope Ranch-style dressing mix
1 teaspoon paprika
1 large egg, lightly beaten
1 tablespoon water
2½ to 3 pounds chicken legs
1 cup Ranch-style dressing

Line a 15- x 10-inch jellyroll pan with heavy-duty aluminum foil; lightly grease foil.

Stir together first 3 ingredients. Whisk together egg and water. Dip chicken into egg mixture; dredge in biscuit mixture. Place chicken in prepared pan.

Bake, uncovered, at 425° for 45 to 50 minutes or until done. Serve with salad dressing. Yield: 6 servings. Kim Hart

Sharing Recipes from Green Road Baptist Church
Green Road Baptist Church
Green Road, Kentucky

Grilled Citrus-Ginger Chicken

¼ cup low-sugar orange marmalade
1 tablespoon prepared mustard
¾ teaspoon ground ginger
⅛ teaspoon ground red pepper
4 bone-in skinned chicken breast halves
3 tablespoons butter or margarine, softened
½ teaspoon grated orange rind
¼ teaspoon ground ginger

Whisk together first 4 ingredients in a small bowl.

Lightly grease food rack; place on grill over medium-high heat (350° to 400°). Brush half of marmalade mixture over chicken. Grill chicken, covered with grill lid, 30 minutes or until done, basting twice with remaining marmalade mixture.

Stir together butter, orange rind, and ginger. Spoon about 1 tablespoon butter mixture on top of each chicken breast. Yield: 4 servings.

Faye Washington

The Club's Choice . . . A Second Helping
Fuquay-Varina Woman's Club
Fuquay-Varina, North Carolina

Chicken in Tomato and Basil Cream

This recipe is a must-try for fresh basil lovers. We suggest an accompaniment of buttered penne pasta and hot garlic bread to top off this quick and easy dish.

½ cup finely chopped onion
1 tablespoon butter or margarine, melted
1 (16-ounce) can whole tomatoes, coarsely chopped
½ cup heavy whipping cream
½ cup shredded fresh basil
1 teaspoon salt
½ teaspoon freshly ground pepper
6 skinned and boned chicken breast halves

Cook chopped onion in melted butter over medium heat 5 minutes or until onion is tender. Increase heat to high, and add chopped tomatoes; cook until liquid is almost absorbed. Add whipping cream, and cook until slightly thickened. Remove sauce from heat; add basil, salt, and pepper.

Place chicken in an 11- x 7-inch baking dish; pour sauce over chicken. Bake, uncovered, at 450° for 16 to 20 minutes or until done. Yield: 6 servings.

Linen Napkins to Paper Plates
The Junior Auxiliary of Clarksville, Tennessee

Greek-Style Baked Chicken

This Greek-inspired dish cooks up in only 25 minutes and is topped with Mediterranean staples such as feta cheese, tomato, mint, and, of course, olive oil.

4 skinned and boned chicken breast halves
¼ cup crumbled feta cheese
1 plum tomato, diced
2 tablespoons chopped fresh parsley
2 tablespoons diced yellow or red bell pepper
1½ teaspoons chopped fresh mint or ½ teaspoon dried mint
¾ teaspoon chopped fresh oregano or ¼ teaspoon dried oregano
¼ teaspoon pepper
1 teaspoon extra-virgin olive oil

Arrange chicken in a lightly greased 11- x 7- inch baking dish.

Combine cheese and next 6 ingredients; stir well. Spoon tomato mixture over chicken; drizzle with oil. Bake, uncovered, at 375° for 25 to 30 minutes or until done. Yield: 4 servings. Toni Smith

Angels in the Kitchen
Grace Episcopal Church
Anderson, South Carolina

Mexican Chicken Rolls

Green chiles and Monterey Jack cheese are rolled up in chicken breasts and sautéed until golden. Crushed tortilla chips make up the breading and carry out the Mexican theme.

4 skinned and boned chicken breast halves
1 (1.62-ounce) envelope enchilada sauce mix
½ cup water
1 (16-ounce) can Mexican stewed tomatoes, undrained
1 (4.5-ounce) can chopped green chiles, drained
¼ cup sliced ripe olives
½ cup (2 ounces) shredded Monterey Jack cheese
1 large egg, lightly beaten
1 cup finely crushed tortilla chips
¼ cup vegetable oil
½ cup (2 ounces) shredded Cheddar cheese

Place chicken between 2 sheets of heavy-duty plastic wrap; flatten to ¼-inch thickness, using a meat mallet or rolling pin.

Stir together enchilada sauce mix, water, and stewed tomatoes in a small bowl; set aside.

Stir together green chiles, olives, and Monterey Jack cheese in a small bowl; toss gently. Spoon mixture evenly onto each breast. Roll up, jellyroll fashion, starting at short side; secure with wooden picks. Dip rolls in egg, and roll in crushed tortilla chips to cover.

Sauté chicken rolls in hot oil in a medium skillet over medium-high heat until lightly browned. Place in an ungreased 8-inch square baking dish. Pour sauce over rolls. Bake, covered, at 350° for 35 to 40 minutes. Uncover and sprinkle with Cheddar cheese; bake 10 more minutes or until cheese melts. Yield: 4 servings. Grace Bermudas

United Church of Tekoa Cookbook
United Church of Tekoa
Tekoa, Washington

Baked Stuffed Chicken with Sweet Pepper Sauce

Stuffed with slices of Monterey Jack cheese and Canadian bacon, these chicken breasts stand out as a striking entrée when sliced and topped with a creamy bell pepper sauce. See for yourself on page 243.

4 skinned and boned chicken breast halves
¼ teaspoon salt
¼ teaspoon pepper
4 (¾-ounce) slices Monterey Jack cheese
4 slices Canadian bacon
1 large egg, lightly beaten
½ cup Italian-seasoned breadcrumbs
2 tablespoons olive oil
Sweet Pepper Sauce

Sprinkle chicken with salt and pepper. Place chicken between 2 sheets of heavy-duty plastic wrap; flatten to ¼-inch thickness, using a meat mallet or rolling pin. Place 1 slice each of cheese and Canadian bacon in center of each chicken breast half; fold ends over, and secure with wooden picks.

Dip each chicken roll in egg, and dredge in breadcrumbs. Place in a greased 11- x 7-inch baking dish; drizzle with olive oil. Bake, uncovered, at 350° for 30 minutes or until done. Slice chicken, if desired, and serve with Sweet Pepper Sauce. Yield: 4 servings.

Sweet Pepper Sauce

¼ cup diced onion
1 garlic clove, minced
1 tablespoon olive oil
¼ cup diced red bell pepper
¼ cup diced green bell pepper
1 cup heavy whipping cream
1 teaspoon dried basil
¼ teaspoon salt
¼ teaspoon freshly ground pepper

Sauté onion and garlic in hot oil in a small saucepan over medium-high heat 1 minute; add bell peppers, and sauté 5 minutes. Add whipping cream and remaining 3 ingredients to pan; bring to a boil. Reduce heat, and simmer, uncovered, 3 minutes, stirring occasionally. Yield: 1½ cups.

Mary Lyall

Alaska's Best
Alaska Telephone Pioneers
Anchorage, Alaska

Santa Fe Chicken Pizza

This southwestern-style pizza gets its sunny personality from fresh cilantro, lime juice, and chunks of spicy grilled chicken.

3 tablespoons chopped fresh cilantro, divided
2 tablespoons olive oil
1 tablespoon fresh lime juice
1½ teaspoons soy sauce
½ teaspoon Worcestershire sauce
½ teaspoon honey
¼ teaspoon ground cumin
¼ teaspoon dried crushed red pepper
2 skinned and boned chicken breast halves
1½ tablespoons butter
1 large onion, cut into ⅛-inch-thick slices and separated into rings
¼ teaspoon red wine vinegar
1 teaspoon soy sauce
1 (10-ounce) Italian bread shell (we tested with Boboli)
2 cups (8 ounces) shredded mozzarella cheese

Stir together 1 tablespoon cilantro, oil, and next 6 ingredients in a bowl. Add chicken; cover and chill 15 minutes. Drain chicken, discarding marinade. Lightly grease food rack; place on grill over medium-high heat (350° to 400°). Grill chicken, without grill lid, 6 minutes on each side or until done. Cut chicken into ½-inch pieces; cover and chill.

Melt butter in a large skillet over medium-high heat. Add onion; cook 3 minutes or until onion begins to brown. Add vinegar; reduce heat to medium-low, and cook 10 minutes, stirring constantly. Add 1 teaspoon soy sauce, and cook 5 to 10 more minutes, stirring constantly.

Spread onion mixture over bread shell. Sprinkle with ¾ cup cheese; add chicken. Sprinkle with remaining 1¼ cups cheese. Bake, uncovered, at 475° for 8 to 10 minutes or until cheese is bubbly. Sprinkle with remaining 2 tablespoons cilantro. Yield: 2 servings.

Sounds Delicious: The Flavor of Atlanta in Food & Music
Atlanta Symphony Orchestra
Atlanta, Georgia

Chicken Basque

Chock-full of zucchini, roasted red peppers, Italian sausage, and chicken, this Mediterranean-inspired dish is easily served as a one-dish meal.

2 pounds zucchini, cut into ¾-inch-thick slices
2 tablespoons olive oil
1½ teaspoons salt
1 teaspoon pepper
¾ pound mild or hot Italian link sausage
1 tablespoon butter or margarine, melted
1 medium onion, chopped
8 ounces small fresh mushrooms
1 garlic clove, minced
¼ cup olive oil
1½ pounds skinned and boned chicken breast halves, cut into 1-inch pieces
1 cup all-purpose flour
1 cup dry vermouth
1 (15-ounce) jar roasted red peppers, chopped
1 tablespoon chopped fresh parsley
1 bay leaf
½ teaspoon dried basil
½ teaspoon dried thyme

Sauté zucchini in 2 tablespoons hot olive oil in a large skillet over high heat 3 minutes or until browned. Sprinkle with salt and pepper; stir well. Remove from skillet with a slotted spoon; set aside.

Reduce heat to medium-high. Add sausage to skillet; cook 8 minutes or until browned. Drain, reserving 1 tablespoon drippings in skillet. Cut sausage into ½-inch-thick slices; set aside.

Add butter and next 3 ingredients to skillet; cook, stirring often, until onion is tender and mushroom liquid evaporates. Remove vegetables from skillet, using a slotted spoon.

Heat ¼ cup olive oil in same skillet over medium-high heat. Dredge chicken in flour; cook chicken in hot oil 8 minutes or until done, turning once. Stir in vermouth, roasted red pepper, reserved sliced sausage, reserved vegetables, parsley, bay leaf, basil, and thyme; bring to a boil. Reduce heat, and simmer, uncovered, 5 minutes; discard bay leaf. Yield: 10 cups.

Gracious Gator Cooks
The Junior League of Gainesville, Florida

Quick Mexican Chicken Fajitas

1 large onion, sliced
1 red or yellow bell pepper, thinly sliced
3 tablespoons vegetable oil
¼ teaspoon garlic powder
¼ teaspoon ground cumin
¼ teaspoon paprika
¼ teaspoon ground red pepper
¼ teaspoon dried oregano
¼ teaspoon dried thyme
½ cup chicken broth
4 skinned and boned chicken breast halves, cut into strips
4 (8-inch) flour tortillas
1 tomato, chopped
1 ripe avocado, chopped
1 cup salsa

Sauté onion and bell pepper in hot oil in a large skillet over medium-high heat 10 minutes or until very tender. Add garlic powder and next 5 ingredients; cook 1 minute. Add chicken broth, and bring to a boil; add chicken, and cook 7 minutes or until chicken is done.

While chicken cooks, heat tortillas according to package directions; spoon chicken mixture onto warm tortillas. Top with tomato, avocado, and salsa; roll up tortillas. Yield: 4 servings. Terri Smith

The Monarch's Feast
Mary Munford PTA
Richmond, Virginia

Canyonlands Chicken Pot Pie

Green chiles, black beans, and cilantro give this pot pie a southwestern kick.

1 cup chicken broth, divided
4 skinned and boned chicken breast halves, cut into ¾-inch pieces
3 Yukon gold potatoes, chopped (about ½ pound)
3 tablespoons cornstarch
1 (14½-ounce) can stewed tomatoes, undrained and chopped
1 (15-ounce) can black beans, rinsed and drained
1 (8¾-ounce) can whole kernel corn, drained
1 (4.5-ounce) can chopped green chiles
½ cup chopped fresh cilantro
¾ teaspoon salt
½ (15-ounce) package refrigerated piecrusts

Cook ½ cup chicken broth, chicken, and potato in a large skillet over medium-high heat 5 minutes or until chicken is done, stirring often. Combine remaining ½ cup broth and cornstarch; stir cornstarch mixture into chicken mixture. Bring to a boil, stirring constantly; cook 1 minute. Remove from heat, and stir in tomatoes and next 5 ingredients. Pour mixture into a shallow 1½-quart baking dish.

Roll piecrust into a 12-inch circle. Place over chicken mixture; fold edges under, and crimp. Cut slits in crust for steam to escape.

Bake at 350° for 1 hour or until chicken mixture is hot and bubbly and crust is golden. (Cover with strips of aluminum foil during last 10 minutes of baking to prevent excessive browning, if necessary.) Let stand 10 minutes before serving. Yield: 4 servings.

Always in Season
The Junior League of Salt Lake City, Utah

Chicken Tetrazzini

4 ounces uncooked spaghetti
2 cups chopped cooked chicken
1 (4-ounce) can mushroom stems and pieces, drained
2 tablespoons chopped pimiento
3 tablespoons chopped onion
¼ cup butter or margarine, melted
1 (14.25-ounce) can cream of chicken soup, undiluted
1 (5-ounce) can evaporated milk
½ teaspoon celery salt
¼ teaspoon Worcestershire sauce
½ cup (2 ounces) shredded Cheddar cheese
¼ cup grated Parmesan cheese

Cook spaghetti according to package directions; drain. Stir together spaghetti, chicken, mushrooms, and pimiento.

Cook onion in butter in a large skillet over medium heat until tender and lightly browned. Add soup and next 3 ingredients to onion mixture. Stir together onion mixture and spaghetti mixture; place in a greased 11- x 7-inch baking dish. Sprinkle with cheeses. Bake, uncovered, at 350° for 20 to 25 minutes or until thoroughly heated. Yield: 4 to 6 servings. Donna Kraft

Cooking with Class
Timber Lake Booster Club
Timber Lake, South Dakota

Amaretto Turkey

1 (15-pound) turkey
8 garlic cloves, divided
2 bay leaves
1 medium-size orange, quartered
2 teaspoons pepper, divided
1 large onion, chopped
2 cups amaretto
1 cup orange juice

Remove giblets and neck, and rinse turkey with cold water; pat dry. Place 3 garlic cloves, 1 bay leaf, and orange in cavity; sprinkle cavity with ½ teaspoon pepper. Tie ends of legs together with string; lift wingtips up and over back, and tuck under bird.

Rub skin of turkey with 2 garlic cloves; sprinkle with remaining 1½ teaspoons pepper. Place turkey in a roasting pan with remaining 3 garlic cloves, remaining bay leaf, and onion.

Place amaretto in a long-handled saucepan; heat until just warm. Remove pan from heat, and ignite amaretto with a long match; allow flame to burn 2 minutes. Pour amaretto and orange juice over turkey. Bake, covered, at 325° for 3 to 3¾ hours or until a meat thermometer inserted in meaty part of thigh registers 180°, basting often with pan drippings. Uncover turkey during the last half hour of baking. Remove turkey from roasting pan; cover and let stand 15 minutes before carving. Yield: 12 to 15 servings.

Note: For a delicious gravy, strain drippings from roasting pan through a wire-mesh strainer; skim and discard fat. Pour drippings into a medium saucepan; simmer over medium-high heat until reduced by half.

A Taste of Tradition
Temple Emanu-El
Providence, Rhode Island

Grilled Turkey Tenderloins and Veggies

¼ cup soy sauce
2 teaspoons minced garlic, divided
1½ pounds turkey tenderloins
4 to 6 small zucchini, sliced lengthwise
4 to 6 small yellow squash, sliced lengthwise
1 small eggplant, sliced lengthwise
2 teaspoons salt, divided
⅓ cup extra-virgin olive oil
½ teaspoon pepper
2 small onions, halved
4 portobello mushroom caps
⅓ cup balsamic vinegar

Place soy sauce, 1 teaspoon minced garlic, and turkey in a large heavy-duty, zip-top plastic bag; seal securely, and marinate in refrigerator 2 hours, turning bag occasionally.

Place zucchini, yellow squash, and eggplant in a colander. Sprinkle with 1 teaspoon salt. Let stand 2 hours. Rinse and pat dry.

Stir together remaining 1 teaspoon garlic and 1 teaspoon salt, olive oil, and pepper in a small bowl. Place squash, eggplant, onion, and mushrooms in a large bowl. Drizzle oil mixture over vegetables, tossing to coat well. Remove onion from bowl, and wrap in heavy-duty aluminum foil.

Remove turkey from marinade, discarding marinade. Coat food rack with cooking spray; place on grill over medium-high heat (350° to 400°). Place turkey on rack, and grill, covered with grill lid, 8 to 10 minutes on each side or until a thermometer inserted into thickest portion registers 170°. Remove turkey from grill rack, and keep warm.

Place onion (in foil) and vegetables on grill rack, and grill, covered, 10 minutes or to desired degree of doneness, turning and basting (all but onion) often with oil mixture. Remove foil from onion. Return all vegetables to bowl, and drizzle with vinegar; toss gently. Transfer vegetables to a serving platter. Slice turkey, and arrange around vegetables. Yield: 4 to 6 servings.

Down by the Water
The Junior League of Columbia, South Carolina

Cornish Hens with Wild Rice Stuffing

¼ cup finely chopped celery
¼ cup finely chopped onion
2 tablespoons finely chopped green bell pepper
2 tablespoons butter or margarine, melted
1⅓ cups chicken broth
2 tablespoons chopped fresh parsley
1 teaspoon herb seasoning*
⅔ cup uncooked wild rice
2 Cornish hens (about 1 to 1¼ pounds each)
½ teaspoon salt
¼ teaspoon pepper
¼ cup butter or margarine
½ cup red currant jelly
¼ cup brandy

Sauté celery, onion, and green pepper in 2 tablespoons butter in a medium saucepan over medium heat until tender. Stir in chicken broth, parsley, and herb seasoning; bring to a boil. Stir in wild rice; cover, reduce heat to medium-low, and simmer 25 minutes or until tender. Set aside.

Remove giblets from hens, and discard giblets. Rinse hens with cold water, and pat dry. Sprinkle cavity with salt and pepper. Stuff hens lightly with rice mixture, and close cavities. Secure with wooden picks; truss. Place hens, breast side up, in a shallow pan.

Melt ¼ cup butter in a small saucepan. Brush hens lightly with melted butter; reserve remaining butter for sauce. Bake hens at 375° for 30 minutes. Meanwhile, combine jelly and brandy with reserved butter; cook over low heat, stirring until jelly melts. Brush hens with jelly mixture. Bake, covered, 35 to 45 more minutes or until juices run clear, basting every 10 minutes. Yield: 2 servings.

*For herb seasoning, we used dried basil, marjoram, parsley, thyme, celery, tarragon, and oregano.

Note: If you have basting sauce left over, place in a saucepan, and boil 1 minute to reduce slightly; spoon over each hen. Sharon Riley

Carnegie Hall Cookbook
Carnegie Hall, Inc.
Lewisburg, West Virginia

Duck with Blackberry Sauce

The smooth and spirited blackberry sauce that accompanies this rich duck gets a sweet note from pure maple syrup.

2 tablespoons butter or margarine
3 tablespoons sugar
⅓ cup dry white wine
⅓ cup orange juice
2 tablespoons raspberry vinegar
1¼ cups fresh blackberries or 1 (14-ounce) package frozen blackberries, thawed and drained
1 cup beef broth
¾ cup chicken broth
2 tablespoons Cognac
1 tablespoon pure maple syrup
4 boned duck breast halves
½ teaspoon salt
¼ teaspoon pepper
1 tablespoon butter or margarine

Melt 2 tablespoons butter in a nonstick skillet over medium heat; add sugar, and cook, stirring constantly, 5 minutes or until sugar melts and turns a light golden brown. Add wine, orange juice, and vinegar. Bring to a boil, stirring constantly, until caramelized sugar dissolves. Add blackberries and broths. Bring to a boil; reduce heat, and simmer, uncovered, 15 minutes or until reduced to 1 cup. Pour mixture through a wire-mesh strainer into a 3-quart saucepan, discarding seeds. Stir in Cognac and syrup; set aside.

Sprinkle duck breast halves with salt and pepper; cook, skin side down, in a hot ovenproof skillet over high heat 7 to 8 minutes or until lightly browned, turning once. Bake, uncovered, at 400° for 18 to 20 minutes or until a meat thermometer inserted into thickest part of breast registers 180°. Remove duck from skillet, discarding drippings.

Add reserved blackberry mixture to skillet, and cook over high heat 2 minutes, stirring constantly to loosen particles from bottom of skillet. Add 1 tablespoon butter, stirring until butter melts. Slice duck, and serve with sauce. Yield: 4 servings.

Bay Tables
The Junior League of Mobile, Alabama

Smothered Quail

A savory gravy of sherry and chicken broth smothers these quail before baking and makes a delicious sauce to spoon over rice on the side.

8 quail, dressed
½ cup butter or margarine
¼ cup all-purpose flour
2 cups chicken broth
½ cup dry sherry
1 teaspoon salt
¾ teaspoon pepper

Brown quail, in batches, in butter in a large skillet over medium-high heat. Place quail, breast side up, in a lightly greased 9-inch square baking dish.

Add flour to skillet, stirring until smooth. Cook 2 minutes, stirring constantly over medium heat. Gradually stir in broth and sherry; cook over medium heat, stirring constantly, until mixture is thickened and bubbly. Stir in salt and pepper. Pour sauce over quail. Bake, covered, at 350° for 1 hour. Yield: 4 servings. V. V. Thompson

'Pon Top Edisto
Trinity Episcopal Church
Edisto Island, South Carolina

Salads

Pear-Walnut Salad, page 270

Apple-Strawberry Spinach Salad

Crisp bacon crumbles, slices of sweet strawberries, and cubes of tart apple flatter tender spinach leaves dressed in a tangy vinaigrette.

1 pound fresh spinach (12 cups loosely packed torn spinach)
2 Granny Smith apples, cubed
1 cup sliced fresh strawberries (9 large)
½ cup fresh bean sprouts (optional)
6 slices bacon, cooked and crumbled
Tangy Vinaigrette

Remove stems from spinach; wash leaves thoroughly, and pat dry. Layer spinach, apple, strawberries and, if desired, bean sprouts in a large salad bowl. Cover and chill. Top with bacon, and drizzle with Tangy Vinaigrette just before serving. Yield: 12 servings.

Tangy Vinaigrette

¾ cup vegetable oil
½ cup sugar
⅓ cup white vinegar
1 small onion, grated (about ½ cup)
1 teaspoon salt
2 teaspoons Worcestershire sauce

Whisk together all ingredients in a bowl. Cover and chill. Whisk again just before drizzling over salad. Yield: 1¾ cups.

Simply the Best . . . Recipes by Design
Columbus Area Visitors Center
Columbus, Indiana

Apple-Orange-Avocado Salad with Crème Fraîche

Crème fraîche is a thickened cream with a velvety texture and tangy flavor. You can make your own crème fraîche by combining 4 teaspoons sour cream, 4 teaspoons whipping cream, and 1½ teaspoons powdered sugar in a custard cup. Cover and chill it 8 hours to thicken slightly.

8 leaves Romaine lettuce
8 leaves Red Leaf lettuce
8 leaves Green Leaf lettuce
4 medium oranges, sectioned
2 ripe avocados, sliced
2 medium Braeburn apples, sliced
Crème Fraîche Raspberry Vinaigrette

Line individual salad plates with lettuce leaves. Arrange orange sections, avocado slices, and apple slices over lettuce leaves; drizzle with Crème Fraîche Raspberry Vinaigrette. Serve immediately. Yield: 8 servings.

Crème Fraîche Raspberry Vinaigrette

3 tablespoons crème fraîche
3 tablespoons raspberry vinegar
2 teaspoons Dijon mustard
½ teaspoon salt
½ teaspoon freshly ground pepper
½ teaspoon sherry or port
½ cup olive or vegetable oil

Process first 6 ingredients in a blender until smooth, stopping to scrape down sides. Turn blender on high; gradually add oil in a slow, steady stream. Blend until thickened. Cover and chill. Yield: 1 cup.

A Thyme to Remember
Dallas County Medical Society Alliance
Dallas, Texas

Broccoli and Orange Salad

¾ cup mayonnaise
¼ cup sugar
2 tablespoons white vinegar
1 large bunch broccoli, cut into flowerets, or 1 (16-ounce) package broccoli flowerets
½ cup golden raisins
½ small purple onion, thinly sliced and separated into rings
4 slices bacon, cooked and crumbled
1 (11-ounce) can mandarin oranges, drained
⅓ cup sliced almonds, toasted

Stir together mayonnaise, sugar, and vinegar in a large bowl. Add broccoli and raisins; toss well. Cover and chill thoroughly. Top with onion, crumbled bacon, mandarin oranges, and toasted almonds. Yield: 10 servings.

Peggy Boyd

The Monarch's Feast
Mary Munford PTA
Richmond, Virginia

Chopped Cilantro Salad

6 fresh tomatillos, husked
⅔ cup loosely packed fresh cilantro leaves
6 tablespoons fresh lime juice (about 3 limes)
2 garlic cloves, halved
2 teaspoons chopped jalapeño pepper (about 1 small)
¾ cup vegetable oil
1 cup finely chopped green onions
1 teaspoon salt
½ teaspoon pepper
5 cups loosely packed, coarsely chopped Romaine lettuce
4 cups loosely packed, coarsely chopped cabbage
2 medium tomatoes, seeded and chopped (about 1½ cups)
1½ cups chopped, peeled jícama
1½ cups fresh corn kernels (about 3 ears)
½ cup crumbled feta cheese
2 ripe avocados, chopped
Tortilla chips (optional)

Cut tomatillos into quarters. Process tomatillos, cilantro, and next 3 ingredients in a blender 20 seconds or until pureed; pour into a medium bowl. Whisk together cilantro puree and oil; add green onions, salt, and pepper, stirring well.

Stir together Romaine lettuce and next 5 ingredients in a large bowl. Gently toss avocado and lettuce mixture with cilantro mixture. Serve with tortilla chips, if desired. Yield: 8 servings.

Sounds Delicious: The Flavor of Atlanta in Food & Music
Atlanta Symphony Orchestra
Atlanta, Georgia

Fiesta Salad

A colorful trio of orange, avocado, and purple onion slices sparkles on a bed of buttery Boston lettuce leaves.

½ cup dry white wine
½ cup olive or vegetable oil
¼ cup fresh lemon juice
2 teaspoons paprika
¾ teaspoon salt
½ teaspoon ground white pepper
½ teaspoon sugar
½ teaspoon dry mustard
2 small heads Boston lettuce, separated into leaves
2 large oranges, peeled and sliced crosswise
1 large avocado, sliced
1 purple onion, thinly sliced and separated into rings

Combine first 8 ingredients in a jar; cover tightly, and shake vigorously. Chill dressing.

Arrange lettuce leaves evenly on individual salad plates; arrange orange slices, avocado slices, and onion rings over lettuce leaves. Serve with dressing. Yield: 6 servings. Lisa Pelegrin Jefferson

Noel Bluffin' We're Still Cookin'
Noel Area Chamber of Commerce
Noel, Missouri

Fruit Salad with Fresh Mango Sauce

Nine fresh fruits mingle in this colorful salad capped with a mango and orange puree. Leave the skins on the nectarine if you'd like, to distinguish the pretty slices from their identical twin peach slices.

2 ripe nectarines, sliced
2 ripe peaches, peeled and sliced
2 plums, sliced
1 firm ripe mango, peeled and coarsely chopped
1 firm ripe pear, peeled and sliced
½ small honeydew melon, peeled, seeded, and cubed
¼ cup fresh lemon juice
¼ cup fresh blueberries
¼ cup fresh raspberries
Fresh Mango Sauce
Garnish: fresh mint sprigs

Arrange first 6 ingredients on a large platter; drizzle with lemon juice. Cover and chill up to 3 hours before serving.

Divide fruit among individual chilled salad plates. Spoon blueberries and raspberries over fruit. Drizzle ½ cup Fresh Mango Sauce over fruit. Garnish, if desired. Serve with remaining Fresh Mango Sauce. Yield: 6 servings.

Fresh Mango Sauce

1 large mango, peeled and chopped
1 tablespoon grated orange rind
¾ cup fresh orange juice (about 2 oranges)
2 tablespoons sugar

Process all ingredients in a blender until pureed, stopping to scrape down sides. Pour mixture through a wire-mesh strainer into a bowl, discarding solids. Cover and chill. Yield: 2½ cups.

Made in the Shade
The Junior League of Greater Fort Lauderdale, Florida

Mixed Greens with Roquefort and Dried Fruit Terrine

½ pound Roquefort cheese, softened
6 tablespoons butter, softened
1 cup chopped mixed dried fruit
½ cup chopped pecans, toasted
10 cups mixed salad greens
Lemon Dressing

Process cheese and butter in a food processor just until blended. Transfer mixture to a bowl; fold in fruit and pecans. Spoon into a 5- x 3-inch loafpan lined with heavy-duty plastic wrap. Press down tightly to remove air. Cover and chill at least 8 hours.

Invert terrine onto a platter. Slice loaf into ½-inch-thick slices with a warm knife. Cut each slice diagonally into triangles.

Toss salad greens with Lemon Dressing. Divide greens evenly among salad plates; top each serving with terrine slices. Yield: 10 servings.

Lemon Dressing

¼ cup lemon juice
2 tablespoons honey
½ teaspoon pepper
¼ teaspoon salt
¼ teaspoon dried basil
¼ teaspoon dried tarragon
½ cup olive oil

Whisk together first 6 ingredients. Slowly add oil, whisking constantly. Yield: ¾ cup.

Simply Divine
Second-Ponce de Leon Baptist Church
Atlanta, Georgia

Papaya Salad

Coarsely ground papaya seeds add a peppery punch to the dressing for papaya and avocado-topped lettuces.

2 ripe papayas
½ cup sugar
½ cup chopped onion
½ cup white vinegar
½ cup vegetable oil
2 teaspoons salt
½ teaspoon dry mustard
1 head Romaine lettuce, torn
1 head Bibb lettuce, torn
2 large avocados, sliced

Peel papayas, and cut in half lengthwise. Remove 2 tablespoons papaya seeds; discard remaining papaya seeds. Cut papaya into thin slices; set aside.

Process sugar and next 5 ingredients in a blender until smooth, stopping to scrape down sides. Add reserved papaya seeds, and process until seeds are coarsely ground. Remove ½ cup dressing, and set aside.

Toss together Romaine and Bibb lettuces in a salad bowl; drizzle with remaining dressing, and toss to coat.

Divide lettuce mixture among individual salad plates; top with reserved papaya and avocado slices. Drizzle reserved ½ cup dressing over fruit. Yield: 8 servings.

What Can I Bring?
The Junior League of Northern Virginia
McLean, Virginia

Pear-Walnut Salad

Toasted walnuts and crumbled Gorgonzola add texture and tang to this gourmet salad of mixed greens and red pears.

6 cups loosely packed mixed salad greens
6 red Bartlett pears, cut into wedges
½ cup walnut pieces, toasted
4 ounces Gorgonzola cheese, crumbled
½ cup olive oil
2 tablespoons balsamic vinegar
1 tablespoon Dijon mustard
¼ teaspoon salt
¼ teaspoon freshly ground pepper

Divide salad greens among individual salad plates. Arrange pear wedges over salad greens; sprinkle with walnuts and cheese.

Combine olive oil and remaining 4 ingredients in a jar; cover tightly, and shake vigorously. Drizzle dressing over salads. Yield: 6 servings.

Back to the Table
Episcopal Church Women—Christ Church
Raleigh, North Carolina

Fresh Tomato Salad

4 large tomatoes, cut into ¼-inch-thick slices
4 to 5 garlic cloves, minced
½ cup chopped fresh parsley
¼ cup shredded basil leaves
½ cup olive oil
¼ cup water
½ teaspoon salt
¼ teaspoon dried oregano
¼ teaspoon pepper
Crusty Italian bread (optional)

Arrange tomato slices in a 13- x 9-inch dish.

Stir together garlic and next 7 ingredients. Pour parsley mixture over tomato slices. Serve with slices of crusty Italian bread, if desired. Yield: 8 servings. Margaret DelloStritto

The Official Cookbook of Central New York's TomatoFest
TomatoFest of Central New York, Inc.
Auburn, New York

Grilled Vegetable Salad with Goat Cheese Croutons

Croutons topped with warm goat cheese and fresh thyme nestle in a medley of grilled vegetables and gourmet mixed baby salad greens.

3 tablespoons balsamic vinegar
1 tablespoon minced purple onion
1 tablespoon honey
½ teaspoon salt
½ teaspoon freshly ground pepper
½ cup olive oil
4 new potatoes
2 cups fresh broccoli flowerets
1 red bell pepper, quartered
1 yellow bell pepper, quartered
1 zucchini, cut into ¼-inch-thick lengthwise slices
1 yellow squash, cut into ¼-inch-thick lengthwise slices
1 baby eggplant (about 8 ounces), cut lengthwise into ¼-inch-thick slices
¼ cup olive oil
4 cups loosely packed gourmet mixed baby salad greens
Goat Cheese Croutons

Process first 5 ingredients in a blender 20 seconds, stopping to scrape down sides. Turn blender on high; gradually add ½ cup olive oil in a slow, steady stream. Cover dressing; chill at least 1 hour.

Cook potatoes in boiling salted water to cover 15 to 20 minutes or until tender. Drain; cool and cut into ¼-inch-thick slices.

Cook broccoli in boiling water to cover 3 minutes; drain. Plunge into ice water to stop the cooking process; drain.

Brush potato, broccoli, red pepper, and next 4 ingredients with ¼ cup olive oil. Grill vegetables, covered with grill lid, over medium-high heat (350° to 400°) 6 minutes; remove potato and broccoli. Grill remaining vegetables 4 to 6 more minutes or until tender, turning once. Peel skins from peppers, if desired. Toss vegetables with ¼ cup dressing.

Toss salad greens with ¼ cup dressing; divide among individual salad plates. Top with grilled vegetables and Goat Cheese Croutons. Serve with remaining dressing. Yield: 4 servings.

Goat Cheese Croutons

8 (½-inch-thick) slices French baguette
2 tablespoons olive oil
¼ teaspoon salt
½ teaspoon freshly ground pepper, divided
8 (¼-inch-thick) slices goat cheese (about 4 ounces)
1 tablespoon chopped fresh thyme

Place baguette slices on a baking sheet, and brush with oil; sprinkle with salt and ¼ teaspoon pepper. Bake at 350° for 5 minutes or until toasted, turning once. Top with sliced goat cheese; sprinkle with remaining ¼ teaspoon pepper and thyme. Bake 3 to 4 more minutes or until goat cheese is warm. Yield: 8 croutons.

Always in Season
The Junior League of Salt Lake City, Utah

Baked Sweet Potato Salad

This isn't your mother's potato salad! Baked sweet potatoes, mango chutney, and yogurt put a new spin on an old favorite.

3 medium-size sweet potatoes (about 2½ pounds)
2 tablespoons mango chutney
1 tablespoon minced purple onion
1 tablespoon fresh lime juice
1 (8-ounce) container plain nonfat yogurt
1½ teaspoons curry powder
1 teaspoon salt
½ teaspoon pepper
1 red bell pepper, chopped
2 celery ribs, chopped
½ cup thinly sliced purple onion

Prick sweet potatoes several times with a fork. Bake at 400° for 1 hour. Let stand 15 minutes. Peel and chop sweet potatoes.

Combine mango chutney and next 6 ingredients in a large bowl; mix well. Stir in chopped sweet potato, bell pepper, celery, and sliced purple onion. Serve warm or chilled. Yield: 4 to 6 servings.

Sounds Delicious: The Flavor of Atlanta in Food & Music
Atlanta Symphony Orchestra
Atlanta, Georgia

Conspiracy Two-Tone Slaw

A green cabbage slaw with red bell pepper and a red cabbage slaw with green bell pepper charm you into sampling both versions.

⅔ cup buttermilk
⅔ cup light mayonnaise
1 teaspoon grated lemon rind
1½ tablespoons fresh lemon juice
1 bunch green onions, diagonally sliced and divided
¼ cup chopped fresh dill
½ green cabbage, shredded (about 4½ cups)
½ red bell pepper, cut into thin strips
1 cup shredded carrot
½ teaspoon salt
½ teaspoon pepper
½ red cabbage, shredded (about 4½ cups)
½ green bell pepper, cut into thin strips
Green Leaf lettuce leaves
Chopped fresh parsley

Whisk together first 4 ingredients. Stir in about 1¼ cups green onions and dill. Cover and chill dressing.

Toss together green cabbage, red bell pepper, and half each of carrot, salt, and pepper. Add half of dressing; toss gently. Cover and chill. Repeat procedure with red cabbage, green pepper, and remaining carrot, salt, and pepper. Add remaining half of dressing; toss gently. Cover and chill.

Serve slaws side by side on lettuce leaves; top with remaining green onions and chopped parsley. Yield: 8 to 10 servings.

Savoring the Southwest Again
Roswell Symphony Guild
Roswell, New Mexico

Marinated Rotini Salad

2 (12-ounce) packages rotini (corkscrew pasta)
1 tablespoon olive oil
8 ounces Genoa salami, sliced
1 (5-ounce) package sliced pepperoni
4 ounces mozzarella cheese, cubed
4 ounces Cheddar cheese, cubed
1 medium-size purple onion, sliced
½ cup sliced ripe olives
½ cup sliced pimiento-stuffed olives
¼ cup freshly grated Parmesan cheese
½ cup olive oil
¼ cup dry white wine
1 teaspoon red wine vinegar
½ teaspoon sugar
½ teaspoon chopped fresh dill
¼ teaspoon pepper

Cook rotini according to package directions; drain. Rinse rotini with cold water, and drain. Combine rotini, 1 tablespoon oil, and next 8 ingredients; toss gently.

Combine ½ cup olive oil and remaining 5 ingredients. Pour over rotini mixture; toss gently. Cover and chill at least 2 hours. Toss gently before serving. Yield: 16 servings. Corrie Scranton

Cook Bookery
The University of Illinois College of Medicine at Peoria
Peoria, Illinois

Bev's Tortellini Salad

¾ cup olive oil
¼ cup red wine vinegar
1 tablespoon dried basil
1 tablespoon Dijon mustard
¼ teaspoon salt
¼ teaspoon pepper
1 garlic clove
2 (9-ounce) packages refrigerated cheese tortellini
1 (6-ounce) jar marinated artichoke hearts, drained and chopped
1 (2¼-ounce) can sliced ripe olives, drained
½ cup dried tomato halves in oil, drained and cut into strips
¼ cup chopped fresh parsley
¼ cup freshly grated Parmesan cheese
1 green bell pepper, coarsely chopped

Process first 7 ingredients in a blender until smooth, stopping to scrape down sides.

Cook tortellini according to package directions; rinse with cold water, and drain. Add artichoke hearts and remaining 5 ingredients; pour dressing over salad, and toss gently. Cover and chill at least 2 hours. Yield: 8 servings. L. Kay Schultheis

Olivet Heritage Cookbook
Olivet Presbyterian Church
Charlottesville, Virginia

Greek Orzo Salad with Shrimp

1 pound unpeeled, large fresh shrimp
3 cups water
¾ cup uncooked orzo
1 (4-ounce) package crumbled feta cheese
1 cup cherry tomatoes, quartered
12 kalamata olives, pitted and halved
2 green onions, thinly sliced
3 tablespoons chopped fresh dill or 1 tablespoon dried dill
3 tablespoons olive oil
3 tablespoons fresh lemon juice
1½ tablespoons red wine vinegar
2 garlic cloves, minced
½ teaspoon salt
¼ teaspoon pepper

Peel shrimp, and devein, if desired. Bring water to a boil; add shrimp, and cook 3 to 5 minutes or just until shrimp turn pink. Drain.

Cook orzo according to package directions; drain. Rinse with cold water; drain well. Combine shrimp, orzo, feta cheese, and next 3 ingredients in a large bowl.

Stir together dill and remaining 6 ingredients. Drizzle dressing over shrimp mixture; toss to coat. Yield: 4 servings. Julie French

United Church of Tekoa Cookbook
United Church of Tekoa
Tekoa, Washington

Curried Rice and Chicken Salad

Win favor with this curried salad that's easy on the cook because it's a make-ahead dish.

1⅓ cups uncooked long-grain rice
2 chicken bouillon cubes
2 tablespoons curry powder
2 tablespoons butter or margarine
2 cups diced cooked chicken breast
1 (14-ounce) can artichoke hearts, drained
1 onion, chopped
½ cup cashews
¼ cup raisins
½ teaspoon salt
½ teaspoon pepper
1 cup mayonnaise
1 tablespoon lemon juice
½ teaspoon curry powder

Cook rice according to package directions, adding bouillon cubes, 2 tablespoons curry powder, and butter. Let cool.

Combine rice mixture, chicken, and next 6 ingredients.

Whisk together mayonnaise, lemon juice, and ½ teaspoon curry powder. Pour dressing over rice mixture; stir well. Cover and chill 2 hours. Yield: 10 servings. Jackie Adams

'Pon Top Edisto
Trinity Episcopal Church
Edisto Island, South Carolina

Louise Mathew's Chutney Chicken Salad

Curry and chutney work in tandem to provide sweet spiciness to this chunky chicken salad.

¾ cup mayonnaise
½ cup chutney
½ cup sour cream
¼ cup fresh lime juice
1 teaspoon curry powder
½ teaspoon salt
4 cups cubed cooked chicken breast
2 celery ribs, chopped
¾ cup seedless green grapes, halved
½ cup chopped green onions
1 (2.25-ounce) package slivered natural almonds, toasted

Stir together first 6 ingredients in a large bowl. Stir in chicken and remaining 4 ingredients. Yield: 6 to 8 servings.

Note: To make ahead, combine all ingredients as directed except almonds. Cover and chill. Stir in almonds just before serving.

Cookin' with Friends
National Presbyterian School Class of 2000
Washington, D.C.

Caesar Salad Dressing

Salty anchovies, tangy lemon juice, and zesty Dijon mustard spark this classic salad dressing.

⅓ cup grated Parmesan cheese
⅓ cup fresh lemon juice
1 (2-ounce) can anchovy fillets
3 garlic cloves
2 tablespoons Dijon mustard
1 teaspoon sugar
1 teaspoon Worcestershire sauce
1 cup olive oil
2 tablespoons chopped fresh parsley

Process first 7 ingredients in a blender or food processor until smooth, stopping to scrape down sides. Turn blender on high; add oil in a slow, steady stream. Add parsley; process until blended. Serve over salad greens. Yield: 1½ cups. Denise Dunkin

Doggone Good Cookin'
Support Dogs, Inc.
St. Louis, Missouri

Simply Scrumptious Salad Dressing

⅓ cup honey
⅓ cup olive oil
⅓ cup blackberry wine

Whisk together all ingredients in a bowl. Cover and chill. Whisk again just before serving over fruit. Yield: 1 cup. Lawra Conklin

Carnegie Hall Cookbook
Carnegie Hall, Inc.
Lewisburg, West Virginia

Raspberry Vinaigrette

½ cup vegetable oil
¼ cup sugar
¼ cup raspberry wine vinegar
1 tablespoon poppy seeds
1 tablespoon minced onion
1 teaspoon dry mustard
½ teaspoon salt

Whisk together all ingredients in a bowl. Cover and chill. Whisk again just before serving over salad greens, grapefruit sections, or melon balls. Yield: ¾ cup.

Simply the Best . . . Recipes by Design
Columbus Area Visitors Center
Columbus, Indiana

Vinaigrette Salad Dressing

1 cup vegetable oil
½ cup cider vinegar
1 garlic clove, minced
1 teaspoon sugar
1 teaspoon dry mustard
1 teaspoon paprika
1 teaspoon Worcestershire sauce
½ teaspoon salt
¼ teaspoon pepper

Whisk together all ingredients in a bowl. Cover and chill. Whisk again just before serving over salad greens. Yield: 1½ cups. Jane Baldwin

Scent from P.E.O. Sisterhood
Philanthropic Educational Organization, Chapter AG
Newcastle, Wyoming

Sauces & Condiments

Pineapple-Mango Salsa, page 286

Berry Sauce

This simple, no-cook topper is ideal for fresh summer berries on warm summer days.

2 cups whole fresh strawberries
¼ cup unsweetened apple juice
2 tablespoons frozen unsweetened apple juice concentrate, thawed
¼ teaspoon vanilla extract

Process all ingredients in a blender until smooth, stopping to scrape down sides. Serve sauce over vanilla ice cream, pound cake, poached fruit, or custard. Store in an airtight container in refrigerator. Yield: 1⅔ cups.

Donna Tetley

Culinary Tastes of Blue Mountain Cooks
Grand Terrace Branch Library: Friends
Grand Terrace, California

Cranberry-Horseradish Sauce

Spread this zesty sauce over slices of bread to add zip to a turkey sandwich.

2 cups fresh cranberries
1 small onion, quartered
¾ cup sour cream
½ cup sugar
2 tablespoons prepared horseradish
½ teaspoon salt

Pulse cranberries and onion in a food processor until coarsely chopped, stopping to scrape down sides.

Stir together cranberry mixture, sour cream, and remaining 3 ingredients in a medium bowl. Serve with roast beef or turkey. Store in an airtight container in refrigerator. Yield: 2½ cups.

A Cookery & Memories from Old Bourne
The Bourne Society for Historic Preservation
Bourne, Massachusetts

Orange Sauce for Pork Roast

Bitters are a solution of aromatic herbs, barks, roots, and plant products used to add a bittersweet note to foods and mixed drinks.

⅓ cup sugar
1 tablespoon cornstarch
⅛ teaspoon salt
1 teaspoon grated orange rind
1 cup fresh orange juice
1 tablespoon lemon juice
½ cup butter or margarine
1 tablespoon orange liqueur
3 dashes of aromatic bitters (we tested with Angostura)

Combine first 4 ingredients in a small saucepan. Gradually add juices, stirring well. Bring to a boil; reduce heat to medium, and cook, stirring constantly, until thickened and bubbly. Remove from heat; add butter, liqueur, and bitters, stirring until butter melts. Serve warm over roast pork, chicken, or veal. Yield: 2 cups.

Plummer House Museum
Traill County Historical Society
Hillsboro, North Dakota

Super Barbecue Sauce

2 cups Worcestershire sauce
1¼ cups ketchup
1 cup cola soft drink
½ cup butter or margarine
1½ tablespoons sugar
1 tablespoon salt
2 teaspoons freshly ground pepper

Combine all ingredients in a medium saucepan. Bring to a boil; reduce heat, and simmer, stirring constantly, 30 minutes. Serve warm with chicken, pork, or beef. Yield: 3¼ cups. Carol Haas

Deborah Heart and Lung Center
75th Anniversary National Cookbook
Deborah Hospital Foundation
Browns Mills, New Jersey

Hollandaise Sauce

Serve this rich, velvety-smooth French classic to dress up delicate, pencil-thin asparagus, brunch egg dishes, and fish.

2 egg yolks
½ teaspoon dry mustard
⅛ teaspoon salt
⅛ teaspoon ground red pepper
1 teaspoon fresh lemon juice
¼ cup whipping cream
¼ cup butter or margarine, cut into 4 pieces

Whisk together first 4 ingredients in top of a double boiler; gradually stir in lemon juice, stirring constantly. Add whipping cream and one-fourth of butter to egg mixture; cook over hot, not boiling, water, stirring constantly with a wire whisk until butter melts. Add another fourth of butter, stirring constantly. As sauce thickens, stir in remaining butter. Cook until temperature reaches 160°, stirring constantly.

Remove sauce from double boiler, and serve immediately. Yield: ½ cup.

A Taste of Washington State
Washington Bed & Breakfast Guild
Seattle, Washington

Mushroom Sauce

Spoon this velvety fresh mushroom sauce over your favorite grilled meat for a decadent delight.

1 (8-ounce) package sliced fresh mushrooms
3 tablespoons butter or margarine, melted
2 tablespoons all-purpose flour
1¼ cups chicken broth
1¼ cups half-and-half
½ cup freshly grated Parmesan cheese
½ teaspoon salt
½ teaspoon freshly ground pepper

Sauté mushrooms in butter in a large skillet over medium-high heat 5 minutes or until tender. Reduce heat to low; sprinkle mushroom mixture with flour, and cook, stirring constantly, 2 minutes. Whisk in broth and half-and-half. Bring to a boil; reduce heat, and simmer, uncovered, 15 minutes or until thickened, stirring often. Stir in cheese, salt, and pepper; simmer 2 minutes. Serve warm over chicken, beef, pork, or seafood. Yield: 2 cups. George E. Williams, Jr.

A Dab of This and a Dab of That
Bethlehem Baptist Church Senior Missionary
Ninety Six, South Carolina

Pesto

Pine nuts are found in the pine cones of several varieties of pine trees. Because of their high fat content, store them in an airtight container in the refrigerator or freeze them up to nine months.

½ cup pine nuts
1½ cups freshly grated Parmesan cheese
4 garlic cloves
⅛ teaspoon salt
¾ cup olive oil
2 cups loosely packed fresh basil leaves

Bake pine nuts in a shallow pan at 350°, stirring occasionally, 5 minutes or until toasted.

Pulse pine nuts, Parmesan cheese, garlic, and salt in a food processor 10 to 15 times or until a paste forms. With processor running, gradually pour olive oil through food chute. Add basil, and process until blended. Store in an airtight container in refrigerator. Serve pesto over hot cooked pasta, stir into soups, or use as a sauce for pizza. Yield: 1½ cups. Paseur Family

Cookin' with Friends
National Presbyterian School Class of 2000
Washington, D.C.

Pineapple-Mango Salsa

3 cups finely chopped fresh pineapple
1 medium mango, chopped (about 1¼ cups)
1 cup chopped celery
½ cup chopped purple onion
¼ cup chopped red bell pepper
1 (4.5-ounce) can chopped green chiles, undrained
¼ cup chopped fresh cilantro
¼ cup lime juice

Stir together first 6 ingredients in a large bowl. Stir in cilantro and lime juice. Cover and chill. Serve with grilled chicken or fish. Yield: 6 cups.

Always in Season
The Junior League of Salt Lake City, Utah

Devonshire Cream

Brew a fresh pot of tea, and enjoy this British specialty with a batch of scones.

1 (3-ounce) package cream cheese, softened
1 tablespoon powdered sugar
½ teaspoon vanilla extract
⅓ cup whipping cream

Beat cream cheese at medium speed with an electric mixer until fluffy. Stir in powdered sugar and vanilla. Gradually add whipping cream, beating until spreading consistency (do not overbeat). Cover and chill. Serve with fresh fruit or scones. Yield: 1 cup. Katy Weir

Feeding the Flock
St. Philips Episcopal Church
Topeka, Kansas

Cranberry-Apple Relish

Wondering how many bags of berries to buy? A 12-ounce bag of fresh cranberries contains about 3 cups, so you'll need to buy 2 bags to have enough cranberries for this recipe.

4 cups fresh cranberries
½ cup raisins
2 cups diced unpeeled Granny Smith apple
1 cup sugar
½ cup chopped walnuts, toasted
1 teaspoon fresh lemon juice

Pulse cranberries and raisins in a food processor 3 or 4 times or until coarsely ground. Stir together cranberry mixture, apple, and remaining ingredients. Cover and chill. Serve with pork, chicken, duck, or turkey. Yield: 5 cups.

Hearthside: A Country Community Cookbook
Christ Community Church
Weare, New Hampshire

New-Fashioned Corn Relish

1 small onion, chopped (about 1 cup)
½ cup sugar
½ cup apple cider vinegar
2 teaspoons celery seeds
½ teaspoon mustard seeds
1 (15.25-ounce) can whole kernel corn, drained
½ cup chopped celery
¼ cup sweet pickle relish
1 (2-ounce) jar diced pimiento, drained

Stir together first 5 ingredients in a 3-quart saucepan; bring to a boil. Reduce heat, and simmer, uncovered, 10 minutes.

Stir together corn and remaining 3 ingredients in a large bowl; pour hot vinegar mixture over corn mixture, and stir gently. Let cool completely (about 2 hours). Store in an airtight container in refrigerator. Yield: 2½ cups. Jeanne Hancock

Recipes for Champions
Shebas of Khiva Temple Oriental Band
Amarillo, Texas

Honey Butter

Spoon this sweet delight into a pretty container, and tie with a ribbon to give as a homespun hostess gift.

½ cup butter, softened
¼ cup honey
1 teaspoon grated orange rind
½ teaspoon ground cinnamon

Combine all ingredients in a mixing bowl; beat at medium speed with an electric mixer until smooth. Store in an airtight container in refrigerator. Serve with bread, biscuits, English muffins, pancakes, waffles, or scones. Yield: ¾ cup. Lisa Terry

North Country Cooking
51st National Square Dance Convention
St. Paul, Minnesota

Homemade Mustard

1 large egg, lightly beaten
¼ cup water
¼ cup white vinegar
3 tablespoons sugar
1 tablespoon all-purpose flour
1 tablespoon dry mustard
⅛ teaspoon salt
1 tablespoon butter or margarine

Combine first 7 ingredients in a small saucepan. Bring to a boil, stirring constantly. Remove from heat; add butter, stirring until butter melts. Cover and chill 8 hours. Yield: ¾ cup. Terri Cooper

Scent from P.E.O. Sisterhood
Philanthropic Educational Organization, Chapter AG
Newcastle, Wyoming

Rhubarb-Cherry Jam

6 cups chopped fresh rhubarb
5 cups sugar
1 (6-ounce) package cherry gelatin
1 (21-ounce) can cherry pie filling

Stir together rhubarb and sugar in a large Dutch oven. Bring to a boil over medium-high heat; reduce heat, and simmer, uncovered, 10 minutes or until rhubarb is tender, stirring often.

Stir in gelatin; cook 1 to 2 minutes or until gelatin dissolves, stirring often. Stir in pie filling, and cook until thoroughly heated. Pour into hot, sterilized jars, filling to ¼ inch from top; wipe jar rims. Cover at once with metal lids, and screw on bands. Cool; store in refrigerator up to 1 month. Yield: 8 half-pints. Signe L. Tol

Blest Recipes
Our Redeemer Lutheran Church
Chugiak, Alaska

Spiced Peach Jam

You can substitute frozen peaches for fresh. Use 4 cups finely chopped frozen peaches that have been thawed and drained.

3 pounds peaches, finely chopped (about 4 cups)
7½ cups sugar
¼ cup lemon juice
1 teaspoon ground cinnamon
½ teaspoon ground cloves
½ teaspoon ground allspice
1 (3-ounce) package liquid pectin

Combine first 6 ingredients in a Dutch oven; bring to a boil, stirring often. Boil 1 minute, stirring constantly.

Add liquid pectin to peach mixture; return to a boil, and boil 1 minute, stirring constantly. Remove from heat, and skim off foam with a metal spoon.

Pour hot jam into hot, sterilized jars, filling to ¼ inch from top; wipe jar rims. Cover at once with metal lids, and screw on bands.

Process in boiling-water bath 5 minutes. Let stand 1 week before serving. Yield: 9 half-pints. Ashley Venable

All We Need Is Love
Columbus-Lowndes Humane Society
Columbus, Mississippi

Zucchini Bread and Butter Pickles

This is a wonderful recipe to use if you have an abundance of zucchini from your garden. You'll need a large stockpot (about 20-quart size) to cook all the zucchini, onion, and pepper. If you don't have a pot big enough, you can easily cut this recipe in half.

25 to 30 medium zucchini (about 16 to 17 pounds)
8 onions, thinly sliced
1 green bell pepper, cut into thin strips
1 red bell pepper, cut into thin strips
5 cups sugar
5 cups apple cider vinegar (5% acidity)
½ cup salt
2 tablespoons mustard seeds
1 teaspoon ground turmeric
½ teaspoon ground cloves

Thinly slice zucchini, and place in a large bowl. Cover with ice, and let stand at room temperature 2 hours (add more ice as needed). Drain.

Combine onion and remaining 8 ingredients in a large stockpot; bring to a boil, and turn off heat. Add drained zucchini, and stir gently.

Pack hot zucchini mixture into hot jars, filling to ½ inch from top. Remove air bubbles; wipe jar rims. Cover at once with metal lids, and screw on bands. Process jars in boiling-water bath 12 minutes. Yield: 17 pints. Mary Johnson Sargent

Favorite Recipes
Friends of Memorial Hospital
Weiser, Idaho

Soups & Stews

Frogmore Stew, page 303

Chilled Fruit Soup

This bubbly sipping soup is a refreshing start to a summer meal when watermelons are at their peak.

1½ cups chopped cantaloupe
1½ cups chopped honeydew melon
1 cup chopped watermelon, seeded
2 cups fresh orange juice
⅓ cup lime juice
¼ cup honey
3 tablespoons sugar
3 cups Asti Spumante or other sweet sparkling wine

Process first 7 ingredients in a blender until smooth, stopping to scrape down sides. Cover and chill 8 hours. Stir in sparkling wine before serving. Yield: 8 cups. Jill Brethauer

Sesquicentennially Delicious
The Western Pennsylvania Hospital
Pittsburgh, Pennsylvania

Brie Cheese Soup

Serve this silky soup as an elegant appetizer at your next special-occasion dinner.

12 ounces Brie
¼ cup butter or margarine
½ cup all-purpose flour
6 cups chilled chicken broth (we tested with Swanson's ⅓-less-sodium)
⅓ cup dry white wine
¾ cup diced fresh mushrooms
½ cup diced carrot
½ cup diced celery
¼ cup whipping cream
⅛ teaspoon ground white pepper

Remove and discard rind from Brie. Cube cheese, and let stand at room temperature to soften.

Melt butter in a Dutch oven; add flour, and cook oven over medium heat, whisking constantly, until roux is caramel-colored (about 2 minutes). Whisk in chicken broth. Bring to a boil, reduce heat, and simmer, uncovered, until mixture reduces by one-third (about 20 minutes). Skim any butter or matter that may collect on top, and discard. Add wine and vegetables; simmer, uncovered, 10 minutes or until vegetables are tender. Add softened Brie, and stir until melted. (Do not let boil.) Stir in cream and pepper. Serve immediately. Yield: 6 cups. Gerald Bonsey

Rave Reviews
Ogunquit Playhouse
Ogunquit, Maine

Curried Carrot Soup

Complexly flavored curry kisses this creamy carrot soup.

1 medium onion, chopped
1 teaspoon dried thyme
1 bay leaf
2 tablespoons vegetable oil
4 medium carrots, cut into ½-inch pieces
3 (14½-ounce) cans chicken broth
1 (8-ounce) package cream cheese, softened
3 tablespoons chopped fresh parsley
1½ tablespoons curry powder
¼ teaspoon salt
Dash of ground red pepper

Sauté first 3 ingredients in hot oil in a large saucepan over medium-high heat until onion is tender. Add carrot and chicken broth; bring to a boil. Reduce heat, and simmer, uncovered, 30 minutes or until carrot is tender. Discard bay leaf.

Process half of carrot mixture and half of cream cheese in a blender until smooth. Repeat procedure with remaining half of carrot mixture and cream cheese. Stir in parsley, curry, salt, and red pepper. Return puree to saucepan, and cook until thoroughly heated. Yield: 6 cups. Clinky Seabrook

Angels in the Kitchen
Grace Episcopal Church
Anderson, South Carolina

Chanterelle Velvet Soup

Chanterelle mushrooms have a distinctive orange flesh and a sweet fruity-nutty flavor. Fresh chanterelles are generally available at gourmet markets during the late summer through early winter months. If you can't find them at your market, we suggest substituting fresh oyster mushrooms.

¼ cup butter or margarine
¼ cup all-purpose flour
5 cups chicken broth
1 small onion, chopped
1 celery rib, chopped
1 medium carrot, chopped
2 garlic cloves, minced
2 tablespoons olive oil
1 pound fresh chanterelle mushrooms, chopped
½ cup dry sherry
2 cups whipping cream
1½ tablespoons Worcestershire sauce
1 tablespoon balsamic vinegar
½ teaspoon salt
¼ teaspoon freshly ground pepper

Melt butter in a Dutch oven; add flour, and cook over medium heat, whisking constantly, until roux is caramel-colored (about 2 minutes). Whisk in broth; bring to a boil.

Meanwhile, sauté onion and next 3 ingredients in hot oil in a large skillet over medium-high heat 5 minutes. Add mushrooms; sauté 4 minutes. Add sherry; simmer 2 minutes.

Process vegetable mixture in a blender until smooth, stopping to scrape down sides. Add pureed vegetables, whipping cream, and remaining 4 ingredients to boiling broth mixture. Return to a boil. Reduce heat, and simmer, uncovered, 10 minutes, stirring occasionally. Yield: 9 cups.

Sherry Ludwig

Sharing Our Best
Bull Run Parent Teacher Club
Sandy, Oregon

Thai Peanut Soup

This soup gets its kick from lemon grass, an ingredient in Thai cooking. The fragrant herb is reed shaped with a scallionlike base and can be found in Oriental markets.

1 tablespoon butter or margarine
⅓ cup finely chopped onion
⅓ cup finely chopped celery
2 tablespoons finely chopped red bell pepper
2 tablespoons all-purpose flour
1 tablespoon finely chopped fresh lemon grass (white part only)
¼ teaspoon ground red pepper
1 (14½-ounce) can chicken broth
1 (14-ounce) can coconut milk
½ cup creamy peanut butter
1 tablespoon soy sauce
¼ teaspoon salt
Garnishes: chopped peanuts, red bell pepper strips

Melt butter in a large Dutch oven over medium heat; add onion, celery, and chopped bell pepper, and sauté until tender. Stir in flour, lemon grass, and ground red pepper. Gradually stir in chicken broth and coconut milk; bring to a boil. Reduce heat; add peanut butter, soy sauce, and salt. Cook until thoroughly heated, stirring constantly. To serve, ladle soup into individual bowls. Garnish, if desired. Yield: 4 cups.

Beth Grosvenor

Tasty Treasures
Immanuel Lutheran Church Ladies Aid
Leland, Michigan

Bistro Onion Soup

Soft, oozing Gruyère cheese enticingly encloses a caramelized onion broth and toasty French bread slices.

4 large onions (about 2 pounds), sliced
¼ cup butter or margarine, melted
2 tablespoons all-purpose flour
5¼ cups water
½ cup dry white wine
½ cup dry red wine
4 chicken bouillon cubes
4 beef bouillon cubes
2 bay leaves
½ teaspoon salt
½ teaspoon dried sage
¼ teaspoon pepper
8 (½-inch) diagonally sliced French bread slices, toasted
8 slices Gruyère cheese

Sauté onion in butter in a Dutch oven over medium heat, stirring often, 15 minutes or until golden. Stir in flour; cook 1 minute. Add water and next 8 ingredients. Bring to a boil; reduce heat, and simmer, partially covered, 30 minutes. Discard bay leaves.

Ladle soup into 4 individual ovenproof soup bowls. Place on a baking sheet. Add 2 bread slices to each bowl, and cover with 2 slices cheese. Broil 5½ inches from heat 4 minutes or until cheese is bubbly. Serve immediately. Yield: 4 servings (6 cups).

Gracious Gator Cooks
The Junior League of Gainesville, Florida

Yellow Pepper Soup

½ cup chopped onion
1 celery rib, chopped
1 medium carrot, chopped
1 tablespoon olive oil, divided
4 yellow bell peppers, chopped (about 2½ pounds)
2 large potatoes, peeled and chopped (about 1½ pounds)
1 bay leaf
3 to 4½ cups water
1½ teaspoons salt
¼ teaspoon pepper
1 cup (¼-inch) cubed Italian bread (about 4 [1-ounce] slices)
4 teaspoons grated Parmesan cheese
1 teaspoon finely chopped parsley

Sauté onion, celery, and carrot in 1 teaspoon oil in a Dutch oven over medium-high heat 10 minutes or until tender. Add bell pepper and next 3 ingredients. Bring to a boil; reduce heat, and simmer, uncovered, 25 minutes or until potato is tender. Discard bay leaf.

Process mixture, in batches, in a food processor, stopping to scrape down sides. Return mixture to heat; add salt and pepper. Bring mixture to a boil; reduce heat, and simmer, uncovered, 5 minutes.

Heat remaining 2 teaspoons oil in a nonstick skillet over medium-high heat until hot. Add ½ cup bread cubes, and cook in hot oil, stirring constantly, 2 minutes or until golden. Remove from heat, and repeat procedure with remaining bread cubes. Sprinkle croutons with Parmesan cheese and parsley. Serve immediately over soup. Yield: 6½ cups.

Tom and Nancy Campbell

Sesquicentennially Delicious
The Western Pennsylvania Hospital
Pittsburgh, Pennsylvania

Baked Potato Soup

This family-pleaser is the ever-popular loaded and stuffed baked potato–soup style.

4 large baking potatoes
⅔ cup butter or margarine
⅔ cup all-purpose flour
7 cups milk
4 green onions, sliced
1 (12-ounce) package bacon, cooked and crumbled
1¼ cups (5 ounces) shredded Cheddar cheese
1 (8-ounce) container sour cream
¾ teaspoon salt
½ teaspoon pepper

Bake potatoes at 400° for 1 hour or until done; cool. Cut potatoes in half lengthwise; scoop out pulp, and reserve. Discard shells.

Melt butter in a Dutch oven over low heat. Whisk in flour until smooth. Cook 1 minute, whisking constantly. Gradually whisk in milk; cook over medium heat, whisking constantly, until mixture is thickened and bubbly.

Stir in potato pulp and green onions; bring to a boil. Cover, reduce heat, and simmer 10 minutes. Add bacon and remaining ingredients; stir until cheese melts. Serve immediately. Yield: 14 cups.

Simple Pleasures: From Our Table to Yours
Arab Mothers' Club
Arab, Alabama

Golden Sweet Potato and Pear Soup

1½ pounds sweet potatoes, cut into small pieces
4 cups water
1 (3-inch) cinnamon stick
1¼ teaspoons salt
2 tablespoons butter or margarine
3 medium Comice pears, peeled and cut into thin slices
⅓ cup dry white wine
⅓ cup half-and-half
¼ teaspoon ground white pepper

Combine first 4 ingredients in a Dutch oven; bring to a boil. Cover, reduce heat, and simmer 15 minutes or until sweet potato is tender. Simmer, uncovered, 5 minutes. Discard cinnamon stick, and set potato mixture aside.

Melt butter in a large skillet over medium heat; add pear, and sauté 5 minutes. Add wine; cover, reduce heat, and simmer 10 minutes.

Process potato mixture and pear mixture, in batches, in a food processor 1 minute or until smooth, stopping to scrape down sides. Return pureed mixture to Dutch oven; stir in half-and-half and pepper. Cook over medium heat until thoroughly heated, stirring often. Yield: about 8 cups.

Perennial Palette
Southborough Gardeners
Southborough, Massachusetts

Italian Sausage Soup

1½ pounds Italian sausage links, cut into ½-inch slices
2 medium onions, chopped
2 garlic cloves, minced
3 (10½-ounce) cans beef broth
1 (28-ounce) can whole tomatoes, undrained and chopped
1½ cups dry red wine
1 medium-size green bell pepper, chopped
3 tablespoons fresh parsley
½ teaspoon dried basil
3 cups uncooked farfalle (bow tie pasta)
2 zucchini, cut in half lengthwise and sliced
Grated Parmesan cheese

Brown sausage in a large skillet over medium heat; remove sausage, and drain well, reserving 1 tablespoon drippings in skillet.

Sauté onion and garlic in drippings in skillet over medium-high heat 3 minutes or until tender. Combine sausage, onion mixture, broth, and next 5 ingredients. Bring to a boil; cover, reduce heat, and simmer 1 hour. Add pasta and zucchini. Cover and simmer 12 minutes.

To serve, ladle soup into individual bowls. Sprinkle with cheese, and serve immediately. Yield: 13 cups. Marsha Liakos

Tried and True from Riverview
Riverview Hospital Auxiliary
Wisconsin Rapids, Wisconsin

Southwestern Soup

Here's a sure-to-satisfy soup that comes together in a hurry, thanks to canned products. Taco seasoning mix and green chiles give it extra kick!

2 pounds ground turkey
1 medium onion, chopped
2 (1¼-ounce) envelopes taco seasoning mix
1 (1-ounce) envelope Ranch-style dressing mix
2 (15¼-ounce) cans whole kernel corn, undrained
2 cups water
1 (16-ounce) can pinto beans, undrained
1 (15½-ounce) can black beans, undrained
1 (15¼-ounce) can kidney beans, undrained
1 (14½-ounce) can diced tomatoes, undrained
1 (10-ounce) can diced tomatoes and green chiles, undrained
Shredded Cheddar cheese
Sliced green onions
Sour cream
Tortilla chips

Cook turkey and onion in a Dutch oven, stirring until turkey crumbles and is no longer pink. Stir in taco seasoning mix and dressing mix. Add corn and next 6 ingredients. Bring to a boil; reduce heat, and simmer, uncovered, 1 hour.

To serve, ladle soup into individual bowls. Top with cheese, green onions, sour cream, and tortilla chips. Yield: 15 cups.

Symphony of Flavors
The Associates of the Redlands Bowl
Redlands, California

Spicy Black-Eyed Pea Soup

1 pound ground hot pork sausage
1 cup chopped onion
1 cup chopped celery
1 cup chopped green bell pepper
2 (15-ounce) cans jalapeño black-eyed peas, undrained
2 (10-ounce) cans diced tomatoes with green chiles
1 (11-ounce) can white shoepeg corn, drained
1 (10-ounce) package frozen sliced okra
1 teaspoon salt
½ teaspoon pepper

Cook sausage in a Dutch oven, stirring until it crumbles and is no longer pink. Drain sausage on paper towels, reserving ¼ cup drippings in pan; return sausage to drippings in pan. Add onion, celery, and bell pepper; sauté in drippings over medium-high heat 5 minutes or until tender. Add peas and remaining 5 ingredients. Bring to a boil; cover, reduce heat, and simmer 30 minutes or until okra is tender. Yield: 11 cups.

Simple Pleasures: From Our Table to Yours
Arab Mothers' Club
Arab, Alabama

Mushroom and Potato Chowder

2 tablespoons butter or margarine
1 small onion, chopped
1 celery rib, chopped
½ small green bell pepper, chopped
1 (8-ounce) package sliced fresh mushrooms
2 cups medium-size red potatoes, peeled and cut into ½-inch cubes
2 cups chicken broth
½ teaspoon dried thyme
2 cups milk, divided
1½ teaspoons salt
½ to 1 teaspoon pepper
3 tablespoons all-purpose flour

Melt butter in a Dutch oven over medium heat; add onion, celery, and bell pepper, and sauté 5 minutes or until tender. Add mushrooms; sauté 3 minutes. Add potato, broth, and thyme; bring to a boil. Cover, reduce heat, and simmer 30 minutes or until potato is tender, stirring occasionally. Stir in 1½ cups milk, salt, and pepper; return to a simmer.

Whisk remaining ½ cup milk and flour in a small bowl until smooth. Whisk mixture into soup. Bring to a boil; reduce heat, and simmer, uncovered, 5 minutes or until thickened and bubbly. Yield: 5½ cups.

Secrets of Amelia
McArthur Family Branch YMCA
Fernandina Beach, Florida

Christmas Eve Oyster Corn Chowder

1 large onion, chopped
2 celery ribs, chopped
¼ cup butter
2 new potatoes, cut into ¼-inch cubes
2 medium carrots, cut into ¼-inch cubes
¼ cup chopped fresh Italian parsley
3 cups half-and-half, divided
1 (7-ounce) can cream-style corn
1 teaspoon salt
½ teaspoon sugar
¼ teaspoon freshly ground pepper
1 to 2 (12-ounce) containers fresh oysters, undrained
Garnish: chopped fresh Italian parsley

Sauté onion and celery in butter in a Dutch oven over medium heat until tender. Add potato, carrot, and ¼ cup parsley; cook 1 minute. Add 2 cups half-and-half, and bring to a boil. Reduce heat, and simmer, uncovered, 15 minutes or until potato is tender. Stir in remaining 1 cup half-and-half, corn, and next 4 ingredients. Bring to a boil; reduce heat, and simmer, uncovered, 5 minutes or until edges of oysters curl. Serve immediately. Garnish, if desired. Yield: 8 cups.

Yuletide on Hilton Head: A Heritage of Island Flavors
United Way of Beaufort County
Hilton Head Island, South Carolina

Island Shrimp Gumbo

1 pound unpeeled, medium-size fresh shrimp
3 slices bacon
1 large onion, chopped (about 2 cups)
1 cup chopped green bell pepper
2 tablespoons all-purpose flour
1 teaspoon salt
¼ teaspoon pepper
2 (14½-ounce) cans diced tomatoes, undrained
½ cup hot water
2 cups sliced fresh okra
Hot cooked rice

Peel shrimp, and devein, if desired; set aside.

Cook bacon in a large skillet until crisp; remove bacon, reserving 2 tablespoons drippings in skillet. Crumble bacon, and set aside. Cook onion in drippings, stirring constantly, until browned. Add green pepper; cook until tender. Add flour, stirring until smooth. Stir in salt and pepper; cook 1 minute. Add tomatoes and water. Bring to a boil; add reserved bacon and okra. Cover, reduce heat, and simmer 20 minutes or until okra is tender. Add shrimp; cook 5 more minutes or until shrimp turn pink. Serve over rice. Yield: 8 cups.

Secrets of Amelia
McArthur Family Branch YMCA
Fernandina Beach, Florida

Frogmore Stew

For an extra-spicy stew, substitute Cajun sausage for regular smoked sausage.

10 quarts water
1 (5-ounce) package crab boil
2 large onions, quartered
3 pounds smoked sausage, cut into 1-inch pieces
3 pounds new potatoes
12 ears fresh corn, cut in half
3 pounds unpeeled, large fresh shrimp

Bring water to a boil in a large stockpot. Add crab boil, onion, sausage, and potatoes; return to a boil, and cook 35 minutes or until potatoes are tender. Remove onion, sausage, and potatoes with a slotted spoon to a large shallow bowl or platter; keep warm.

Add corn to stockpot; return to a boil, and cook 10 minutes. Add shrimp; cook 3 more minutes. Remove corn and shrimp with a slotted spoon to bowl with potato mixture. Serve immediately with cocktail sauce, if desired. Yield: 10 to 12 servings.

W. Frank Cason

A Dab of This and a Dab of That
Bethlehem Baptist Church Senior Missionary
Ninety Six, South Carolina

West Indian Beef Stew

This thick and exotic stew has a consistency similar to Hungarian goulash or beef stroganoff. It's delicious served over fruited rice (see Note).

½ cup all-purpose flour
1 teaspoon ground ginger
2½ pounds sirloin steak, cut into 1½-inch chunks
⅓ cup vegetable oil
1 large onion, coarsely chopped
1 medium-size red bell pepper, cut into strips
1 medium-size yellow bell pepper, cut into strips
1 medium-size green bell pepper, cut into strips
2 jalapeño peppers, finely chopped
3 garlic cloves, chopped
1½ teaspoons minced fresh ginger
1 (10½-ounce) can condensed beef broth, undiluted
3 tablespoons tomato paste
2 tablespoons molasses
1½ teaspoons salt
½ teaspoon pepper
3 medium tomatoes, cut into chunks
¼ cup pimiento-stuffed olives, halved
3 tablespoons dark rum (optional)
2 tablespoons fresh lime juice
Chopped fresh cilantro

Combine flour and ground ginger in a large heavy-duty, zip-top plastic bag; seal bag, and shake well. Add beef to bag, a few chunks at a time; seal bag, and shake to coat.

Brown one-third of beef in one-third of hot oil in a Dutch oven over high heat about 3 minutes. Remove beef from skillet; set aside. Repeat procedure twice with remaining beef and oil. Reduce heat to medium-high, and add onion to pan; sauté 2 minutes. Add red bell pepper and next 5 ingredients; sauté 5 minutes or until vegetables are tender. Stir in beef broth, tomato paste, and molasses; bring to a boil. Reduce heat; simmer, uncovered, 30 minutes, stirring occasionally.

Add beef, salt, and pepper to vegetable mixture; cook, uncovered, 10 minutes. Add tomato and olives; cook 5 more minutes (meat should be medium rare). Stir in rum, if desired, and lime juice. Sprinkle individual servings with cilantro. Yield: 10½ cups. Jeanne Salmon

Note: Simply stir orange rind, golden raisins, and coarsely chopped peanuts into hot cooked rice.

Rave Reviews
Ogunquit Playhouse
Ogunquit, Maine

Black Bean-Chicken Chili

2 skinned and boned chicken breast halves, cut into 1-inch pieces
1 medium onion, chopped
1 green bell pepper, chopped
2 garlic cloves, minced
2 tablespoons chicken broth
2 (28-ounce) cans stewed tomatoes, undrained
2 (15-ounce) cans black beans, rinsed and drained
2 cups medium salsa
2 tablespoons chili powder
1 teaspoon salt
1 teaspoon ground cumin
½ teaspoon hot sauce
Shredded Cheddar cheese (optional)

Cook first 4 ingredients in broth in a Dutch oven over medium-high heat 3 minutes or until onion is tender.

Add tomatoes and next 6 ingredients; bring to a boil. Reduce heat, and simmer, uncovered, 30 to 35 minutes, stirring often.

To serve, ladle chili into individual bowls. Top with shredded cheese, if desired. Yield: 13 cups.

Seaboard to Sideboard
The Junior League of Wilmington, North Carolina

Santa Fe-Style Chicken Chili

2 large onions, diced
2 medium-size green bell peppers, diced
1 medium-size red bell pepper, diced
8 garlic cloves, minced
¼ cup olive oil
2 teaspoons chili powder
2 teaspoons ground cumin
⅛ teaspoon ground red pepper
2 (14½-ounce) cans chicken broth
1 (28-ounce) can whole tomatoes, undrained and chopped
2 pounds skinned and boned chicken breast halves, cut into ½-inch cubes
2 (16-ounce) cans pinto beans, rinsed and drained
1 (15-ounce) jar medium salsa
1 (10-ounce) package frozen whole kernel corn
1 tablespoon brown sugar
1 tablespoon white vinegar
1 teaspoon pepper
¾ teaspoon salt
Hot cooked rice

Sauté first 4 ingredients in hot oil in a Dutch oven over medium heat 5 minutes or until tender. Add chili powder, cumin, and ground red pepper; cook, stirring constantly, 1 minute.

Add broth and tomatoes; bring to a boil. Reduce heat, and simmer, uncovered, 15 minutes. Add chicken and next 3 ingredients; bring to a boil. Reduce heat, and simmer, uncovered, 5 minutes. Add brown sugar and next 3 ingredients; simmer, uncovered, 20 minutes. Serve over rice. Yield: 10 cups.

Symphony of Flavors
The Associates of the Redlands Bowl
Redlands, California

Vegetables

Asparagus Dijon, page 309

Grilled Artichokes

This beurre blanc (white butter) sauce is a French classic that accents poultry, seafood, and eggs as well as grilled and steamed vegetables.

1 large artichoke
1 lemon, cut into wedges
2 tablespoons olive oil
¼ cup water
2 garlic cloves, coarsely chopped
⅛ teaspoon salt
⅛ teaspoon pepper
Basil-Garlic Beurre Blanc

Wash artichoke by plunging up and down in cold water. Cut off stem end, and trim about ½ inch from top. Remove any loose bottom leaves. With scissors, trim one-fourth off top of each outer leaf, and rub cut edges with a lemon wedge. Cut artichoke in half; snip around fuzzy thistle (choke), and remove with a spoon. Rub cut sides with lemon wedges. Squeeze juice from lemon wedges, and reserve juice.

Place artichoke halves on a large piece of heavy-duty aluminum foil. Drizzle with lemon juice and olive oil; add water. Sprinkle with garlic, salt, and pepper. Fold aluminum foil over artichoke halves to seal in juices.

Place on grill rack. Grill, without grill lid, over medium heat (300° to 350°) 20 minutes. Serve with Basil-Garlic Beurre Blanc. Yield: 2 servings.

Basil-Garlic Beurre Blanc

½ cup dry white wine
3 tablespoons white wine vinegar
1 tablespoon minced shallot
1 tablespoon minced garlic
½ cup heavy whipping cream
½ cup butter, cut into pieces
¼ cup chopped fresh basil

Combine first 4 ingredients in a small saucepan. Bring to a boil; reduce heat, and simmer, uncovered, 6 minutes or until liquid is reduced by half. Stir in cream. Return to a boil; reduce heat, and simmer, uncovered, 6 minutes or until liquid is reduced by half. Remove from heat; add butter, stirring until butter melts and sauce is smooth. Stir in basil. Yield: ¾ cup.

Bay Tables
The Junior League of Mobile, Alabama

Asparagus Dijon

1½ pounds fresh asparagus
¼ cup whipping cream
2 tablespoons mayonnaise
2 tablespoons sliced green onions
1½ tablespoons Dijon mustard
1 hard-cooked egg, finely chopped (optional)

Snap off tough ends of asparagus; arrange asparagus in a steamer basket over boiling water. Cover and steam 8 minutes or until crisp-tender; keep warm.

Beat whipping cream at high speed with an electric mixer until stiff peaks form. Fold in mayonnaise, green onions, and mustard; sprinkle with egg, if desired. Spoon sauce over warm asparagus. Serve immediately. Yield: 6 servings.

Kathy Ingram

Panthers' Pantry
Children's Educational Foundation
Madera, California

Roasted Asparagus

Roasting intensifies the fresh asparagus flavor of these delicate spears.

1 pound fresh asparagus
½ cup freshly grated Parmesan cheese
1 tablespoon grated lemon rind
¼ teaspoon salt
¼ teaspoon freshly ground pepper
¼ cup olive oil

Snap off tough ends of asparagus; arrange asparagus in a single layer in a nonstick 15- x 10-inch jellyroll pan. Sprinkle with cheese, lemon rind, salt, and pepper. Drizzle with oil. Bake, uncovered, at 350° for 10 minutes or until tender. Yield: 4 servings.

International Home Cooking
The United Nations International School Parents' Association
New York, New York

Broccoli and Cheese Skins

These ultimate skins aren't for the faint of appetite. Nestled inside each crispy potato skin is a bounty of fresh vegetables, brown rice, and cheese. Sunflower kernels and seasonings make this dish stand out.

10 (8-ounce) baking potatoes, unpeeled
Shortening
1 (16-ounce) package fresh broccoli flowerets
½ cup chopped fresh mushrooms
½ cup minced onion
1 garlic clove, minced
2 tablespoons butter, melted
2 cups cooked brown rice
1¾ cups (7 ounces) shredded Cheddar cheese, divided
2 large eggs, beaten
¼ cup sour cream
2 tablespoons chopped fresh parsley
2 tablespoons soy sauce
¼ teaspoon seasoned salt
¼ teaspoon pepper
⅛ teaspoon ground nutmeg
¼ cup sunflower kernels
Paprika

Scrub potatoes; pat dry. Rub potatoes with shortening, and place on an ungreased baking sheet. Bake at 450° for 1 hour. Cut a 1-inch lengthwise strip from top of each potato. Scoop out pulp, leaving shells intact; reserve pulp for other uses. Place shells on ungreased baking sheet; bake at 450° for 10 minutes or until crisp and brown.

Meanwhile, process broccoli in a food processor in 3 batches until finely chopped. Arrange broccoli in a steamer basket over boiling water. Cover and steam 3 minutes or until crisp-tender.

Sauté mushrooms, onion, and garlic in butter in a large skillet over medium-high heat 5 minutes or until tender. Stir in broccoli; cook 1 minute, stirring constantly. Remove from heat, and stir in rice. Combine 1 cup cheese, eggs, and next 6 ingredients; add to broccoli mixture, stirring constantly. Spoon ½ cup broccoli mixture into each reserved potato shell. Sprinkle with remaining ¾ cup cheese and sunflower kernels; sprinkle with paprika. Cover loosely with aluminum foil. Bake at 350° for 15 minutes; uncover and bake 5 more minutes or until a thermometer inserted into center of each potato registers 160°. Yield: 10 servings.

Melinda Porter

The Flavors of Mackinac
Mackinac Island Medical Center
Mackinac Island, Michigan

Breaded Cauliflower

Coated with seasoned breadcrumbs, these flowerets are fried until golden for a crunchy appetizer or side dish. Serve them with a dipping sauce if you'd like.

- **1 medium cauliflower, broken into flowerets**
- **1 cup water**
- **4 egg yolks**
- **1 teaspoon garlic powder**
- **1 teaspoon onion powder**
- **1 teaspoon minced fresh parsley**
- **½ teaspoon sugar**
- **½ teaspoon salt**
- **¼ teaspoon pepper**
- **1 cup Italian-seasoned breadcrumbs**
- **3 tablespoons freshly grated Parmesan cheese**
- **½ cup butter, divided**

Combine cauliflower and water in a large skillet. Bring to a boil; cover, reduce heat, and simmer 8 minutes or until crisp-tender. Drain and set aside.

Combine egg yolks and next 6 ingredients in a medium bowl. Combine breadcrumbs and Parmesan cheese in a zip-top plastic bag. Add half of cauliflower to egg yolk mixture; toss to coat. Place cauliflower in bag with breadcrumb mixture; seal bag securely, and shake gently to coat.

Melt ¼ cup butter in a large skillet over medium heat; add coated cauliflower to skillet, and cook 4 minutes or until golden. Drain cauliflower on paper towels. Repeat procedure with remaining half of cauliflower and ¼ cup butter. Serve immediately. Yield: 5 to 7 servings.

Tyrelle Schweitzer

Cooking with Class
Timber Lake Booster Club
Timber Lake, South Dakota

Carrot Soufflé

A sprinkle of cinnamon sweetly spices this simple soufflé.

2 pounds carrots, chopped
½ cup butter or margarine, softened
1 cup sugar
3 large eggs, lightly beaten
2 tablespoons all-purpose flour
1 teaspoon baking powder
Ground cinnamon

Cook carrot in boiling water to cover 20 to 25 minutes or until tender; drain. Mash carrot and butter with a potato masher. Add sugar and egg; beat at medium speed with an electric mixer 2 minutes. Stir in flour and baking powder. Pour into a greased 11- x 7-inch baking dish. Sprinkle with cinnamon. Bake, uncovered, at 350° for 1 hour or until set. Yield: 8 servings. Lore Wootton

Favorite Recipes
Friends of Memorial Hospital
Weiser, Idaho

Sautéed Fennel and Carrots

1 (1-pound) fennel bulb
2 medium carrots
1 tablespoon olive oil
¼ cup dry white wine
¼ cup water
1 tablespoon sugar
¼ teaspoon salt
¼ teaspoon pepper

Rinse fennel thoroughly. Trim stalks to within 1 inch of bulb. Discard hard outside stalks; reserve leaves for other uses. Cut a slice off bottom of bulb. Cut out tough core from bottom of bulb. Starting at 1 side, cut bulb lengthwise into ¼-inch-thick slices. Cut slices into ¼-inch strips. Cut carrots in half crosswise, and cut into ¼-inch strips.

Sauté fennel and carrot in hot oil in a large skillet over medium-high heat 5 minutes or until lightly browned. Add wine and remaining ingredients. Bring to a boil; cover, reduce heat, and simmer 4 minutes. Uncover and cook until almost all liquid evaporates and vegetables are glazed. Yield: 6 servings. Jewell Vroonland

Of Books and Cooks
Woman's Book Club
Harrison, Arkansas

Grilled Portobello Steaks

4 large portobello mushrooms (about 3 to 4 ounces each)
½ cup olive oil
2 garlic cloves, minced
1 teaspoon salt
2 teaspoons Worcestershire sauce
½ teaspoon freshly ground pepper

Cut stems off mushrooms near the cap. Reserve stems for other uses. Place mushroom caps, gill side up, on a plate. Combine olive oil and remaining 4 ingredients. Spoon oil mixture evenly into gills of each mushroom. Cover and chill until ready to grill. Place mushrooms, gill side up, on grill rack. Grill, covered with grill lid, over medium heat (300° to 350°) 4 minutes. Turn mushrooms; grill, covered, 4 minutes or just until tender. Yield: 4 servings. Jory Family

Cookin' with Friends
National Presbyterian School Class of 2000
Washington, D.C.

Caramelized Onion Pudding

Be patient when preparing this pudding. The key to creating sweetly caramelized onions is stirring them often.

½ cup butter or margarine
6 cups sliced onions (about 3 large onions)
6 large eggs
2 cups heavy whipping cream
¼ cup sugar
3 tablespoons all-purpose flour
2 teaspoons baking powder
2 teaspoons salt

Melt butter in a Dutch oven over medium heat. Add onion; sauté 45 minutes or until onion is browned. Remove from heat; set aside.

Stir together eggs and remaining 5 ingredients; add to onion. Pour mixture into a greased 13- x 9-inch baking dish.

Bake, uncovered, at 350° for 45 minutes or until golden. Let stand 5 minutes before serving. Yield: 10 servings. Kathy Cary

Look Who's Cooking in Louisville
Pitt Academy
Louisville, Kentucky

Lovin' Onions

Cheddar and Monterey Jack cheeses plus a little jalapeño pepper spice up things a bit–what's not to love about these onions?

1 tablespoon butter or margarine
7 medium onions, coarsely chopped (about 2¾ pounds)
½ cup self-rising flour
½ teaspoon salt
¼ teaspoon pepper
1¼ cups (5 ounces) shredded Cheddar cheese
1¼ cups (5 ounces) shredded Monterey Jack cheese
1 tablespoon chopped canned jalapeño pepper

Melt butter in a large skillet over medium heat; add onion, and sauté 10 minutes or until tender.

Combine flour, salt, and pepper. Combine cheeses. Add 1 cup cheese to flour mixture; stir well. Add onion and jalapeño pepper to flour mixture; stir well. Pour into a greased 3-quart baking dish. Top with remaining cheese mixture. Bake, uncovered, at 350° for 30 minutes or until cheese melts and mixture is bubbly. Yield: 6 servings. Dolly Sloan

We're Cooking Up Something New:
50 Years of Music, History, and Food
Wichita Falls Symphony League
Wichita Falls, Texas

Sugar Snap Peas with Mint Dressing

This fresh sugar snap pea salad is bathed in a fresh mint vinaigrette. Team it with lamb at a spring dinner celebration.

1 pound fresh sugar snap peas, trimmed
1½ cups fresh mint leaves, chopped
3 tablespoons finely chopped shallot
3 tablespoons rice wine vinegar
1 teaspoon Dijon mustard
1 teaspoon honey
¼ teaspoon salt
⅛ teaspoon freshly ground pepper
6 tablespoons olive oil

Cook peas in a small amount of boiling salted water 1 to 2 minutes or until crisp-tender; drain. Immediately plunge peas into ice water to stop the cooking process; drain. Stir together mint and next 6 ingredients. Gradually whisk in olive oil. Let dressing stand at room temperature 10 minutes. Pour dressing over peas, and toss. Yield: 5 servings.

Sharing Our Best
The Arrangement Hair Salon
Columbus, Ohio

Mediterranean Potatoes

3 medium onions, chopped
2 large garlic cloves, minced
2 tablespoons olive oil
2 cups chopped fresh tomato (about 2 large)
1 (6-ounce) can tomato paste
⅓ cup chopped fresh parsley
1 bay leaf
1½ teaspoons salt
1 to 1½ teaspoons dried basil
½ to 1 teaspoon dried oregano
¼ to ½ teaspoon dried thyme
¼ teaspoon freshly ground pepper
3 pounds baking potatoes

Sauté onion and garlic in hot oil in a large skillet over medium-high heat 6 to 8 minutes or until tender. Add tomato and next 8 ingredients, stirring well. Cover, reduce heat, and simmer 15 minutes, stirring occasionally. Remove bay leaf.

Cut potatoes into bite-size pieces, and place in a greased 3-quart baking dish. Pour tomato mixture over potato, spreading evenly. Bake, uncovered, at 350° for 55 to 60 minutes or until potato is tender. Yield: 8 to 10 servings.

Simply Divine
Second-Ponce de Leon Baptist Church
Atlanta, Georgia

Bourbon Sweet Potatoes

4 pounds sweet potatoes
½ cup firmly packed brown sugar
½ cup butter or margarine, softened
½ cup bourbon
⅓ cup orange juice
1 teaspoon salt
½ teaspoon apple pie spice
⅓ cup pecans, chopped

Cook sweet potatoes in boiling water to cover 30 to 45 minutes or until tender; drain. Let cool to the touch. Peel potatoes, and place pulp in a large bowl; mash well. Stir in sugar and next 5 ingredients. Spoon mixture into a greased 13- x 9-inch baking dish. Sprinkle with pecans. Bake, covered, at 350° for 45 minutes. Yield: 8 servings.

Lighthouse Secrets: A Collection of Recipes from the Nation's Oldest City
The Junior Service League of St. Augustine, Florida

Spinach with Herbs

2 pounds fresh spinach
3 slices bacon
2 medium onions, thinly sliced
½ cup chopped fresh parsley
2 tablespoons white wine vinegar
1 teaspoon chopped fresh rosemary
1 teaspoon salt
¼ teaspoon pepper

Remove stems from spinach. Wash leaves thoroughly, and pat dry with paper towels; tear into large pieces. Set aside.

Cook bacon in a large Dutch oven until crisp. Remove bacon; drain on paper towels, reserving 2 tablespoons drippings in Dutch oven. Crumble bacon, and set aside.

Sauté onion in hot drippings in pan over medium heat until tender. Add spinach, parsley, and remaining 4 ingredients; sauté 3 to 5 minutes or until spinach wilts and is tender. Top with crumbled bacon. Serve immediately. Yield: 8 servings.

Flavors of Hawaii
Child and Family Service Guild
Honolulu, Hawaii

Squash and Apple Casserole

A brown sugar and spice topping sprinkled over butternut squash and apples creates a sweet side dish that pairs deliciously with pork.

1¼ pounds butternut squash, peeled and cut into 1-inch pieces
4 to 5 medium Granny Smith apples, peeled and cut into 8 wedges each
½ cup firmly packed brown sugar
1 tablespoon all-purpose flour
1 teaspoon salt
¼ teaspoon ground cinnamon
¼ teaspoon ground nutmeg
¼ cup butter or margarine

Combine squash and apple in an ungreased 13- x 9-inch baking dish. Stir together brown sugar and next 4 ingredients in a small bowl. Cut in butter with a pastry blender until mixture is crumbly.

Sprinkle sugar mixture over squash mixture. Bake, uncovered, at 350° for 50 to 60 minutes or until squash and apple are tender. Yield: 8 servings.

Out of the Ordinary
The Hingham Historical Society
Hingham, Massachusetts

Baked Green Tomatoes, Sicilian Style

1 cup Italian-seasoned breadcrumbs
¼ cup olive oil
3 tablespoons water
2 garlic cloves, crushed
2 teaspoons freshly grated Parmesan cheese
3 medium-size green tomatoes, sliced

Combine first 5 ingredients in a small bowl; stir well.

Coat a 15- x 10-inch jellyroll pan with cooking spray. Place tomato slices in a single layer in pan. Top each tomato slice with crumb mixture. Bake, uncovered, at 350° for 35 to 40 minutes or until crumb mixture is lightly browned. Yield: 6 servings. Phyllis Lamantia

Tutto Bene
Salvatore Mancini Lodge #2440
North Providence, Rhode Island

Winter White Puree

The buttery cream base of this puree tames the earthy, intense essence of three root vegetables.

4 quarts water
1½ teaspoons salt, divided
1 pound turnips, peeled and cut into 1-inch pieces
1 pound parsnips, cut into 1-inch pieces
2 cups cauliflower flowerets
1 Granny Smith apple, peeled and diced
10 tablespoons butter, cut into small pieces
¾ cup heavy whipping cream
¼ teaspoon freshly ground white pepper
½ cup grated Parmesan cheese

Bring water and 1 teaspoon salt to a boil in a Dutch oven. Add turnip, parsnip, cauliflower, and apple. Bring to a boil; cook 15 minutes or until turnip is tender. Drain well.

Process vegetables, remaining ½ teaspoon salt, butter, cream, and pepper in a food processor until smooth. Spoon mixture into an ungreased 9-inch square baking dish. Sprinkle with cheese.

Bake, uncovered, at 350° for 20 minutes or until golden. Serve immediately. Yield: 6 servings.

Sounds Delicious: The Flavor of Atlanta in Food & Music
Atlanta Symphony Orchestra
Atlanta, Georgia

Yams and Cranberries

Leave the skin on the orange to add a wonderful citrus flavor.

2 (29-ounce) cans yams, drained and sliced
1 (12-ounce) package fresh cranberries
1½ cups sugar
1 small orange, thinly sliced
¼ cup orange juice
¾ teaspoon ground cinnamon
¼ teaspoon ground nutmeg
⅛ teaspoon ground mace
½ cup pecan halves

Place yams in an ungreased 2-quart baking dish; set aside.

Combine cranberries and next 6 ingredients in a medium saucepan.

Bring to a boil; cover, reduce heat, and simmer until cranberry skins pop. Pour cranberry mixture over yams; top with pecans. Bake, uncovered, at 350° for 45 minutes. Serve with a slotted spoon, if desired. Yield: 6 to 8 servings.

Plummer House Museum
Traill County Historical Society
Hillsboro, North Dakota

Zucchini Patties

1½ cups shredded zucchini (about 2 medium)
¼ cup all-purpose flour
¼ cup grated Parmesan cheese
2 large eggs, lightly beaten
2 tablespoons finely chopped onion
2 tablespoons mayonnaise
½ teaspoon salt
¼ teaspoon pepper
¼ teaspoon dried oregano
1 tablespoon butter

Pat shredded zucchini between layers of paper towels to remove excess moisture. Combine zucchini, flour, and next 7 ingredients in a bowl; stir well.

Melt butter in a large skillet over medium heat; spoon 2 tablespoons batter for each patty into skillet. Cook until browned on both sides. Yield: 4 servings.

Terri Mullins

Culinary Tastes of Blue Mountain Cooks
Grand Terrace Branch Library: Friends
Grand Terrace, California

Acknowledgments

Each of the community cookbooks listed is represented by recipes appearing in *America's Best Recipes*. The copyright is held by the sponsoring organization whose mailing address is included.

202's Totally Tempting Treasures, American Legion Auxiliary Green-Pierce Unit 202, 1101 E. Scott St., Wichita Falls, TX 76301

Alaska's Best, Alaska Telephone Pioneers, 600 Telephone Ave., MS 10, Anchorage, AK 99503

The Albany Collection: Treasures and Treasured Recipes, Women's Council of the Albany Institute of History and Art, 125 Washington Ave., Albany, NY 12210

All We Need Is Love, Columbus-Lowndes Humane Society, 13 Airline Rd., Columbus, MS 39701

Always in Season, Junior League of Salt Lake City, Inc., 526 E. 300 S., Salt Lake City, UT 84102

Ambrosia, Junior Auxiliary of Vicksburg, P.O. Box 86, Vicksburg, MS 39180

. . . And It Was Very Good, Temple Emeth, 1666 Windsor Rd., Teaneck, NJ 07666

Angels in the Kitchen, Grace Episcopal Church, 711 S. McDuffie St., Anderson, SC 29624

Angels in the Kitchen Cookbook, Community Presbyterian Church, P.O. Box 470053, Celebration, FL 34747

Apron Strings: Ties to the Southern Tradition of Cooking, Junior League of Little Rock, Inc., 3600 Cantrell Rd., Ste. 102, Little Rock, AR 72202

The Art of Cooking, Muscle Shoals District Service League, P.O. Box 793, Sheffield, AL 35660

Back to the Table, Episcopal Church Women—Christ Church, P.O. Box 25778, Raleigh, NC 27611-5778

Bay Tables, Junior League of Mobile, 57 N. Sage Ave., Mobile, AL 36608

Best and Blessed, Sweet Spirit Singers, 135 Main St., Liberty, MS 39645

Beyond Cotton Country, Junior League of Morgan County, 109 2nd Ave. NE, Decatur, AL 35601

Black Tie & Boots Optional, Colleyville Woman's Club, P.O. Box 181, Colleyville, TX 76034

Blended Blessings, First Presbyterian Church, 308 W. Fisher St., Salisbury, NC 28144

Blest Recipes, Our Redeemer Lutheran Church, P.O. Box 670150, Chugiak, AK 99567

Bravo! Recipes, Legends & Lore, University Musical Society, 881 N. University Ave., Ann Arbor, MI 48109-1011

Bread from the Brook, The Church at Brook Hills, 3145 Brook Highland Pkwy., Birmingham, AL 35242

Café Weller . . . Tastes to Remember, Apple Corps of the Weller Health Education Center, 325 Northampton St., Easton, PA 18042

Capital Celebrations, Junior League of Washington, 3039 M St. NW, Washington, DC 20007

Carnegie Hall Cookbook, Carnegie Hall, Inc., 105 Church St., Lewisburg, WV 24901

A Century of Serving, Junior Board of Christiana Care, Inc., P.O. Box 1668, Wilmington, DE 19899

Chautauqua Celebrations, Wythe Arts Council, Ltd., P.O. Box 911, Wytheville, VA 24382

Chautauqua Porches–A Centennial Cookbook, Colorado Chautauqua Cottagers, Inc., ℅ Valerie Hess, Colorado Chautauqua, Cottage #10, Boulder, CO 80302

Classic Italian Cooking, Italian American Society of San Marco Island, 366 Wales Ct., Marco Island, FL 34145

The Club's Choice . . . A Second Helping, Fuquay-Varina Woman's Club, 612 E. Academy St., Fuquay-Varina, NC 27526

Cook Bookery, The University of Illinois College of Medicine at Peoria, One Illini Dr., Peoria, IL 61605

The Cookbook of the Museum of Science, Boston, The Volunteer Service League of the Museum of Science, Boston, Science Park, Boston, MA 02114-1099

Cookbook Seasoned with Love, Upsala Community Presbyterian Church, 101 Upsala Rd., Sanford, FL 32771

The Cookbook Tour, Good Shepherd Lutheran Church, P.O. Box 355 Hwy. 42, Plainview, MN 55964

A Cookery & Memories from Old Bourne, The Bourne Society for Historic Preservation, 22 Sandwich Rd., Bourne, MA 02532

Cooking Up Memories, Tazewell County Genealogical and Historical Society, 719 N. 11th, Pekin, IL 61555-0312

Cooking with Class, Timber Lake Booster Club, P.O. Box 62, Timber Lake, SD 57656

Cooking with Pride, Madison Park/Camelview PTO, 1431 E. Campbell, Phoenix, AZ 85014

Cookin' in the Canyon, Jarbidge Community Hall, P.O. Box 260081, Jarbidge, NV 89826

Cookin' with Friends, National Presbyterian School Class of 2000, 4121 Nebraska Ave. NW, Washington, DC 20016

Culinary Tastes of Blue Mountain Cooks, Grand Terrace Branch Library: Friends, 22795 Barton Rd., Grand Terrace, CA 92313

A Dab of This and a Dab of That, Bethlehem Baptist Church Senior Missionary, 303 E. Main St., Ninety Six, SC 29666

Deborah Heart and Lung Center 75th Anniversary National Cookbook, Deborah Hospital Foundation, Cymrot Center, 212 Trenton Rd., Browns Mills, NJ 08015

De Nuestra Mesa: Our Food, Wine, and Tradition, New Hope Charities, Inc., 626 N. Dixie Hwy., West Palm Beach, FL 33401

Designer's Recipes for Living, East Tennessee Interior Design Society, 1527 W. Woodshire Dr., Knoxville, TN 37922

Diamond Delights, Diamond Hill Elementary School, 104 Lake Secession Rd., Abbeville, SC 29620

Dining by Design: Stylish Recipes, Savory Settings, Junior League of Pasadena, 149 South Madison Ave., Pasadena, CA 91101

The Dining Car, Service League of Denison, 418 W. Main, Denison, TX 75020

Doggone Good Cookin', Support Dogs, Inc., 9510 Page Ave., St. Louis, MO 63132

Down by the Water, Junior League of Columbia, Inc., 2926 Devine St., Columbia, SC 29205

Down Home Dining in Mississippi, Mississippi Homemaker Volunteers, Inc., 715 Markette St., Water Valley, MS 38965

Exclusively Broccoli Cookbook, Coventry Historical Society, Inc., P.O. Box 534, Coventry, CT 06238

Favorite Recipes, Friends of Memorial Hospital, 645 E. 5th, Weiser, ID 83672

Favorite Recipes Taste of Tradition, B.A. Ritter Senior Citizen Center, 914 Boston, Nederland, TX 77627

Feeding the Flock, St. Philips Episcopal Church, 3860 S.E. California, Topeka, KS 66609

Flavors of Falmouth, Falmouth Historical Society, 55-65 Palmer Ave., Falmouth, MA 02541

Flavors of Hawaii, Child and Family Service Guild, 200 N. Vineyard Blvd., Building B, Honolulu, HI 96817

The Flavors of Mackinac, Mackinac Island Medical Center, P.O. Box 536, Market St., Mackinac Island, MI 49757

From the Kitchens of Lake Wynonah, Civic Association of Lake Wynonah, Navajo Dr., Auburn, PA 17922

Fruits of Our Labor, St. Joseph Parish, 7607 Trendwood Dr., Lincoln, NE 68506

Gator Championship Recipes, Florida Goal-Liners, 6270 West City Rd. 320, McIntosh, FL 32664

Generations of Good Food, Jeannette Public Library, Sixth and Magee Sts., Jeannette, PA 15644

Gracious Gator Cooks, Junior League of Gainesville, 430-A N. Main St., Gainesville, FL 32605

Great Expectations, Assistance League of Southeastern Michigan, 3128 Walton Blvd., Ste. 247, Rochester Hills, MI 48309

Hearthside: A Country Community Cookbook, Christ Community Church, P.O. Box 391, Weare, NH 03281

The Heart of Pittsburgh, Sacred Heart Elementary School PTG, 325 Emerson St., Pittsburgh, PA 15206

Heaven's Bounty, Long Beach Catholic School Parents' Club, Long Beach Catholic School, 735 W. Broadway, Long Beach, NY 11561

Home Furniture's 50th Anniversary 1949-1999: Secret Family Cookbook, Make a Wish Foundation, 200 N. Durkee, Appleton, WI 54915

Homemade with Love, Swanton-Missisquoi Valley Lions Club, P.O. Box 376, Highgate Center, VT 05459

International Home Cooking, The United Nations International School Parents' Association, 24-50 Franklin D. Roosevelt Dr., New York, NY 10010

Iowa: A Taste of Home, Iowa 4-H Foundation, 32 Curtiss Hall-Iowa State University, Ames, IA 50011

It's a Snap, Haven of Grace, 1133 Benton St., St. Louis, MO 63106

Keittokirja: Kaleva Centennial Cookbook, Project Kaleva/Kaleva Historical Society, 14551 Wuoksi Ave., Kaleva, MI 49645

Lighthouse Secrets: A Collection of Recipes from the Nation's Oldest City, Junior Service League of St. Augustine, Inc., P.O. Box 374, St. Augustine, FL 32085

Linen Napkins to Paper Plates, Junior Auxiliary of Clarksville, Inc., P.O. Box 30, Clarksville, TN 37041

Look Who's Cooking in Louisville, Pitt Academy, 4605 Poplar Level Rd., Louisville, KY 40213

Madalene Cooks–50 Years of Good Taste, Church of the Madalene, 3188 E. 22nd St., Tulsa, OK 74114

Made in the Shade, Junior League of Greater Fort Lauderdale, 704 S.E. 1st St., Fort Lauderdale, FL 33301

McInnis Bobcat Favorites, McInnis Elementary PTA, 5175 N. U.S. Hwy. 17, DeLeon Springs, FL 32130

The Monarch's Feast, Mary Munford PTA, 211 Westmoreland Rd., Richmond, VA 23227

Noel Bluffin' We're Still Cookin', Noel Area Chamber of Commerce, 108 S. Railroad, P.O. Box 173, Noel, MO 64854

North Country Cooking, 51st National Square Dance Convention, 7125 River Shore Ln., Champlin, MN 55316-2134

Notable Feasts, Friends of the Cape Cod Symphony Orchestra, 712-A Main St., Yarmouth Port, MA 02675

NPT's Community Cookbook, Neighborhood Pride Team, 7455 S.E. 52nd Ave., Portland, OR 97206

Of Books and Cooks, Woman's Book Club, 202 Magnolia, Harrison, AR 72601

The Official Cookbook of Central New York's TomatoFest, TomatoFest of Central New York, Inc., P.O. Box 1611, Auburn, NY 13021

Olivet Heritage Cookbook, Olivet Presbyterian Church, 2575 Garth Rd., Charlottesville, VA 22901

Our Country Christmas Collection, Skaggs Community Health Center, 251 Skaggs Rd., Branson, MO 65615

Our Family's Favorite Recipes, University Family Fellowship, 1125 Stanford Way, Sparks, NV 89431

Our Favorite Recipes, Claremont Society for the Prevention of Cruelty to Animals Serving Sullivan County, Inc., Rte. 3 Box 337, Claremont, NH 03743

Our Heritage Cookbook, First Baptist Church, 218 N. 34th, Billings, MT 59101

Our Saviour's Lutheran Church 75th Anniversary Cookbook, Our Saviour's Lutheran Church, 318 E. 6th St., Casper, WY 82604

Out of the Ordinary, The Hingham Historical Society, P.O. Box 434, Hingham, MA 02043

Over the Bridge, Corpus Christie Women's Guild, 324 Quaker Meetinghouse Rd., East Sandwich, MA 02537-2170

Panthers' Pantry, Children's Educational Foundation, 16436 Paula Rd., Madera, CA 93638

Past to Present: A Pictorial Cookbook, Washington School Restoration Committee, P.O. Box 587, Oakland, OR 97462

Perennial Palette, Southborough Gardeners, P.O. Box 184, Southborough, MA 01772

A Perfect Measurement of Love, Little Flower Children's Services of New York, P.O. Box 9000, Wading River, NY 11792

Pick of the Crop, Two, North Sunflower Academy PTA, 148 Academy Rd., Drew, MS 38737

Picnics, Potlucks & Prizewinners, Indiana 4-H Foundation, Inc., 225 South East St., Ste. 760, Indianapolis, IN 46202

Plummer House Museum, Traill County Historical Society, 308 Caledonia Ave. W., Hillsboro, ND 58045

'Pon Top Edisto, Trinity Episcopal Church, 1589 Hwy. 174, P.O. Box 425, Edisto Island, SC 29438

Rave Reviews, Ogunquit Playhouse, Route One North, Ogunquit, ME 03907

Recipes & Remembrances, Frank P. Tillman Elementary PTO, 230 Quan Ave., Kirkwood, MO 63122

Recipes and Remembrances, Otsego County Historical Society, 320 W. Main St., Gaylord, MI 49735

Recipes for Champions, Shebas of Khiva Temple Oriental Band, 5804 Briar St., Amarillo, TX 79109-6238

Recipes from the Kitchens of Family & Friends, Gresham Women of Elks, P.O. Box 42, Gresham, OR 97030

Savoring the Southwest Again, Roswell Symphony Guild, P.O. Box 3078, Roswell, NM 88202

Savory Secrets, Runnels School, 17255 S. Harrell's Ferry Rd., Baton Rouge, LA 70816

Scent from P.E.O. Sisterhood, Philanthropic Educational Organization, Chapter AG, 109 Forest Hill Way, Newcastle, WY 82701

Seaboard to Sideboard, Junior League of Wilmington, 3803 Wrightsville Ave., Downey Branch Office Park, Unit 9, Wilmington, NC 28403

Secrets of Amelia, McArthur Family Branch YMCA, 1915 Citrona Dr., Fernandina Beach, FL 32034

Sesquicentennially Delicious, Western Pennsylvania Hospital, 4800 Friendship Ave., Pittsburgh, PA 15224

Shalom on the Range, Shalom Park, 14800 E. Belleview Dr., Aurora, CO 80015

Sharing Our Best, The Arrangement Hair Salon, 2982 E. Broad St., Columbus, OH 43209

Sharing Our Best, Bull Run Parent Teacher Club, 41515 SE Thomas Rd., Sandy, OR 97055

Sharing Recipes from Green Road Baptist Church, Green Road Baptist Church, HC 83 Box 210, Green Road, KY 40946

Silver Spoons, Kaiser Rehabilitation Center, 1125 S. Trenton, Tulsa, OK 74120

Simple Pleasures: From Our Table to Yours, Arab Mothers' Club, P.O. Box 884, Arab, AL 35016

Simply Divine, Second-Ponce de Leon Baptist Church, 2715 Peachtree Rd., Atlanta, GA 30327

Simply the Best . . . Recipes by Design, Columbus Area Visitors Center, 506 5th St., Columbus, IN 47201

Sounds Delicious: The Flavor of Atlanta in Food & Music, Atlanta Symphony Orchestra, 1293 Peachtree St., Ste. 300, Atlanta, GA 30309-3552

Southern Elegance: A Second Course, Junior League of Gaston County, Inc., 2950 S. Union Rd., Ste. A, Gastonia, NC 28054

Southern . . . On Occasion, Junior League of Cobb-Marietta, Inc., One Depot St., Ste. 300, Marietta, GA 30060

Spice It Up!, Baton Rouge Branch of American Association of University Women, 10345 Barbara St., Baton Rouge, LA 70815

St. Andrew's Cooks Again, Presbyterian Women of St. Andrew, 1350 N. 23rd St., Beaumont, TX 77706

St. Philomena's Jr. Beta Delicious Recipes of the Future, St. Philomena School's Junior Beta Club, 120 Convent St., Labadieville, LA 70372

A Sunsational Encore, Junior League of Greater Orlando, 125 N. Lucerne Cir. E, Orlando, FL 32801

Sweet Memories, Holy Covenant United Methodist Women, 22111 Morton Ranch Rd., Katy, TX 77449

Symphony of Flavors, The Associates of the Redlands Bowl, P.O. Box 492, Redlands, CA 92373

Taste Buds–A Collection of Treasured Recipes, Alliance of the Illinois State Dental Society, 101C S. Second St., Springfield, IL 62704

A Taste of Tradition, Temple Emanu-El, 99 Taft Ave., Providence, RI 02906

A Taste of Washington State, Washington Bed & Breakfast Guild, 2442 N.W. Market St., Seattle, WA 98107

The Tastes and Tales of Moiliili, Moiliili Community Center, 2535 S. King St., Honolulu, HI 96826

Tasty Treasures, Immanuel Lutheran Church Ladies Aid, 303 E. Pearl, Leland, MI 49654

Tested by Time, Porter Gaud Parents Guild, P.O. Box 30431, Charleston, SC 29417

A Thyme to Remember, Dallas County Medical Society Alliance, 5500 Swiss Ave., Dallas, TX 75214

Today's Special: 25th Anniversary Cookbook from the Kitchens of Empire, Empire State Chapter FMCA, 9 Hickory Ln., Scotia, NY 12302

Tried and True from Riverview, Riverview Hospital Auxiliary, 410 Dewey St., Wisconsin Rapids, WI 54494

Tutto Bene, Salvatore Mancini Lodge #2440, 8 Hunter Run, North Providence, RI 02904

United Church of Tekoa Cookbook, United Church of Tekoa, 301 S. Crosby St., Tekoa, WA 99033

Victorian Secrets, The Chiselers, Inc., P.O. Box 14494, Tampa, FL 33690-4494

Walking with Christ, First Baptist Church, 714 N. Main St., Mount Airy, NC 27030

We Cook Too, Women's Committee, Wadsworth Atheneum, 66 Middlebrook Rd., West Hartford, CT 06119

We're Cooking Up Something New: 50 Years of Music, History, and Food, Wichita Falls Symphony League, 4500 Seymour Hwy., Wichita Falls, TX 76309

What Can I Bring?, Junior League of Northern Virginia, Inc., 7921 Jones Branch Dr., Ste. 320, McLean, VA 20165

Yuletide on Hilton Head: A Heritage of Island Flavors, United Way of Beaufort County, P.O. Box 22961, Hilton Head Island, SC 29925

Index

Your Community Cookbook Could Win an Award

The McIlhenny Company of Avery Island, Louisiana, generates a great deal of enthusiasm among service organizations nationwide by sponsoring the Tabasco® Community Cookbook Awards Competition each fall at the company headquarters in Avery Island. These awards were established 11 years ago to recognize the role community cookbooks play in chronicling and preserving local culinary traditions. All community cookbooks published within the last two years are eligible for entry.

The editors of *America's Best Recipes* salute the winners of the 2000 Tabasco® Community Cookbook Awards competition, some of which have recipes featured in this volume. The McIlhenny Company awarded a total of $10,000 to the winners of the 2000 competition. The first place winner received $3,500, followed by $2,000 for second place, and $1,000 for third. Each regional winner was given $500, and special merit winners received $100. The sponsoring organizations of the winning cookbooks, in turn, donated the prize money to charities of their choice.

The 2000 Tabasco® Community Cookbook Awards winners were:

- **First Place Winner:** *Good Food Served Right,* Traditional Arts in Upstate New York, Canton, NY
- **Second Place Winner:** *Seasons of Santa Fe,* Kitchen Angels, Santa Fe, NM
- **Third Place Winner:** *Crescent City Collection: A Taste of New Orleans,* Junior League of New Orleans, LA
- **Northeast:** *Cooking with Music,* Boston Symphony Association of Volunteers, Boston, MA
- **Mid-Atlantic:** *The Kosher Palette,* Joseph Kushner Hebrew Academy, Livingston, NJ
- **South:** *Splendor in the Bluegrass,* Junior League of Louisville, KY
- **Midwest:** *Breakfast in Cairo, Dinner in Rome,* International School of Minnesota Foundation, Eden Prairie, MN
- **Southwest:** *Settings on the Dock of the Bay,* The Assistance League of the Bay Area, Webster, TX
- **West:** *Flavor it Greek!,* Philoptochos Society of Holy Trinity Greek Orthodox Church, Portland, OR
- **Special Merit Award:** *Help Yourself! There's a God's Mighty Plenty,* Cathorne-Brooks Family Association, Richmond, VA
- **Special Merit Award:** *A Peach Flavored Past,* Altrusa International, Inc., Palisade, CO
- **Walter S. McIlhenny Hall of Fame 2000:** *Celebrate San Antonio,* San Antonio Junior Forum, San Antonio, TX
- **Walter S. McIlhenny Hall of Fame 2000:** *Out of Our League,* Junior League of Greensboro, NC

For information on the Tabasco® Community Cookbook Awards or for an awards entry form send a self-addressed stamped #10 (legal size) envelope to

Tabasco Community Cookbook Awards
℅ Hunter & Associates, Inc.
41 Madison Ave.
New York, NY 10010-2202

For a free booklet about producing a community cookbook send a self-addressed stamped #10 (legal size) envelope to

Compiling Culinary History
℅ Hunter & Associates, Inc.
41 Madison Ave.
New York, NY 10010-2202